Tales from
the
Great Lakes

Tales from the Great Lakes

Based on C.H.J. Snider's
"Schooner Days"

Introduced and Edited
By Robert B. Townsend

Dundurn Press
Toronto • Oxford

Edited by Tom Kluger
Cover design and digital colour rendition: Ron & Ron Design & Photography
Book design: Ron & Ron Design & Photography
Printed and bound in Canada by Webcom

The publisher wishes to acknowledge the generous assistance and ongoing support of the **Canada Council**, the **Book Publishing Industry Development Program** of the **Department of Canadian Heritage**, the **Ontario Arts Council**, the **Ontario Publishing Centre** of the **Ministry of Citizenship, Culture and Recreation**, and the **Ontario Heritage Foundation**.

J. Kirk Howard, Publisher

Canadian Cataloguing in Publication Data

Snider, C.H.J. (Charles Henry Jeremiah), 1879–1971.
   Tales from the Great Lakes

Selected articles written for Toronto's The evening telegram, 1931–1954.
ISBN 1-55002-234-2

1. Great Lakes – History. 2. Ships – Great Lakes – History. I. Townsend, Robert B. II. Title.

F551.S55 1995   977   C95-931358-3

Dundurn Press Limited	Dundurn Distribution	Dundurn Press Limited
2181 Queen Street East	73 Lime Walk	1823 Maryland Avenue
Suite 301	Headington, Oxford	P.O. Box 1000
Toronto, Canada	England	Niagara Falls, N.Y.
M4E 1E5	OX3 7AD	U.S.A. 14302-1000

Schooner Days

The *Albatross* and the *Albacore*,
The *Hydrabad* and the *Bangalore*;
And timber droghers by the score,
In "Schooner Days" are pictured.

Those ships were built of oak and iron,
No engines there, nor boilers firin',
But men and muscle, never tiring,
Stowed their loads and hoisted sail

Could I but see those sights again,
Those gallant ships and sailor men:
No four hours on, and eight off then,
'Twas many years ago.

Now they're gone, almost forgotten,
Officers and men and sails of cotton;
Their hulks abandoned, timbers rotten,
A memory of by-gone days.

Charles Joyce, Meldrum Bay, to "Schooner Days"
February 1951

The *Madeline*.

Contents

Acknowledgements 10

Introduction 13

Charles Henry Jeremiah Snider, 1879–1971, "The Skipper" 16

About the Old Schooners 22

Building a Schooner 23

Rigs 24

Stonehookers 25

Registration 28

The Fore-'n'-After 29

Whatchacallit 30

Fitting-Out Time Fifty Years Ago .33

Seagoing Teamsters 37

Making Hay in December 43

Port Credit 45

Sunday Scorching 46

Last Coal of Last Century 51

Brave Boat Work at Century's End 54

Chasing a *Lithophone* 57

Snider Mysteries 61

At the Foot of the Highlands 61

The *Marysburgh* 64

Perhaps This Solves the Highlands' Secret 66

Little Lady of Fifty-five Years Ago 70

Highland Creek and Rouge River .72

Port Union 74

Frenchman's Bay 76

A "Hesperus" out of Frenchman's Bay 79

A Credit to the *Maple Leaf* 82

Six-Men Lassie 86

Gunboat Times on the Great Lakes 88

The Hickory Jib Boom 91

Port Oshawa 94

Port Darlington 95

Where "Schooner Days" Come From 97

Port Britain 100

Millhaven and the *Oliver Mowat* 102

Nosey O'Brien 105

New Wine in an Old Bottle 107

The Pickled Prince 111

Toronto's Timbermen 115

Grafton Harbour 117

"Out of Cat Hollow" 120

Weller's Bay 121

The *Belle Sheridan* 122

Vienna at Needle's Eye 130

Hunting Out a Hidden Port 133

Sails Still Shimmer on Napanee River 134

Snow Bird 137

Port Milford 140

Jib Picnic in the *Picton* 142

A Prince of Prince Edward 145

Blue Bottom of Last Century 148

Why the Topmasts Were Sent Down 149

Oswego – a Dangerous Place 152

Wrecked at Oswego Was Fate of Many 154

Axe to the Root of a Mystery 156

Bridgeport 159

Last over Jordan Was the *Flying Dutchman* 160

Riding It Out with the *Queen of the Lakes* 161

What Is a Shellback? 164

Lake Fishboats 165

Spences of Saugeen 169

"Riddle of the Sands" Gave Collingwood a Railway 173

The Beaver Mormons 177

Passing Hails: The *Lyman M. Davis* 181

Sending a Schooner over Niagara Falls 182

Mary and Lucy 186

Why Ships Capsize 187

Hallowe'en off Point Traverse 189

The *Persia* and Her Pet 'Coon 193

Schooners on Lake Simcoe 194

Caledonia's Gear Goes into Guns for Britain

    and $$$ for *Telegram* Fund 197

Sold under the "Broad Arrow" 200

Acknowledgements

Words alone cannot express my appreciation to the many friends who have made it possible for me to fulfil the dreams of those who were acquainted with the career of the late C.H.J.Snider, that at least portions of his "Schooner Days" be published in book form.

Kenneth Macpherson, former provincial archivist, and a close, personal friend and confidant of C.H.J. Snider, acting as a trustee of his estate, was responsible for the preservation of Snider's material in accessible form. As a consequence of his efforts generations of marine and historical researchers will have available to them this valuable source of material. His hearty endorsement of our efforts to produce this book is gratefully acknowledged.

Thanks to Don Withrow, a past commodore of the Provincial Marine 1812. I first met Don Withrow at the final meeting of a very small group who had tried to form a Marine Heritage Society of Ontario. Under the Leadership of Dr. Bryan Kerman, five or six individuals had a dream to build a replica of the *Prince Regent*, the first war vessel built in Toronto (1812) for Ontario's bicentennial in 1992. At that time I was also spearheading an effort to salvage the original plan of the Harbourfront Corporation to build a proper nautical centre and marine museum at Maple Leaf Quay, on Toronto's Harbourfront. At that last meeting Dr. Kerman had suggested the need for the preparation of a keyword index database of Snider's "Schooner Days" material. Don Withrow took up the challenge and did the organization and follow up with many volunteers that made the preparation of the "Schooner Days" database possible. His constant telephone calls, visits to my office, and our meetings together with Dr. Paul Bator of the Ontario Heritage Foundation (whose encouragement is also acknowledged), provided me with the enthusiasm necessary for the preparation of this book.

A very special thanks to Lorne Joyce, "the world's leading authority on stonehookers sailing out of Port Credit"; who, like Ken Macpherson, was a personal friend of Snider in his later years, and was with him to the end.

Lorne Joyce was born and grew up in the area adjacent to Port Credit Harbour. From early childhood he had a love of the vessels of Lake Ontario, and has spent a lifetime researching and photographing vessels – sail and steam – of schooner days. He has prepared thousands of slides of photographs, paintings and drawings of the ships, harbours, and people associated with schooner days – all of which he has freely made available to artists and authors for many years, not asking for, and seldom receiving, the acknowledgment or credit that he so justly deserves. He has provided a number of the photographs as well as much help and support in the preparation of this book, for which I am grateful.

Appreciation is also extended to the Marine Museum of the Great Lakes at Kingston and the Ontario Archives and the Metropolitan Toronto Reference Library, Baldwin Room, for their cooperation and for providing photographs which we have reproduced in this book.

Robert B. Townsend
June 1995

Introduction

The surface of the Great Lakes is 95,275 square miles. By comparison, the land surface of Great Britain and Ireland is 88,781 square miles.

It is 1,166 miles (not knots) from the city of Kingston, Ontario, at the mouth of the mighty St. Lawrence River, to Duluth, Minnesota, which is at the western end of Lake Superior. Trips of an additional five hundred miles would be required to ply Lake Michigan and Georgian Bay of Lake Huron. This is straight line sailing. The coastline of the Great Lakes is about 3,075 miles or more. That extensive coastline surrounds more than half the fresh water on the globe.

Lake Ontario is 216 miles long and at one point is some 54 miles wide. While its tides are of no real concern for day-to-day sailing, and its unmarked rocks few and far between, it unfortunately can boast of some five thousand shipwrecks in its comparatively short maritime history. Ships no longer attempt to sail during the winter months (yachts are restricted by their insurance policies to sailing between April 1 and November 15) and their captains have great respect for it during a storm.

This book is about the sailing vessels, schooners and yachts that have sailed these Great Lakes, their builders, the people who have sailed them, and the ports to which they have sailed during the early years of the province of Ontario, from the very early 1800s to the early days of the twentieth century. It is based on the writings and marine research of the late C.H.J. Snider. Much of this information was reported by him in a series of columns called "Schooner Days" in *The Evening Telegram* between 1931 and 1956.

An important part of the "Schooner Days" column was the "Passing Hails" – letters of comment and inquiry he received from his many readers. On a number of occasions his readers asked when "Schooner Days" would be published in book form, always with the promise that it would be done. In his final column, he stated:

"New Year's resolve No. 1957 – To get 'Schooner Days' into a presentable book this year if we do nothing else."

Snider passed away in 1971, at the age of 92, with no indication that he had kept that New Year's resolution.

After reading some 1,300 of the "Schooner Days" columns, and preparing a database of the vessels, places, and people named in the articles, it became apparent that the material was so significant that it should be published.

The format in this book is to present as many of the columns as possible in their original style, with a minimum of comment, and yet provide the reader with an accurate sampling both of Snider's writing, a portrayal of life in schooner days, the vessels he wrote about, and a history of some communities not well-known to a large population in 1995.

Courtesy of Lorne Joyce.

C.H.J. Snider (1879 – 1971).

On a few occasions we have merged a number of the columns into one, omitting some duplication, and keeping the story to a single theme. Many worthwhile stories, particularly those of Snider's Evergreen Club, a group of elderly sea captains and early sailors, who related to Snider many of their experiences, have been omitted. The thread of many of those stories run from column to column, and would be better grouped together in a further book. Famous boat builders, such as Louis Shipkula, the Muir Brothers, Tait of Garden Island, Capt. James Andrew of Oakville, Capt. Alexander Cuthbert of Cobourg and others, and stories of sailing yachts and races of the schooner days era similarly have been limited or eliminated in the belief that there are sufficient stories in each of these categories to justify separate books.

It is unfortunate that space precluded the inclusion of many interesting and historically significant columns; such as those concerned about the loss of HMS *Speedy*; many of the vessels of the War of 1812; Snider's search for and identification of significant old vessels; and stories of WWII naval vessels built in Ontario and comparisons with those naval vessels built in Ontario in schooner days.

Snider Collection, Archives of Ontario

The *Albacore*, one of the schooners that Snider served on in the early 1890s.

Charles Henry Jeremiah Snider
1879 – 1971
"The Skipper"

This book has been produced to give this generation an insight into the genius of a great Canadian sailor, marine artist, historian, and one ot its most prolific marine writers. In modern times he would have been made an officer of the Order of Canda and have would have received many other notable awards. In his own day he had the respect and admiration of every sailor in Ontario and beyond – not to mention the thousands of dedicated regular readers of his weekly column.

Charles Henry Jeremiah Snider was a fifth generation Canadian. The Snider family were Palatines who left Hanover in 1742; first for Holland, the later to the American Colonies, eventually settling in Pennsylvania. The family migrated with the United Empire Loyalists, trekking northward in a two-year wagon journey and reached Vaughan Township, York County, Ont., in 1797.

Born May 26, 1879, at Sherwood, a hamlet near Maple, Ont., C.H.J. Snider – known to his many close frinds simply as Jerry Snider – was 10 when he jour-neyed to Weston (now part of Metropolitan Toronto) to write his high school

Snider Collection, Archives of Ontario

The bow of the *Albacore*.

entrance examinations. He passed with honours. He had one term at the Auditorium of Art, situated at the corner of Queen and James Streets in Toronto, which was later the site of Eaton's store. He graduated from Toronto Collegiate Institute (now Jarvis Collegiate Institute), with the highest marks in French of any matriculant in Ontario.

While still a junior in high school he "descended the lower reaches of Jarvis Street till stopped by the stench of the open sewer mouth at the bottom of that stately thoroughfare," where he observed the *Barque Swallow* of Port Credit. "Are you going to Port Credit sir?" asked the knee-panted junior. "Kin you steer?" "Yes" "If I take ye to the Credit how'll ye git back?" "Shanks Mare and the radial,"(referring to the electric railway that at that time ran from Long Branch to the Toronto city limits) answered the 13 year old. He made the trip at the helm of the schooner while the captain did all the heavy work, usually done by the crew who had, it turned out, deserted him for a local tavern. So started his love of the sea.

In boyhood he "sailed before the mast" in the lake schooners *Albacore, Vienna, Loretta Rooney, Oliver Mowat, Antelope*, and *Stuart H. Dunn*, and knew many

Snider researched and located the remains of HMS *Nancy,* a hero of the war of the 1812. Here, third from the right, he attends the opening of the HMS Nancy Museum, in which he was instrumental in founding, at Wasaga Beach, 1928. They are holding a model of the *Nancy*.

other vessels, the people who sailed them, their stories, and the ports into which they sailed.

Snider drew a sketch of the *Barque Swallow*, (the name of the schooner-rigged stonehooker,) and before he got his senior matric had sold it to John Ross Robertson, MP, founder of the *Toronto Evening Telegram*, along with an illustrated article on the ancient landmark of the stonehooker fleet. This was the start of his voyage through the broad ocean of newspaper life, which saw him become city editor, managing editor, and, as a trustee of the John Ross Robertson Estate, a publisher of the *Telegram*.

In 1893 he saw and sketched replicas of Columbus' discovery vessels, the *Nina*, *Pinta* and *Santa Maria* which had been built, outfitted and sent as a gift from the Queen of Spain to the World's Fair in Chicago. These three ships sailed from Spain without benefit of auxiliary engines, and were laid up for a few days in the Royal Canadian Yacht Club's basin off Toronto Island.

He loved and gloried in the serious racing of sailing yachts, and he wrote, sketched, painted, and talked about them.

It was in 1896 that Amelius Jarvis, long-time commodore of the Royal Canadian Yacht Club, Toronto, skippered *Canada* in an international race off Toledo, Ohio, for what has since been called the Canada's Cup. That started his coverage of thrilling sailing events.

In 1900 came his first, big, away-from-Toronto, all-expenses-paid assignment when he described that year's America's Cup so dramatically when the U.S. *Velsheda* outsailed the *Shamrock* off Sandy Hook, N.Y. He later described how Lord Dunraven, a dour Scot who was said to be the most unpopular (with Americans) America's Cup challenger of all time, sailed his *Valkyrie* against the U.S. *Genesta*, *Galatea* etc., as well as Sir Thomas Lipton, equally well-known and loved as the most popular loser of all time, as *Shamrocks* *I*, *II*, *III* and *IV*, tried in vain to take the cup back to Britain.

At the time when the America's Cup was the biggest sporting event of the year and he covered every race in person, he organized street shows at the *Telegram* office at Bay and Melinda Streets, Toronto, where the race could be followed by watching the moving models of the participating yachts operated on wires across Bay Sreet.

As he climbed up the rungs of the old *Toronto Telegram*, from cub police reporter to City Hall and city desk, he covered on the side every yacht race, and every marine event he possibly could. He illustrated his own books and articles of men and ships, and the shoals and storms that wrecked them. His spare time was spent talking to the owners, skippers, and crew of the many schooners, stonehookers, and other vessels of the Great Lakes, as well as their families. His encyclopedic mind acquired a knowledge of the maritime heritage of his adopted

Toronto and of the Great Lakes, that was to make him an outstanding historian of the Great Lakes, and the men and ships that sailed them, and of Ontario.

In 1911, after much research, he dived deep into the murky depths of the Nottawasaga River and located the remains of HMS *Nancy* which had been burned and sunk during the War of 1812 without ever firing a shot for Canada.

Later he was instrumental in having her raised, restored and placed for all to see to this day at Nottawasaga. An exact four-foot model he made of her, complete in every detail even to her guns, is encased in splendour at the Marine Museum in the CNE Grounds of Toronto. As well, he was involved in numerous marine archaeological surveys, including extensive analyses of wrecks thought to be remnants of La Salle's *Griffon* and the early French-English fleets of the Seven Years' War.

He published a number of books based on his extensive research. In the year 1912 saw *In the Wake of the Eighteen Twelvers* published, the first of a series of historic novels, written in his own wonderful style, lavishly illustrated, about marine action in the War of 1812. In due course followed *Faded Flags of Fadeless Fame*, *The Glorious* Shannon's *Old Blue Duster* (both in 1923), *The Story of the* Nancy *and other 1812ers* (1927),

Under the Red Jack (1928). *The Log of the* Nancy, *Tarry Breeks and Velvet Garters* a story of the French ships on the Great Lakes, and *The Lucky Penny, Privateer* (1929). His article "The Flag and How to Fly It" (1931) was reprinted twelve times. He was also the principle author of the *Annals of the Royal Canadian Yacht Club, 1852–1937*.

Blinded in one eye, he did not serve in the armed forces during World War I or World War II, but he did stints as a war correspondent, and he did make a significant contribution to the war effort of Canada. In WWI he started a special "Watch Fire" edition of the *Telegram* at 10 p.m. to keep Torontonians up to date on the ebb and flow of the overseas action. During WWII he was a War Correspondent in Britain, did a stint as an air raid warden in London. This latter experience led to his being the founder of the British War Victims Fund, a highly successful venture which won the hearts of the British people.

He crossed the ocean seventeen times, including being the only Canadian on board the lighter-than-air dirigible *R100* on her fifty-seven hour journey from Canada to England in August 1930. He sailed the length of the Great Lakes at one time or another, in winter and in summer, in both steam and sail.

He owned eight sailing vessels from the *Blue Peter* to the *Kingarvie*. He raced and cruised thousands of miles in every kind of sailing craft from dinghies to Banks fishermen and three-masted schooners, and that included participation in a dozen hard-fought contests in the champion Nova Scotia schooner *Bluenose*, and four successive season championships as owner of the *Gardenia*.

Ships and sailing were in his blood. His knowledge of the sailing ships of the Great Lakes, both Canadian and American, their rigs, their captains, their builders, the ports where they were built and the ports where they sailed was, for lack of a better word, outstanding.

Commodore T.K. Wade of the Royal Canadian Yacht Club, in making Mr.Snider a Life Member of the club called him a great describer of sailing and yachting events "because you write in such a way as to be understandable by sailor and landlubber alike."

In addition to his writings and his marine research, Snider was an accomplished marine artist. Many of his paintings and sketches are part of the John Ross Robertson collection housed in the Baldwin Room of the Metropolitan Toronto Reference Library. Others are in storage at the Marine Museum of Toronto, at the Canadian National Exhibition grounds (for lack of a better place).

Probably his most significant contribution to society was the 1,303 "Schooner Days" articles that he wrote for the *Toronto Evening Telegram* between 1931 and 1956. In "Schooner Days" Snider not only describes the ships, the men who sailed them, and the ports of the Great Lakes, he describes the history of the develop-

John Ross Robertson Collection, Metropolitan Toronto Reference Library

Besides being a great marine researcher, Snider was also an accomplished artist, as these three drawings show. Above is the HMS *Speedy*.

ment of Ontario during the 1800s and early 1900s. These articles, entertaining in their own right, touched on the many facets of Ontario's (and that part of the U.S. bordering on the Great Lakes) rich and varied marine history. They are based on personal knowledge, notes taken during extensive interviews with lake sailors, captains and their families over sixty years, and literally thousands of letters he received in response to his columns, which he called "Passing Hails."

John Ross Robertson Collection, Metropolitan Toronto Reference Library

The steamer *Corinthian*. The *Corinthian* is the subject of the story "Grafton Harbour."

Probably no other Canadian historian has recorded the growth of this country from such an extensive source of first-hand knowledge and experience. His intellect, training as a marine artist, newspaper reporter and editor, his extensive travel to virtually every port and former port on the Great Lakes both by land and sea, and his personal knowledge of the ships and people he wrote about in "Schooner Days," made him a very unique and extremely accurate historian.

John Ross Robertson Collection, Metropolitan Toronto Reference Library

The HMS *Duke of Gloucester.*

About the Old Schooners

The nineteenth century is often thought of as a period when that lovely creation of man, the merchant sailing ship in all her many different forms, fought a losing battle with the steamship. In fact the real story is quite different from that which is printed in nearly all history books – even those which purport to be histories of shipping and are very much more interesting.

Until the commercial development of the practical compound marine steam engine in the 1860s, steam engines could not compete successfully with sailing vessels in general trade. Compound engines use the same steam twice over to generate power. The simple engines which preceded them used it only once. Put simply, ships equipped with marine engines manufactured before 1860 were, by the time the vessel had loaded enough cargo to provide a profitable return in freight money, so full there was not enough room left for sufficient coal to get them anywhere. The steamships of the day required that rebunkering – refuelling – facilities be readily available. This, of course, eliminated many of the small ports of the Great Lakes. As a consequence, steamships on the Great Lakes during the 1800s were limited to light cargoes and passengers, which offered relatively high returns in fares and freight money, and left a lot of room for fuel.

Before 1860, the great bulk of world trade, and certainly the Great Lakes, was by sailing ships, built of wood, and differing very little from ships built one and two hundred years earlier, although on the Great Lakes, the schooner rig very much predominated. The technology of building wooden ships had not changed materially for a couple of hundred years.

With the gradual change from cordwood to coal as a fuel for steam engines, both shipping and locomotive, which occurred after the 1860s, there was a need for new engineering and design skills. The steamship had to develop a long way from the techniques of wooden shipbuilding to make use of the new engines of the 1860s.

Propulsion of the steamers of the early 1800s was by paddlewheel – rotating paddles on each side of the vessel. These paddles were very vulnerable in bad weather, and they worked inefficiently because of the nature of the wave pattern which forms around any ship moving through the water. The eventual answer was the screw propeller, but this involved the need of a long shaft from the engine to the propeller at the stern of the vessel. This involved many stresses, too many for the wooden ships which were made up of hundreds – in many cases thousands – of small pieces fastened together by various means, which are essentially flexible and likely to leak. That required that steamships, to be practical, had to be built of iron or steel. It was also necessary the steamships be large, to take advantage of the economies of scale which affect merchant shipping. For these reasons, during the 1800s, and even into the early 1900s, wooden sailing ships, which could be readily and economically built and sailed, and which could take advantage of the small harbours and often minimal port facilities along the shores of the Great Lakes, were essential to the growth of Ontario, and in fact the entire Great Lakes region of North America.

In fact wooden sailing ships were commercially active on the Lakes well into the 1900s.

Building a Schooner

In the mid-1800s shipbuilders, skilled craftsmen, would build one, and some times two schooners per season, ranging from 50 to 250 tons.

There were many shipbuilding centres on Lake Ontario, particularly Stella on Amherst Island, Picton, Cat Hollow (Port of Cramhae near the present Lakeview) Oshawa, Port Union, Port Credit and Sixteen-mile creek (Oakville), St. Catharines and Port Dalhousie. Many famous schooners were built at other ports that were at the mouths of small creeks and rivers, the shipbuilders moving from site to site.

Wooden shipbuilders, unlike their steel and fibreglass successors, needed little in the way of permanent equipment. Keel blocks could be cut as and where required as timber was so plentiful – virgin timber at that. So could launching ways. A blacksmith's forge for the spikes, bolts, chainplates, and other ironworks, could be set up in less than a day. A toolhouse for the men's mauls, sledges, adzes, axes, saws, planes, and caulking mallets could be put up in the same time – building permits were then unheard of. If the schooner was being built "in the bush," as so many were, that is, at some spot near deep water at a distance from houses, there might be a bunkhouse for the gang as well. There would usually be sawpits, for many of the early vessels were built directly from the forest trees, and both timbers and planks were sawed or adzed by hand from the logs as required. There was an abundance of white oak, hickory, and other fine woods.

It is a strange fact that many vessels built from green timber lasted as well as those built from timber that had seasoned for seven years. It seemed to depend upon the builder carefully rejecting all the sap-wood when cutting the sticks. There is also record of some builders building salt pockets in the ship's sides, well-packed with rock salt. This, kept soft by the surrounding moisture, pickled the white oak to the hardness of iron.

Dimensions alone do not give strength to wooden vessels. Strength is gained from the method of fastening, and from the soundness of the material. Heavy, unsound timbers, poorly fastened are a weakness instaead of a strength, they come apart by their own weight in the stresses and strains and buffeting every water-borne hull is constantly enduring.

Schooners in the coal trade, for instance, bringing coal form Charlotte (the port of Rochester) or Oswego, N.Y., to ports along the north shore of Lake Ontario, were generally loaded from trestles, the coal pouring throught their hatches from considerable height. This undoubtedly contributed to many casualties, particularly when crossing the lake in heavy fall gales.

Rigs

While differences of rig mean nothing to Landsmen they are easily understood. A ship has three masts, all square-rigged, with yards across. A brig has two masts, both square-rigged. A barque has two square-rigged masts, and a mizzenmast fore-and-aft rigged – its sails are hinged behind the mast, instead of crossing it. A brigantine has one square-rigged mast and one rigged fore-and-aft. A schooner is fore-and-aft rigged on all masts, although she may have some square sails too.

Lake schooners often had three masts. A few, mostly intended to tow, had four.

A sloop has only one mast, fore-and-aft rigged. There were many trading sloops on the lakes in the days of sail particularly in sheltered water like the Bay of Quinte.

Full-rigged ships fought yard-arm to yard-arm in the War of 1812, although that rig disappeared soon afterwards. The first lake sailing vessel, the *Frontenac*, 1687, antedating the better known *Griffon* of mysterious fate, was a schooner rig and the last surviving sailer of the Great Lakes, the *Lyman M. Davis*, was burnt as spectacle to attract people to Sunnyside Amusement park, Toronto in 1934.

Archives of Ontario

The *Lyman M. Davis*, built 1873, the last fully rigged working sailing schooner on the Great Lakes, burned as a spectacle at Sunnyside Beach, Toronto, in 1934.

Many of the barques and brigs in the *Dominion Registry* were really barquentines or three-masted schooners. A barquentine has three or more masts, and is completely square rigged on the foremast. The others are fore-and-aft.

The typical lake barque had fore-and-aft sails on all three masts, but on the foremast she would have an additional yard from which hung a square sail, and above that another yard with a square topsail, and above that again triangular raffees, either singly or in pairs.

The raffee was a characteristic sail of the Great Lakes, and was used on two-masted and three-masted schooners, which often had no other "square" canvas. It was a triangular sail, the peak or head of it hoisted on the topmast, the clews – outer corners – extended by a yard crossing the mast. Sometimes, the lower part of it dropped to a point or points below the yard. It was then called a "diamond raffee." A "single raffee" was a right-angled triangle on half of the yard. The "double raffee" was all in one piece but occupied both halves of the yard or yardarms. Two single raffees, set above the square topsail, on either yard-arm was known as "batwings."

Stonehookers

Special mention must be made about this unique type of vessel, so important to our heritage, and not known by this generation. It has been said that Toronto was built on Dundas Shale. Up until the invention of the cement block and the motor truck, this was essentially true. Dundas Shale was not the stone quarried from the Niagara Escarpment near the town of Dundas, but was the prevalent stone on the near shore bottom of Lake Ontario between Port Whitby and Oakville, and beyond.

During the nineteenth century and into the beginning of this century, stone was essential for the filling of wooden cribs in the construction of harbours, so important in the development of our trade on the lakes. But it was the cities, particularly Toronto, that needed stone for foundations (look at the foundations of most buildings built before 1910) and walls; flat stones for roads and sidewalks; cobblestones for pavements as well as crushed stones for sidewalks.

So came an early Canadian development: the stonehooker. Unique in navigation, and without duplication outside of Lake Ontario.

These were small vessels, usually about 20 to 100 tons burden, mostly scows with very little draft and schooner rigged. These scows were nearly all square ended, unlike the scows of Lake Erie which had V-shaped sterns, or the "Barrel bowed" Bay of Quinte scows. They were wide and shoal, and in light winds were very fast.

The Port Credit scows were designed so they could carry the whole load of stone on the deck, thus affording a great saving in the handling of the cargo. Take

Piersol Collection, Archives of Ontario

The *Maude S.*, a stonehooker out of Port Credit, with her scow that was used to lift stone off the bottom of the lake, alongside.

for instance the *Coronet* which was 53 feet long, 17-foot beam, and had a 4-foot deep hold. When light, and with the centreboard up, she only drew eighteen inches. She would store thirty tons of stone on the deck, but nothing in the hold save stone chips for ballast. She is reported to have sailed well in this trim although the load brought her to within eight inches of the water amidships but three or four feet at the bow and stern. The mainboom projected seventeen feet outboard (half its length).

The trade in stone came out of ports along the coast of Lake Ontario from Belleville to Bronte (Port Nelson and Wellington Square, in the olden days), but it was centred in Port Credit.

The stonehooker would usually anchor as close to the shore as possible and collect its cargo by sending a small, flat scow or barge onto which loads of stone were gathered, sometimes from the beach, but mostly from the lake bottom by using long rakes with prong like forks at right angle to the handle to locate and haul the stone. It was wet work. Men frequently had to wade in the water, prying loose the stone with crowbars, and then lifting the stone onto the barges or small scows. Some barges had hoists and "A" frames to help lift the stones. Many of

Archives of Ontario

The *Wavecrest* a "two-'n'-after," one of the more attractive, yacht-like schooners active on Lake Ontario during schooner days.

these barges or small scows would carry one-third of a toise (16 feet by 12 feet by 3 feet high, for a total of 216 cubic feet, in comparison, a bush cord of wood was four by four by sixteen feet, for a total of 128 cubic feet),.about three tons of stone. It would be about ten to forty scow loads to fill a stonehooker for a full cargo. Gravel was loaded the same way.

Taking the stone from the lake was so prolific that the Three Rod Law was passed – stonehookers were not allowed to take stone from within three perches (49 1\2 feet) of the shore or waters edge. Because of the Three Rod Law, many stonehookers did not put their hailing port on the stern to avoid detection from the shore.

The taking of stone off the Scarborough Highlands [Bluffs], which was close to the entrance to Toronto Harbour by way of the Eastern Gap, was so severe that those Highlands are now famous as the Scarborough Bluffs. Signs were posted in Toronto Harbour imploring skippers not to take stone from that area to prevent erosion. It is strange that in recent years city officials are replacing much of that stone to prevent further erosion.

Stone mostly sold for $5 a toise and three trips a week at two toise a trip was considered good for a two-man crew.

The extent of the stonehooking trade be can envisioned when you consider that in the year 1903 Toronto Harbour port officials registered over one thousand stonehooker loads of stone.

Registration

Prior to 1874, Canadian vessels received British registry at Montreal. There were some registers prior to the *Dominion Register* First Annual List in the Department of Marine at Ottawa in 1874. One of the oldest being the *Thomas Register of Canadian and American Shipping on the Great Lakes and River St. Lawrence*, published in 1864. Snider, in his 1,303 "Schooner Days" articles made frequent reference to those registers, and to the many port records that are still available.

He was able to determine that in 1874 the *Dominion Register* credited Ontario with 20 barques, 2 brigs, 4 barquantines, 5 brigantines, 313 schooners and 211 steamers; in all 815 vessels, 604 of them sailing vessels. It would be within the mark to increase these figures by at least 50 percent to account for the large number of Ontario vessels registered in Montreal prior to 1874, and the even larger number of vessels that were never registered at all, in spite of threats and penalties.

Besides forty-seven schooners, two sloops, one yacht and nineteen steamers, Toronto registered one barque and one brigantine. Incompleteness of the Dominion registration is emphasized by the "one yacht" in the returns. This was the George Gooderham yacht *Oriole*. In fact, many yachts were owned in Toronto at the time, but only one was registered. This can be said of many small craft of commerce.

Archives of Ontario

A "two-'n'-after" schooner showing two single raffees set as batwings.

The *Thomas Register* of 1864 accounts for 681 sailing vessels on the lakes at that time. Of these, 424 were schooners, 157 barquentines, 81 brigantines, 17 sloops, 1 barque and 1 brig, for all sorts of rigs flourished on the lakes in those days.

The Fore-'n'-After

Oh sailor on the steamer,
With the comforts of a landsman,
Did you ever vision those who broke the trail?
Men who braved the foulest weather
While the hooker held together,
Or sailed a race with death before a gale?
With your more than ample free-board,
And your horse-power in the thousands,
You can laugh at storms that used to take their toll
Of the little fore-'n'-afters
With their fearless crews and masters
And a cargo far too heavy in the hold.

From Duluth to Kingston City
With a foot or so of free-board
They'd take a chance like Vikings of the past;
Give their best and trust their Maker,
Where their owners willed they'd take her,
Doughty skippers, and stout hearts before the mast.

They are gone, yes gone forever,
And the rugged roads they travelled,
But the wakes they left behind will never fade:
Not a port that didn't know 'em,
As up and down the lakes they plied their trade.

Now the lakes are just a highway
For the plodding bluff bowed freighters,
Run on schedule from the day they leave the ways;
Though now steel and steam is master
Still my love's the fore-'n'-after,
And the glamour of the old wind jammer days.

S.A. Clarke

Snider commented on this poem in his column:

This poem was read by Rev. P.F. Garner at the mariner's service, Cherry Valley, Sunday, April 19, 1936.

They were written by S.A. Clarke, of Toronto, an old Prince Edward County boy, with a particularly soft spot in his heart for Milford and Black Creek.

His own title for them was "Windjammers," but we have taken the liberty of changing it for this reason: "Windjammer" has been worked to death by landsmen and pulp magazines writers who wouldn't know a sailing vessel if they saw one outside a motion picture theatre, and Mr. Clark knows his schooners, the fore-and-afters of his love, from the truck to keel, and gudgeon strap to stemhead.

In strict practice, on the lakes, we used to confine the term to two-masted schooners only, but that was just our little way of having fun with the greenhorns who wanted to know what was a four-master. We called "three-'n'-afters" for their further bewilderment. As a mater of fact fore-and-after describes accurately any vessel with fore-and-aft sails, no matter how many masts she had, nor how few; and so it embraces comprehensively the thousand sails of schooner whose gleaming wings once surrounded Prince Edward County like flock of grown-up gulls. It is the grown-ups in the gull families who wear white.

August 5, 1950
Whatchacallit

How do you pronounce forecastle? Take a good look before you open your mouth. Once I took a university professor down into a lake schooner, and after a five minute survey he pronounced the word distinctly thus: "I think if you don't mind I'd like to have a look around the deck – immediately." He meant putrid.

That was merely begging off. But if you are a sailor at sea you might say "folksel." On the lakes you might get by with "forksel." In either place you would be tabbed as a greenhorn, or what was worse, a dude, if you said "fore castle." The Lunenburgers, who have a language of their own, say "fawksel" just as they say "fawsel" for foresail and "nothe" for north.

Yet fore castle – two words – was exactly how the thing began; a square platform with wooden walls, shield high, built up on the lofty stemhead of the Viking ships, where the archers shot their arrows and hurled their javelins, stinkpots, and fireballs into the lower waists of their enemies. The platform at the other end of the ship was the after castle.

When both came down in the marine world, the after one was the quarterdeck and the forward one the forecastle head, under which the seamen slept, when they could.

Modern forecastles are of course steel apartments almost anywhere in the ship except the jailshaft tunnel. They can be and ought to be electric lighted, steam heated, air conditioned, chromium plumbed with plenty of toilets, and hot and cold showers. I would like to hold forth briefly, however on schooner forecastles I have known.

My best was the *Oliver Mowat*'s, the three-masted schooner sailed by the late Capt. James Peacock of Port Hope.

"Take the top bunk forward on the port side," said James when I signed on at Oswego.

Forward of the foremast was a square doghouse with a two-leaved door and a sliding top; and the fore scuttle – a big one at forty inches wide. Outside it was painted buff, with pale blue trim. With the double door hooked back and the slide pushed over, the sun streamed down to a yellow-painted floor, eight feet below. The inside walls of the scuttle were painted white and reflected light.

Two long chests, or lidded boxes, on the floor, painted light buff, made good seats, and they were also beds – for a couple of tons of chain cable. The chains, flaked down in long lengths in these lockers, led up through the deck to the windlass barrel and after several turns around it out the hawsepipes and back again to the rings of the anchors, bedded inboard from the catheads. The forecastle was walled with four bunks on each side, two and two, one above the other, the lower ones at the level of the chain lockers.

In the blunt V of the bows and forward of these bunk rows, was the fore peak, where were stowed the lanterns and pieces of spare gear.

The eight bunks were shelves of inch board faced with ledges of a foot deep, required to keep the straw mattresses and their occupants from spilling to the floor when the vessel rolled.

The mattresses were of blue and white ticking, well-stuffed, and one patch quilt and a pillow covered with ticking, was on each of the four bunks used. The spares were filled with coils of rope, spare block and gear.

The paulpost, a central pillar coming up from the keelson, was not concerned with bunks and bed. Above deck it was a lodgment for the heel of the bowsprit on its forward side and aft for the hinged paul which kept the windlass-barrel from backing up.

All the interior woodwork was painted either buff or white or pale blue. A tiny lamp was screwed to the after side of the paulpost, but not needed by day.

On the floor, at the foot of the paulpost, was a pot-bellied little Quebec heater, which could burn anything but ice-cubes. Its tummy was bare, for it got red hot on the least provocation, but all the rest of it was, *mirabile dictu*, varnished black. it was the only polished forecastle stove in captivity. In front of the stove was a square box with flared sides, filled with sawdust, the spit kit, height of Pullman luxury in a laker.

"And see," said red-moustached Tom Paddington, "that you hit it first shot every time, young fellow, for the man who misses has to clean up."

The *Mowat*'s forecastle was the non-pareil of schooner days. Jim Peacock was a clean man, inside and out, and he kept his vessel that way. He made a fortune out of her, where owners who begrudged the price of a paint brush or laundry soap went broke by their own miserliness.

My worst forecastle I shall not name. It was typical of some out of nineteen in lake sailing days, the combined product of owner's niggardliness, master's indifference, and sailor's laziness. They called it the boar pen, and it was.

It was so dark that you could not see into it by day or night without a lantern. The tin lamp on it's paulpost has burned till the oil gave out, without ever having illuminated anything. Its wick was short and rusty and eked out with a strip of torn canvas. Its burner was foul and its chimney was black with soot.

If you swung the lantern like a switchman at a siding you would discover that the wretched hole had never been painted. The wood that went into it was fresh from the plane, or the adze, and was darkened and stained with coaldust, soot, graindust, and iron ore. It was stained with spray and rain through the open scuttle, the sweat of an unventilated enclosure, and the seepage of the five Great Lakes through deck and sides, and the return of bilgewater from the pumps which could not escape through the scuppers.

The bunks were filled with mouldy straw, pounded into a mat by countless uneasy slumbers, and covered with sacks and mildewed bedding.

The stove was a raw red rusted shell of oft-burned iron. The place was alive with bedbugs, and if a bucket of water was spilled on the filthy floor the swung lantern would reveal an insect drama of the Johnstown flood. Rat holes plugged with the broken necks of whiskey bottles served as scuppers.

The slimy bunks were jackknifed with initials and the obscene pictographs then common in the water-closets of country schools. The place stank of burnt-out lamps, bilgewater, nicotine and mustiness. Every corner had its bottle of cure-alls for diseases of men.

Old Capt. W.D. Graham of St. Catharines, who died recently in his nineties, told me that when he was a horseboy in a timber drogher he used to sleep with the horses on deck, rather than in the forecastle.

It was a good tip, but we had no horsebox.

The captain of this other vessel was a decent, silent man of Mohawk blood. He confided in me: "That hellhole forward's too good for them that make it what it is. Some day I'll throw a lighted lantern down there and burn the damn thing out."

His owners did collect fire insurance.

Thank goodness we never had to eat in the forecastle. Lake sailors always dined where the captain and mate dined, at the cabin table and of the same food. The cabin was always clean, or the cook walked the plank.

Snider Collection, Marine Museum of the Great Lakes, Kingston

Typical crew in schooner days. Note the captain with his shirt, vest, and gold watch chain.

April 4, 1942

Fitting-Out Time Fifty Years Ago

The Esplanade was a river of black mud over the boot traps at this time over fifty years ago, but a grand place for all that, in the silver sunshine of April with the pussy willows peeping.

The brave winds that come 'round May 24 were needed to make the muck fordable on foot, but the coal carts could cross it, and kids could hook on behind or hunt for where workmen had raided a car of cedar ties and laid them down for a floating bridge.

The Esplanade, with its lofty name and lowly use, was a wide trackway – officially called Esplanade Street East and Esplanade Street West – that curved along the last line of the beach of Toronto Bay. It had houses, hotels, factories, stable, and railway stations on one side of it; the north, with a wooden sidewalk, and on the other side a web of railway tracks, with no sidewalk, a cinderpath and coal yards and lumber yards, stone yards, boathouses, warehouses, grain elevators, aquatic clubs, basins, slips and wharves. What we called the docks.

Down along the docks was Heaven at this time of the year – or any other time but winter – though the angels were red-nosed bums black-snaking in the sunshine over a community quart from the bars on the north side of the street, or Maggie and Martin, grimy old children of God who lived by picking up coal and bits of wood and railroad iron, or sooty coalheavers, who worked in their bare skins even in April in the dusty holds.

And there were the sailors – steamboat deck hands, looked down upon although they had not sunk to the present-day enormity of wearing gloves – and "real sailors," schooner men from South Bay and the St. Lawrence to the Highlands or Flamborough Head. They were very red of face and long of moustache, and whether home-born or foreigners from Hamilton, Kingston, or the south shore, yea, even Above, they regarded our city with reverence. It was a big place. More'n a hundred thousan' they would say with the judicious air of afar travelled men.

"Above" was the Upper Lakes, "below" the Bay of Quinte east.

From Yonge Street eastward was the best of the waterfront. In the Yonge Street slip the old *Trade Wind* of Whitby would have wintered with the new *Rapid City* of Toronto, an excellent waterfront jest. The *Rapid City* was called after some settlement on the prairies out west, then as little known as Malaysia.

Out West was where we had the North-West Rebellion five years before, but Fort Garry, Fish Creek, Cut Knife, and Batoche were the only landmarks. There was talk of Winnipeg, and a place called Vancouver, but it was doubtful whether that was a town, an island, a strait, or just a name.

Around the corner of Yonge Street the ugly *Laura of Windsor* would be fitting out, a "contrack-built" vessel which was held against her as a bad mark. She was one of the Matthew's fleet, ever painted green above, with red lead below ever fading from submersion, and her name and line name in yellow letters on her quarter.

The sainted *John Wesley*, much littler but no less ugly, a survivor from Mackenzie Rebellion times had been a winter neighbour of the *Laura*'s, but fitted out ahead of her.

Seventeen or eighteen schooners would winter in Toronto, and a dozen passenger steamers and propellers, with part of the ferry fleet. The "big boats," the "palace steamers," of the old Doty fleet and Toronto Ferry Co. (these were the *Primrose* and the *Mayflower*), were too precious to risk in the bay ice and usually wintered with others of the ferry fleet up at Oakville, where Commodore Bob Williams had his home. Ferries ran from Brock Street to the foot of Spadina Avenue, from York Street less often, from Yonge Street, also seldom. From Church Street they ran frequently, and from Parliament Street and the Don. They had funnels which would lower, to let them under the bridges.

The Church Street slip, now buried under a railway viaduct, was the hub of the waterfront. Hence six ferries – the *Arlington*, *John Hanlan*, *Luella*, (even then ancient), *Jessie L. McEdwards*, *Gertrude*, *Truant*, ran regularly for Ward's Island, Island Park, and the Wiman Baths. Brock Street had the *Mascotte*, with her ploughshare bow, the *Sadie* and *Canadian*, with guest artists from Church Street as required.

How the ferries made their landings in the Church Street slip, which was not wider than Church Street itself – sixty-six feet – was a springtime miracle, for then the slip would be already occupied by the *Shickluna*, a green mountain of a propeller, the *James G. Worts*, a three-masted schooner with the deepest hold in Toronto, the big *St. Louis*, with three square sails and two batwings on her foremast, and the excursion steamer *Eurydie*, whose name, of course, was Your-A-Dice, even to Sunday School scholars who did not know the singular number of those spotted cubes used in games of chance.

All these belonged to the Sylvester brothers, retired lake captains who had the wharf and warehouse on the east side of the slip, and did a big business in importing block stone and unloading it with a three horsepower derrick. This was also used for lifting out masts or hoisting in boilers. Their warehouse handled grain, bailed hay, and pressed straw. Their vessels traded everywhere from the head of the lakes to Halifax. Often Toronto would never see them again, after the elabourate spring fitout, until December's ice would freeze them in the bay, and they would be unloading their western wheat into sleighs for the Gooderham Elevator at the east end of the bay.

Fifty years ago last Sunday the stonehooker *White Oak* pushed her square nose through the muddy waters of the Western Gap and opened navigation for 1892 in Toronto Harbour.

The traditional ceremony of awarding the harbourmaster's hat was performed with dexterity and promptitude. Dally Peer of Port Credit, master and owner of the good ship *White Oak*, walked into old Captain Hall's office with fifteen cents in one pocket for harbour dues on three toise of stone for the new cribs for the Eastern Gap. He walked out with three dollar bills in his other pocket in lieu of the "best hat money could buy," a better hat than any stonehooker man could wear.

There were exaggerated reports of a silk "plug" costing as much as $7 "in the States," but that was set down as either traveller's tales or an example of the wickedness of Chicago or the luxury of the *Prince of Wales*.

The Gay Nineties were no gayer than that in Toronto for us who were there.

They were mainly hot in summer, cold in winter, hungry all the time, and happier than now.

The summers were hot because God made them so and man had not yet made electric fans and frigidaires.

The winters were cold because we knew nothing about oil fuel, apartments or insulation, and heated our draughty-halled, high ceilinged houses with reluctant self-feeders and base burners and cast-iron stoves that burned hardwood "cut and split, $4 a cord" with great voracity.

Outside we defended ourselves with fur caps, woollen mitts and overshoes. We were just getting over putting the street cars on sleighs for the winter and heating them with a stingy allowance of peastraw on the floor.

We were hungry because we hadn't heard of vitamins, proteins, and calories, and couldn't buy them if we had, even at the rankly extravagant "corporation" wage rate of 15¢ an hour – which was a sin and a shame, we were told, when plenty of good men were hunting jobs at $1 a day and the work day only began at six in the morning and ended at six at night.

No, the nineties were not so gay in the beginning, when there was talk of war with Portugal and the McKinley bill killed our barley trade, and the great Sir John A. died and left us looking for prosperity from his NP [the National Policy, Macdonald's policy of high tariffs to protect Canadian manufacturers].

The unemployed – there were no reliefees yet hatched – carried the black flag along Front Street in mid-winter and were mollified with a handout of loaves of bread from the old *News* office on Yonge Street and promises at the City Hall of work at laying cedar-block pavements next summer.

The House of Industry, House of Providence, Salvation Army, and a swarm of missions were relief – and the jail. Governor Greene and the Don flats put many a down-and-outer on his feet and kept him there.

Toronto, with 150,000 inhabitants, was in the debris of a busted real-estate boom at the beginning of the decade, and groaned under a tax rate of sixteen mills on the dollar in the middle of it. Beer cost 5¢ a glass, dispensed at a couple of hundred bars and speakeasies.

We saved and saved. The Spanish caravels came to visit us and some of us followed them to the World's Fair at Chicago in 1893, though it cost a king's ransom, $33 return railway fare, and a dollar to get in. And we saved and saved and bought bicycles when they came out, the newfangled safeties, with both wheels the same size, and hard rubber tires that got thicker and softer and hollow as the nineties got gayer in the second half.

The war with Portugal didn't come off, neither did the attempt to coerce Manitoba, the country got the Grits instead of the Tories, the Growing Time moved its head above the horizon, the Full Dinner Pail, and Simcoe and Jarvis Streets – the first asphalted, shone with twinkling handlebars night and morning and noontide.

Bicycle suits, costing $2.50 to $25 and looking better than 1942 war tailoring is likely to look, staved off the high cost of living – temporarily – for males. Everybody wore them to business, whether he came on a wheel or a street car or the first newfangled horseless carriage. Bloomers and divided skirts never made near the same hit, for males or females, but "fibre chamois," to help sleeves puff and skirts flare was a feminine compensation coupled with shirtwaists and high-starched collars, changed every day by the best-dressed ladies.

Muscle men or day labourers continued to wear grey flannel shirts with no collars at all, but the white collar class was rising.

Men making "good money of up to $1,000 a year" – reluctantly passed from paper collars, 15¢ a box of twelve, to celluloid and white rubber – 15¢ apiece, but washable and outlasting linen ones which cost only 5¢ but had to be laundered.

Deficits on the Toronto Exhibition dwindled until surpluses became possible and the country had enough money to make a respectable splash at good Queen Victoria's Diamond Jubilee and "Oom Paul" Kruger's funeral, being the South African [Boer] War, after we had a rather boring preview of a phony war between the United States and Spain.

November 1, 1941
Seagoing Teamsters

Navy stuff was in the kid. His mother was the daughter of an officer in the old square-rigged chequer-sided wooden walls which were *Britannia*'s bulwark, and he had been brought up in Oaklands, the family home between Corunna and Mooretown on the St. Clair River, his childhood flavoured with daily spectacles of great fleets of schooners, in tow or under sail, swimming past shores where tales of the Peninsular War and Trafalgar mingles with the latest reports of the Fenian Raid. He wanted to be a sailor, no tea-kettle tickler, sailor of the sail.

Through judicious political connections he was found a berth in a grocery store in Ottawa. He tried dutifully, for he was an obedient youngster, and found it quite impossible to grow up to be a big butter-and-egg man.

"I'm going to be a sailor," he told his employer.

"You're going to hell," the latter made reply.

Came home, and got a job boring fastenings in Archibald Muir's Port Huron shipyard – an offshoot of the Port Dalhousie yard and dry dock – where they were building the steamer *W.K. Vanderbilt*. A long way from being a sailor, yet, but it was on the road.

Bearded Archie Muir, a fine sailor himself, was sympathetic to the teenage youngster. He told him the brand new schooner *Albatross*, built by his brother Alexander at Port Dalhousie, was upward bound on her maiden voyage, to Bay City, Mich., for timber. She would stop at Port Huron on her way down for a pair of masts for the next of the great "A" fleet of the Muirs, the *Antelope*, whose keel had been laid at Port Dalhousie.

In course of time the *Albatross* alighted, swimming deep with squared oak logs piled as high as the top of the bulwarks. The laddie was told to go home across the river for his clothes. A berth in her was his, on July 11, 1871.

"I'm going to be a sailor," he gleefully told the ferryman as he crossed back from Sarnia.

"You'll only be sorry for it once," said the ferry captain, "and that will be all your life."

It looked as though he was right. The well-bred mannerly boy, small but strong for his sixteen years, and knowing enough about sailing already to shift a gafftopsail sheet or steer a trick, had come to a hard school. Timber-droughing was looked down upon in the old days: the vessels were clumsy boxes, all burthen and no beauty, their crews big brawn and little brains, navies afloat, bossed by foremen and section-bosses masquerading as captains and mates. Some were better and some worse. The Muir brothers, when they sailed the vessels they built, were good seamen and of good stock. If heavy-handed and tightfisted, they were fair and just to all men and generous according to their opportunities. But when they went into the dockyard and timber business they had to take the captains and crews they could get for the wages they could pay. Some of the gangs they got were hard bargains indeed.

The kid was hired as a horseboy, at $12 a month. The *Albatross*, like other timber-droughers, had a team of horses, stabled on deck, forward of the foremast. Their stabling consisted of a manger and a pair of blankets to shelter them from the rain and the spray. They slept standing up and had good sea legs. The horseboy had to feed, water, and groom them, and drive them around the great horse-power capstan when the sticks of oak, weighing tons, were being quilled up and hoisted in, for stowage in the hold and on deck, or for skidding overboard when unloading. He also had to lead the horses on the towpath when they were canalling. He was a seagoing teamster, but on top of that he was slavey messenger and choreboy to men, some of whom called the place where they kennelled, the boarpen, but would have been kicked out of a sty by any self-respecting he-pig.

Aft in the square deck cabin berthed the captain, two mates and cook. All got their meals and a midnight lunch, from the same long dining room table.

The crew lived in the forecastle, sleeping in six bunks, narrow shelves against either bow of the *Albatross*, dark and airless. The shelves had fiddles or weather boards, to keep the straw mattresses from rolling out into the floor.

The horseboy had to sleep on a straw tick laid on a couple of planks stretched across the chainlockers, which formed the seats of the forecastle. They were behind the paulpost, and the dripping anchor cables coming down through the deck hawsepipes, kept his bed damp.

Daylight never entered the pen. The "toilet" was simplicity itself, the lake for a bathtub, a bucket for a hand-basin, and for anything else the wide open spaces of the bowsprit shrouds and jib boom guys, used by all hands in all weathers, with all the privacy of seagulls.

At any hour – day or night – the horseboy would be routed from his sleep and given the work the sailors of the watch should be doing. If the drogher had a royal – some of them had, perched at the tip of the foremast like a pillbox cap – the horseboy would be sent aloft, to set or furl it, half a dozen times in a night. In making or trimming sail he had to hold slack, pull with the rest and coil up after them. If he dozed off from sheer weariness he was roused with the toe of a sea-boot.

Bucko Brennan bent a line to the bale of a bucket with a granny's knot, and hove it overboard. When the strain came on the knot the bucket floated away. It was a calm day and the *Albatross* was standing still, admiring her own wooden image in the smooth water. "Jump overboard and get that bucket," the gigantic timberman bawled to the horseboy.

The kid hesitated and the hero hailed: "Jump over before it drifts astern or I'll throw you overboard."

The lad could swim, and he saw that Bucko meant business. He kicked off his shoes, slipped out of his shirt and trousers, and dove off from the deckload. He caught up with the bucket in a few strokes, but could not well tow it, full of water, so he made it fast to the end of the line which was trailing alongside. His knot held – he knew most of the bends and hitches before he went to the grocery store – and Bucko hauled up the bucket and threw him back the line. He tried to haul himself up by it, but it is one thing to take a ten-foot dive from a solid platform, and another to make a ten-foot soar from the water. It just can't be done; and even holding on to the line with both hands he could not get enough grip on the slabsided timber-drougher with his toes to climb aboard; and he was too weak to haul himself up hand over hand. All he could do was to throw a bowline in the loose end of the line and hang on, calling to the bully to haul him up.

"If you wait till I haul you up you'll hang on there till you drown," answered the brave Bucko.

Then the boy heard a smack ringing above the gurgling of the lake in his ears, and the rope tightened and up he rose out of the water without effort. He was pulled, naked as a fish, over the rail by the schooner's cook, a red-headed virago with arms like the oak timbers of the deckload. She was a sister of one of the crew. Most of the drougher cooks were women. Bucko was gasping with five red stripes across his face where she had smacked him with the open hand. "Don't mind your bare pelt my boy, I've childer of my own," said she, "and that's more than a mule like that Bucko will ever have."

The *Albatross* was a fine, stout vessel, well-built by a good firm of owners, the Muirs, and meant to be a credit to her calling. In spite of her box-like model she was heavily rigged, with four jibs, two gafftopsails, foresail, and a mainsail, and she had a yard across the foremast, with a square sail and raffee as well. All this was to "make time," for time was money. When she reached the Welland Canal her two deck horses were reinforced by four others – the Muirs had their own stable of canal horses – and the six steeds snaked her down the long levels and the twenty-six locks which then formed stairsteps from Lake Erie to Lake Ontario. It takes eight hours to pass the Welland Canal now. Forty-eight hours was a good passage then, and sometimes it took a week.

Rightly named the "raging canal," the Welland gave our boy worse shocks than the *Albatross* had already administered.

The day they arrived in Port Colborne a woman whose husband had been drowned threw herself into the harbour, a man fell from aloft in a nearby vessel and was picked up in pieces, and two Swedes failed to maintain a neutrality pact which existed on board, and jumping out on the dock, went at each other with unsheathed knives.

It blew so hard going down the canal that sometimes a vessel would "take charge" going around a bend and, pitting her thousand tons of weight and windage against the six horsepower on the towpath, would pull the three teams and the horseboys into the canal. To avoid that, the canaller would be moored to the bank to "ride out the gale"

The banks were lined with slippery, muddy towpaths, along which horses, mules, horseboys, and helpers and crews dragged their lines, slipped, swore, fought and disentangled themselves and their vessels as best they could. Timber droughers like the 138-foot *Albatross*, were tight fits for the locks of the "old" canal. Their jib booms had to be run in and topped up, their yards cockbilled, their yawlboats got inboard or overboard, and their taffrail davits and catheads capsized. Even so, ten feet draught and twenty-two foot beam had to be hove through with the capstan, before the canal was entered.

Having survived the canal, the *Albatross* and our hero tackled Lake Ontario and reached Garden Island, opposite Kingston, where the Calvins had their great enterprise. The squared timber was here hoisted out and formed into rafts for Quebec.

This was the round of the *Albatross* all that season – Garden Island to unload, then up Lake Ontario, the canal and Lake Erie, again to Pigeon Bay near Kingsville for another load, and then down to Kingston to unload. It was tough, but it could not kill the ambition of the little lad to be a sailor. That, however, was deferred for a more urgent ambition – to grow heavy enough and strong enough to give his captain the licking of his life.

Yet the same little captain – Charley Staley was his name – had his good points. He felt he was doing the best he could with what the devil sent him and he spared neither himself nor anybody else. He navigated the vessel, hired the crew, paid the bills, managed the ship's business and "worked lumber" in the hold like any stevedore. He always took the starboard side against the first mate's, hustling his watch so as to get the vessel listed with the weight of the incoming timber, so as to make the mate's port side higher and harder to load. He was the "big shot." And he got big pay, $60 per month while the season lasted – eight months at most.

The timber was loaded at anchor, as weather permitted. The oak sticks were floated out to the open sternports, hinged near the deck and hanging down to within a few feet of the schooner's light waterline. Quill-falls, depending from the timber-davits or quills in the schooner's taffrail, were hooked into the chains around the ends of the sticks, and the dripping watersoaked timber was quilled by horses turning the big oak post which was the cylinder or drum of the timber capstan.

It had scores in it to take two messengers, or hailing lines, at once. The horseboy both drove the horses and held the slack, or free ends of the messengers, as the drum wound them in. He had both hands full and was helpless until relieved, if the turns began to slip or anything else went wrong.

The timber entered the hold through the sternports, sliding down brows and persuaded into position in the wings, or sides of the ship, by breasters, short iron bars with one end chisel-edged and the other sharpened into a spike. The spike was stuck into the ceiling or inner lining of the hold, and the chisel end into the stick. The angle trained the timber into its required place, with the aid of canthooks, peavies, rollers, mauls, wedges, and much hard swearing. Men sometimes had their feet crushed under the bit of the square-edged sticks or the slipping of hooks and breasters.

When the vessel was loaded to her port sills, the ports were closed and caulked. Further loading went on through her upper ports, in the taffrail, above the deck, or over the side.

In the fall it was too cold and blew too hard to load lumber on the open shore. The portholes, brows, and skidways of the booms of timber themselves might get frozen up, or go adrift in the hard northerly winds. So the *Albatross* was swept clean of chips and slivers and sawdust and started for Chicago for her share of the gold of the west – a grain cargo. Her new sister, the *Antelope*, once got 27¢ a bushel, a $6,000 freight, for one cargo from Chicago to Kingston – one-third of her whole cost to build.

The *Albatross* started for Chicago. Upward bound in the Welland Canal, there came aboard an Upper Lakes sailor who had stopped off to visit relatives at Port Colborne and wished to work his way home. He was a big man, and a revelation to our abused but unbroken kid. He was groomed and dressed like a prince, broad-brimmed wide-awake hat, blue broadcloth coat, velvet vest, doeskin trousers, fine white shirt without collar or cravat, and shining leather boots, knee-high, with decorated panels of blue leather at the tops. A typical self-respecting and successful long-voyager of the Great Lakes in the 1870s, and as great a contrast to the rag-a-muffin canal jumpers and tough guys of the timber trade as a Mountie to a scarecrow. He carried two beautiful hand-sewn leather bags. When he emptied them in the forecastle he folded up his visiting clothes, packed them neatly, and emerged decently dressed in blue derry smock and overalls, and ready for the hardest job mate or captain could set. And he left hanging handy as good an outfit of oilskins and seaboots as ever caught a cod-fish.

He carried himself with such assurance from the moment he threw his bags over the rail that all the petty bullies of the *Albatross* treated him with respect, recognizing a "big-vessel man" from "up above." He spent his seasons in the large carriers of the Upper Lakes at good wages, and retired each fall for a snug winter at home in the west. Pat Canary was his name.

As they towed out from Port Colborne no one worked harder than Pat at the long job of refitting after canalling and getting the *Albatross'* ten pieces of canvas set and drawing. When this was done the crowd sat themselves down on the forehatch and mopped their brows. They left to the unfortunate horseboy the endless task of coiling down and stowing the miles of rope which had descended to the deck as the mighty sails rose. "And be damn quick about it," Bucko Brennan added.

But Pat Canary had not sat down. He went on flaking the halliards faster than the kid had ever seen them coiled before.

"Why leave it all to the boy?" demanded Pat, "He's worked hard as any of us and I'll bet he's just as tired. Let's all lend a hand."

"Aw, he's paid for that," growled Bucko. "He'll do it or get the toe of the boot."

"It's the toe of my boot will be ticklin' you first," said Pat, cheerfully, hanging another coil on the belaying pin.

The droughermen shamefacedly got off the hatch and went to work.

It was thick weather most of the way up the lakes, and when they got into Lake Michigan the smoke covered the sun by day. Off Milwaukee a tug came panting out, adding her wood smoke to the pall.

"Chicago's on fire and burning to the ground!" hailed her skipper. "I've a wire for you to load in Milwaukee, and I'm to tow you in."

So the *Albatross* put into Milwaukee, and every bridge they towed through someone hailed Pat Canary – "hiya, Pat, how the blank d'ye get in a packet like that? How's all in the east? D'ye know Chicago's burned down?"

He was manifestly a great power where he went. He introduced the kid to wieners and sauerkraut and pretzels and Pabst beer – in judicious quantities, but innumerable places, ashore.

Everywhere he was popular and would be told "you're money's no good here, Pat, you know that!"

And he would pay the shot and leave a quarter for the barman.

"Pat," asked the kid, "why can't I ship in one of these fine big vessels up here?"

"B'y," said Pat, "Them vessels is big and heavy rigged and they drive'em like express trains. They're too heavy for a lad of yor years, and they don't send b'ys to do men's work in 'em. Get some more beef on your bones, and in a year or two mebbe you can get a site in wan. Ye're a good lad, and you'll go far, but don't bite off more than ye can chew."

The *Albatross* loaded scupper deep in Milwaukee, and left Pat there, and sailed for Kingston. Pat's approval of the kid had raised his standing on board. Bucko Brennan ceased to persecute him, and the little captain showed himself somewhat kind. When they were coming down the river St. Clair he said: "We'll pay off in Kingston, but what you'll earn from now till then won't pay your way home to Sarnia. If you like I'll drop you off at Port Huron as we pass, and you can ride across in the ferry and be home a week earlier."

So the kid left timber-droughing – for good. He sailed in many schooners, more happily for the next seven years. Realized that the despised steamkettles had come to stay, got a steamer of his own to command. Many steamers. On his first trip to Chicago he sought Pat Canary. Found him – moored ashore, proprietor of a prosperous bar; and prosperous bars were prosperous in the newly risen Queen of the west.

Now the kid is a brisk young business man of 86 in wholesale hardware in Hamilton. Arrives at the office at nine, leaves at five.

His name? Capt. James W. Baby; same family as came to America with La Salle and left their name on both sides of the Detroit frontier and on Baby Point in Toronto.

His son Stanley Baby, of Toronto, told his father's beginning in sailing to the Shellbacks Club this week, very modestly and very well. It was a fine tribute to a graduate of the old school of the lakes.

January 30, 1943
Making Hay in December

The narrator is the late J.J. O'Connor of Port Arthur, District Magistrate for Thunder Bay, and the time ten years or so ago. He puffed blue rings from a good cigar as he spoke and looked out across the gleaming drifts of new-fallen snow.

"On a fine bright early December day, 1873 or 1874, just after dinner, when a sailor's belt is at the stretch, and he feels that independence which fills him with power beyond anything during the twenty-four hours, I was one of the crew of the brigantine *Fleur-de-Marie*, a French vessel then engaged in the lake trade.

"The *Fleur-de-Marie* was not built in France but at Lanorale, on the St. Lawrence, in 1853. She had black topsides and scarlet petticoat; hemp-rigged, with thick shrouds and stays or tarred roped instead of steel wire, and four yards crossing her foremast, her forward sail-plan culminating in a royal. She had the old style single topsail, which hoisted up on its yard to the top-gallant cross trees, and had to be reefed to be reduced in area. She only measured 156 tons register, and was less than 100 feet long on deck, but with her square rig was quite a handful for a crew of four men forward, captain, two mates and cook aft. Capt. Robert Kent, of Port Whitby, my home port, brought her when she was new, and traded out of Whitby harbour in her for years.

"We were lying at the old Hamilton wharf in Toronto, near the foot of Church Street, and had just finished loading a cargo of wheat for Ogdensburg down the St. Lawrence, at a freight rate of 1 1\2¢ gold.

"American money was then at a discount of 16 percent, and had to pay in gold or its equivalent. It was not an uncommon thing for captains who sailed their own vessels to come home with baking powder tins from the cook's galley filled with gold half-eagles, eagles, and doubles.

"As we had ten thousand bushels under the hatches, this cash freight of $1,250 looked good compared with our own $2.50 a day, which is what we were getting as 'big money' for the fall of the year. In the summer able-bodied seamen worked for $1 a day or $25 a month and often for less. Even in the timber trade and the stave carrying, two of the hardest rackets lake sailors ever had to stand, wages of $14 to $16 a month was common pay seventy years ago.

"After due consideration, I being the youngest pup of the lot and still in my teens, was deputed to meet the captain, my fellow townsmen, and demand an increase of pay to $4 a day.

"On my way aft to where the Old Man smoked in state in the cabin I got out on the snow-covered wharf and walked up and down, rehearsing my speech, hoping to get my courage up, and backing and filling all the time.

"Suddenly my mind was made up for me. The first mate, a typical one of his order, rough and tough, came out on deck and bawled to let go the springline, which led from amidships diagonally across the wharf, and was, like everything else, thickly crusted with snow.

"It flashed on me that it was now or never. If I let go that snow-clad line the next order would be to strike the fly for the tug and lay aloft and cast off the gaskets of the fore topsail; and we would be bound away on a voyage at $2.50 a day from which there would be no chance of change.

"'I've got to see the Old Man before I do another hand's turn,' said I, as gruffly as I could in my boy's bass. 'We may be quitting this hooker.'

"Mr. Mate let go expletives and other kinds of things about d--- sailors and the general weaknesses and wickedness of their kind. But being imbued with the importance of my mission, I proceeded to the seat of the mighty in the smoke-filled cabin and presented – as well as I could – our modest demand.

"The Old Man glared at me, and with the power that was his, as master of the vessel, proceeded to explain to me just what he thought of us as a miserable crew that did not know when we were well-off and added that we were now getting more than we were worth, which was very likely the fact.

"I insisted that all before-the-mast had decided to quit unless we were granted the advance. The fact that it was late in the season, a good freight was in his hold and the brigantine was ready to sail and, being old, had difficulty in shipping hands for late voyages, had more to do, I am sure, than my feeble arguments. He finally sent me forward agreeing to pay us $4 per day, accompanied by language more flowery than the ship's name, with particular application to myself, my forebears and descendants, to many generations. All of which appeared to do him good.

"I came out of the cabin and on deck to meet another explosion from the mate, who still had his mind on the spring line, and again, with many encouraging epithets, ordered me out to let go the snow covered rope.

"This I now did with alacrity, and in my best form as a sailor who was being duly compensated for his highly technical efforts.

My report forward immediately afterwards was so satisfactory that everyone, including the captain and mates, were forthwith in good humor.

"We got away with a tug, towed out through the Western gap, and went spinning down the lake in a spanking nor'wester, spitting snow. We arrived off Kingston in about 16 hours, flying a pilot flag for the river, and with little delay made our destination at Ogdensburg, N.Y. The *Fleur-de-Marie* returned up the river with an easterly slant loaded coal in Oswego and was over in Kingston within a week, making her earnings about $1,750 for the round trip.

"Of course it might have taken a month or might never have been completed, for she could have been frozen in for the winter or lost in the late gales. But that was now these little vessels made bit earning in the schooner days – high freights, and a lot of luck.

"We four forward in the *Fleur-de-Marie* drew $40 each, after stripping her and laying her up for the winter at Kingston. We dispersed on our various ways feeling like millionaires. I returned to my home at what is now Hayden Park at Whitby harbour to strut until the sun-warmed thongs the following spring."

He went on:

"Home coming in the fall was for us sailors like summer holidays to the business man. We looked forward to it all season. Men without homes, who had saved enough money to pay for a winter's keep deposited the whole shot with the old-time Esplanade hotels, such as the Armouries or West Market Street or George Williams or Andy Tymon's at the corner of Church Street, and the other sailors' lodgings on the old Toronto harbourfront; now high and dry behind the viaduct – very dry indeed, and far inland.

"Here they took it easy, sure of three square meals, an odd drink and a pipeful till spring struck into the snowdrift and they were drawn to the outfitting schooners, of which Toronto had a good quota. I always spent my winters at home and early spring would find me along the well-filled wharves of Whitby, on the same quest as those who haunted the Toronto Esplanade site."

"The old time sailor's spring still looks good and I would like to be in it all again. It's charm and glamour I have never found in any other calling. Then the future had to take of itself, but the fond hope beckoned that I would some day tread my own quarterdeck, as the proud possessor of a lake schooner.

"That to my mind – and I haven't changed it – was the height of achievement and enjoyment of life. I never got there – but I have the vision. I went off on another slant, into drugs and insurance, and vessel agencies, and have wound up on the bench, peddling justice, something that is needed and lots of it.

"But I would like to have been master of a schooner!"

Port Credit

Referred to in a map of 1757 as Rivière du Credit, lying between Rivière du Toronto, which is the Humber River, and Rivière des Deux Follies ("River of two Mad Women"), which was Sixteen-Mile Creek at Oakville, Port Credit had been an active fur and brandy trading port in the seventeenth and eighteenth century. It became a government post, Indian reserve, and a very busy harbour, shipping ashes, lumber, cordwood, staves (for making barrels) apples, grains, brick and stone in the nineteenth century.

Towards the end of the nineteenth century, because of a dwindling forest and lack of depth for the bigger grain boats, the harbour traffic and the harbour itself started to die – except for the stonehooker. As many as forty schooner-rigged stonehookers would harbour in Port Credit, raking their stone cargoes from the nearby shale beds of Lake Ontario and delivering their cargoes to the hungry for stone Port of Toronto.

Port Credit had its ups and downs as a harbour, but ever resilient, it is now the centre of a cultured urban community boasting a large marina complex and the nearby Port Credit Yacht Club.

April 1933

Sunday Scorching

Seventy-eight years ago this Easter Sunday Port Credit was swept by its first great fire.

Seventy-eight years is a long time, and yet Abram Block, JP, present day pillar in the Port Credit community, looks back on the Easter fire of 1855 with eyes of remembrance as undimmed as his own steadfast sailor's glance which can catch the light on the Royal York Hotel every evening, twelve miles across the lake water from his home down on the point above the old Credit River mouth.

Seventy-eight years have wrought more changes in Port Credit than they have on Abram Block. He was then a keen-eyed lad of five. He will be 83 this August.

The port then had its fleet of little hookers, in the wood and stone trades, but big vessels, sailing vessels, came in to load lumber and grain and farm produce, and two steamers, the *Highlander* and *City of Hamilton* called daily for passengers and freight.

Beyond the spot where the long abandoned lighthouse stands out in the lake, was a large wharf, connected with the shore by a pier. It had a warehouse on it. You can still see, under water on a clear day, the old line of its outer cribs, running in the direction of the present starch factory.

The "old mouth" of the credit River turned westward in order to reach the lake. When piers which have long since fallen into ruin were built, and the entrance turned to face south-east, the "old mouth" silted up and formed a basin where little hookers used to haul in. It is now dry ground.

The Point, or high land to the west now secured by a stout concrete seawall, from which Mr. Block's house faces the water, once extended lakewards for acres. Lake

Street, still there, turned west on the crumbled point south of Mr. Block's house, and south of Lake Street again were two houses with their orchards and gardens. All this area is now in Lake Ontario.

Steamers did not come into the river, but moored at the wharf and warehouse out beyond the present lighthouse crib. But in the river were wharves and storehouses. Macdonald's Dock was on the west side, with storage for grain. Wooden rails were laid on it, and on these run little trucks which each held twenty-five bushels. Thus grain was dumped into the holds of hungry schooners. There were other wharves and runways and storehouses on the east side of the harbour, in addition to the freight shed out on the pier where the steamboats landed.

On the morning of Easter Sunday, 1855, two men and two boys were sitting on the steamer pier at Port Credit, keenly watching a grain schooner beating up for the harbour against a strong southwester.

Abram Block, senior, ancestor of the Block family – the man who in 1837 discovered the big anchor at Holland Landing, abandoned in the bush – was one of the two men at the pier. Charlie Hare, also a Port Credit pioneer, was the other. The schooner they were watching was the *Raleigh*. She was a smart, white two-master with a little clipper stem-head. Sanford and Moses, Cleveland shipwrights, had built her on Lake Erie in 1848. William Wilson of Oswego, brought her to Lake Ontario, and Captain Hamilton of Toronto, who had the wharf near the foot of Yonge Street bought her. She registered 212 tons (old American measurement) and would carry 12,000 bushels of grain.

It was grain she was after in the Credit, and the oldsters glanced with pride at the two "big vessels" already lying in port, eager to finish loading Peel County barley as soon as the Sabbath was over. Port Credit, they reflected, was becoming a harbour of great importance, with two grain carriers in already this spring and a third on the way.

One of the little youngsters with them was "little Abe" Block, then five years old; now Abram Block, JP.

All was quiet and the watchers leaned their backs comfortable against the sunny east side of the big warehouse, sheltered from the wind. Behind them, in the river, were some fifteen or twenty stonehookers, in all stages of fitting out, for it was an early spring. Beside the two vessels lying at the warehouses ready to load grain for Oswego, there was in port a big dredge. She had wintered in the harbour and was lying upstream a little way. The peace of Easter Sunday lay over the place.

Chales Hare broke the silence.

"I smell something burning," he told Abram Block. The two boys were sent to the corner of the warehouse to see what it was. Their excited yells brought the men to their feet.

"Holy smoke!" exclaimed Charlie Hare, which, considering the day and the deed was rather apt.

C.H.J.Snider photograph courtesy of Lorne Joyce

Port Credit Harbour, 1890s.

Flames were streaming from a big warehouse on the west bank. An early business block on the Lake Shore Road (the present Hamilton highway) was catching, and the stonehooker fleet lay directly in the path of the fire.

"Run home, Abe, and get Jim and tell him to bring the poles!" shouted Abram Block Sr., rushing with Charlie Hare to the fire. To reach it they had to run all around the harbour and cross the old wooden bridge. It was scorching under their feet.

Jim was little Abe's elder brother. The poles were two new setpoles, fresh cut and peeled and spiked and handed with iron, which Abram Block, senior, had prepared for his little topsail schooner *Ann Brown*. She was lying with the other hookers up by the bridge, in the path of the flames.

Like others she hadn't a stitch on her, which is certainly an embarrassing situation for a lady to be in when the firemen call. They had all finished painting, but the sails were down in the cabin, or up in the loft, or laid out on the grass for scrubbing and patching.

Hence the demand for setpoles.

The Blocks then lived on the east side of the river. By the time Abe had panted out his message, and Jim started on a staggering run with the long poles, the flaming shingles, sailing high on the west wind, were falling in the Block's backyard. On Saturday, Abe and the other children had gathered up all the chips in piles, a form of spring cleaning every country boy has had to share. The chip piles began to burn, and Abe

The *Olympia, Reindeer*, and the dredge *Alfred*, at Port Credit.

and his mother were kept on the run with water from the well to extinguish them and keep the house from catching.

Across the bridge a volunteer brigade was working, tossing the water along in an endless chain of buckets from the river to the raging fire. Murray and Cotton's store, the biggest place of business for miles around, went with all its goods. Neeson's Hotel, next door, fell prey to the flames. The wharf and warehouse at Macdonald's Dock caught fire.

Through the smoke and flame the hookermen leapt aboard their little craft lying near the bridge and madly cast off mooring lines and hove up their winter-bedded anchors.

Here was confusion at its wildest for the vessels being without sails there was no adequate means of moving or controlling them. Cast loose they became hopelessly entangled and drifted with the river current, mainbooms fouling railings, bowsprits poking through shrouds, topping-lifts and headstays, until one would have thought the Archangel Michael could not get them free.

To make matters worse this raft of hookers fouled the big blunt nose of the wintering dredge when she was cut adrift, just as the grain carriers were unmooring and heaving out to kedges they had carried out in their yawl boats. The big scow *Rough-and-Ready*, joined in the melee. And there at the pier ends ducked and bobbed the

Raleigh, waiting to come in, having worked far enough to windward to weather the lighthouse with started sheets.

But here, too, the resourcefulness of hookermen showed itself.

"Give a stonehooker a setpole and he'll steer through the Pearly Gates against a headwind," was an old Port Credit proverb, and the boys justified it now.

Thrusting their iron-spiked poles into the bottom they heaved and shoved and walked and winded their craft until the tangle spit up into twos and threes and finally departed into units.

Abram Block and his son, Jim, got the *Ann Brown* clear with the new poles the father had cut in the bush the week before.

Charlie Hare and his helpers pried the *Hunter Rose* loose – she was afterwards called the *Lone Star*, and Charlie often sailed her single-handed, although she would carry fifty or sixty tons.

Bob Collins extracted the old barque *Swallow* with much heaving and sweating. She was such a pioneer that she had carried sand for the site of the old jail, at the foot of Berkeley Street, Toronto, in 1839, and her bilges were quartered logs, hollowed out.

William Naish got the *Mary Ann* clear without capsizing the creek, and Tommy Blowers and the whole Blowers clan hove with might and main on the *Catherine Hays*, the little sloop with the outboard rudder that was their widowed mother's whole fortune. Mrs. Blowers renamed her the *James Abbs* when she was rebuilt and rerigged as a schooner, out of gratitude to Mr. Abbs of Parkdale, a market gardener who was very kind to her and her family.

It was really a piece of good fortune for the hookermen that none of them had so far progressed in fitting out as to have the canvas bent, for the inflammable duck and flax would have caught fire under the rain of sparks, embers, and wind-whirled shingles and the whole fleet would have gone. James Cotton, ignoring his own and has partner's loss, distributed the buckets of the volunteer fire fighter among the fleet when the store was past saving and called to the boys to keep soaking their decks with creek water. This they did and not a vessel caught fire. But they all needed new paint. The blaze stopped on the west bank of the creek for lack of fuel.

Port Credit's second big fire, years afterwards, wiped out the warehouses on the east side of the harbour and virtually destroyed the port. It never built up again. By this time "little Abe" Block was a man grown and master of his own hooker the *Mary E. Ferguson*. It was a night in the late 1880s when he was coming up the lake, and, as he changed watch with his mate, a man named Thompson, the latter drew attention to a blaze on shore. It was the big warehouses going up. This time the wind was offshore and light, so the vessel could not beat up and make the port in time to help the fight.

Flames lit up the whole village and Captain Block could see his new home on the point on the west side clearly, but could only hold his course and hope that it would be saved, as it was, for the fire contented itself with sweeping the busy east bank.

January 20, 1945
Last Coal of Last Century

Three ships were homeward bound up Lake Ontario with Toronto's last coal cargoes of the nineteenth century, on November 25, 1900. The wind was rising to a gale. At dusk snow set in. The leading schooner found Toronto via the Eastern Gap, a fine piece of blind navigation. Another rounded the lighthouse on Gibraltar Point and stood into Humber Bay until the lake shore trains could be heard through the snow, staggered out into the lake again for safety, and anchored, after daylight, Sunday morning in the storm tossed lake off Port Credit. Daylight revealed the third schooner hard and fast aground and close inshore, a mile west of Port Credit lighthouse, with her crew in the rigging, and plugged pickle bottles from the cabin sashing in the surf, enclosing messages imploring help.

The schooner which found Toronto blindfold was the *Antelope*, a fore-and-after. Early in the day Capt. William Wakeley had been surprised to see the three-master astern of him rounding up as though broaching-to, and clewing up her mizzen gafftop-sail before she could be got on her course again. She had been steering wildly before and continued to weave and yaw back and forth like a drunken man.

At dusk it was blowing harder and snow began to fall. Captain Wakeley sighted the glare of Toronto Street lights, mostly gas, in the sky and took careful compass bearing. The snow shut in so thick that nothing could be seen. He squatted the Antelope's mainsail down to the third reef band, and climbed the fore-rigging, kicking snow from the ratlines as he did so, and stared into the smother. A red blur shone to leeward. "Up, hard up!" he sang out to the two men at the wheel, "Jibe over all standing!"

He slid down the rigging in time to gather in the slack of the fore sheet, as the snow filled sail bellowed and thundered and swung over with a bang, followed by the heavy squatted mainsail which came without mishap because it had already been half lowered. The red light then on the pierhead of the Eastern Gap seem to be right over the *Antelope*'s crosstrees as she ploughed through the snow into the shelter of the invisible harbour.

The *Jessie Drummond* was off Whitby at this time. On she came through the snow, with never a glint of light or whimper of whistle to guide her. By ten o'clock her captain, Jimmy Quinn of Oakville, knew he had run his distance to Gibraltar Point and hauled her in for the lee of the Western Sandbar where now the warplanes ride. The foghorn was going every minute and a half and the lighthouse was flashing every fifteen seconds, but neither hoot nor wink reached the *Drummond* smothering in the snow. "Whoo-hoo-hoo!" came a locomotive whistle through the Parkdale cutting, and he knew that in clearing Gibraltar he had missed the anchorage, and would have to face the raging lake again.

He did so, much against the wishes of his crew, who wanted him to beach her. He see-sawed back and forth up the lake, and stood in for the shore when daylight came. The snow cleared just in time to show him the spars of a three-master ahead, hard and fast ashore. He let go two anchors quickly and fetched the *Drummond* up short in the Hamilton steamboat track, away out in the lake off Port Credit. She rolled like a loop-the-loop till she got head-to, and she dragged along the stony bottom and parted one chain, but the other anchor held – what happened after that may be told another time.

The third of the schooners, the one discovered on the beach, was the *Augusta*, Capt. Alex Ure, of Toronto. "Schooner Days" had a New Years call from – who do you think? One of the rescued of forty-four years before.

This was James Henry McGlennon of Toronto, one of the McGlennons from Cat Hollow, which includes Lakeport and the vicinity of Colborne, Ont. McGlennons were to be found in most lake schooners last century, and in this they are masters in steam or in some way connected with the water, if it is only at mariners service's, for theirs is an old lake going family. How Mr. McGlennon was so effectively disguised in the list of *Augusta* survivors was not recognized until he made himself known is curious.

The reporters in 1900 sent the names of the crew in from Port Credit, and by the time they reached the *Telegram* J.H. McGlennon, Colborne, had become "M.C. Chillon, Port Colborne," and was so printed. Newspapers are always fumbling Colborne and Port Colborne, although they are two hundred miles apart by road, but the "Chillon" mess up suggests that they wrote in even worse hands in 1900 than now.

Anyway, that is how it came about and right glad was "Schooner Days" to see Henry McGlennon still in the flesh and none the worse of his harrowing experiences of his twenties. We had already heard from his brother Frank and were hoping for such a call. Mr. McGlennon, clean cut, active graduate of the old lake school, with captains papers, brought along his friend, Captain Brown, and we had a session.

Mr. McGlennon had been with Captain Ure many times in the *W.Y. Emery*, the *Augusta*, and his last charge, the *Reuben Doud* – which promises still another story. The *Augusta*'s last voyage was a grim one from the beginning. Soon after they towed out from Charlotte the head of the rudderpost "broomed," that is broke into splinters so that the steering wheel had no effect on it;

"So how did you get her up the lake?" was asked.

"Hooked tackles on to the backing-chains in the rudder and hove them in through each quarter – and it was a hard job to plough anything like a straight furrow!"

That was what was wrong when she was broaching-to. To get her up the lake at all was a feat of seamanship. She couldn't be steered into shelter under Gibraltar Point apparently, and was lucky to miss standing there. They saw Port Credit light just after they passed it, in a thinning of the snow. Some of them thought it was the last light in Victoria Park, which was then the first sign of Toronto to any coming from the eastward, but Mr. McGlennon knew better. They tried to haul her out into the lake, rough as it was, but her heel touched on the shale bottom off the Port Credit brickyards and she wouldn't come. The first sea that smacked her after she touched washed away her yawlboat from the stern. It tossed alongside for a time, just out of reach, and washed in on the beach near Marigold Point. Poor Captain Ure, whose fate it had been to lose the *Highland Chief*, *Isabella* and *Undine* before this, fought in vain to get the *Augusta* clear, trying to wrench her free as the seas lifted her by booming out her sails. It was cold, wet, killing work and all in vain. When the mizzen began to sway, and half of the after mast twisted and writhed while the forward part remained fast and motionless they knew her back was broken, and she was doomed. That was why the appeals for help were so urgent. Young Doad Martin was only a boy, with a great fear of being drowned. The poor lad made great vows for the future, if he could only be saved, but he went decking in the *Bannockburn* – a man had to work to live in the early 1900s – and the *Bannockburn* disappeared in Lake Superior, so he must have been drowned after all.

When the storm died out efforts were made to save the *Augusta* herself. The *Gordon Jerry*, a steam stonehooker, and the *Mary E. Ferguson*, a sailing one, and several others that had never carried coal in their lives came alongside an dug out a few hundred tons from the *Augusta*'s hold, and brought it to Toronto. Pumps got the water down two feet in her hold, and she began to lift.

But then a gale blew up again and again she pounded. Her masts fell and she broke up into huge bundles of pike-filled timber.

When the *Antelope* got her seven hundred tons of coal unloaded she went up to help lighter the *Augusta* off, but her anchors would not hold. Half the *Augusta*'s coal was salvaged. How the third and last cargo got to Toronto will have to be told next.

January 27, 1945
Brave Boat Work at Century's End

The *Jessie Drummond* black above and red below, third and largest schooner to leave the south shore of Lake Ontario with the last coal cargoes for Toronto in the nineteenth century, was a veteran of the lake marine with thirty-five seasons' service astern of her. She had been to Hamburg and brought back German iron rails to Ontario in 1865. But she never rolled, pitched and plunged more on the Atlantic than she did on Sunday, November 25, 1900. That was when the clearing snowstorm revealed her consort the *Augusta* hard and fast on the north shore, above Port Credit light, and Capt. James Quinn gave the *Drummond* both her anchors in the raging lake to keep her from the *Augusta*'s fate.

All day, through the glasses, he watched the gallant efforts of Toronto and Port Credit volunteers to take the *Augusta*'s crew off. The Toronto men had much the better boat, but not enough manpower to get the boat alongside. The Port Credit lads, stonehookers and fishermen from boyhood, had pluck and skill enough to effect a risky rescue in two trips after many tries.

Meantime, five Toronto yachtsmen had sailed up in a skimming dish that never should have been out in that weather. She was the *Adanac*, a half-decked centreboard sloop, 16 feet long on the waterline and 12 inches freeboard, and she did well to keep them afloat from the Queen's wharf to Port Credit. All honour to these boys who tried, but all the lifesaving they accomplished was their own.

They managed to catch the stern of the tossing *Drummond*, with their boat half full of water and themselves so exhausted with seasickness and bailing that they were not much help to Captain Quinn and his worn out crew. The casting of the windlass had been broken when her big anchor took hold, and it was impossible to weigh anchor again.

The *Drummond* lad had all they wanted with pumping and steering and handling soaked and frozen gear, and some of them were panicky and had begged the captain to run the ship ashore in Humber Bay when they heard the locomotive whistles through the snow. The welcome they gave the yachtsmen to their own reeling decks and wet bunks was not a cordial one. The whole party spent an unhappy night, the ship tossing and grinding frightfully at her anchors, the men pumping and pounding all the running gear, and dousing it and the pump wells with coarse salt to keep them from freezing solid.

By Monday morning the wind was going around to the north, while the sea still ran in tremendous greybacks from the east, and the *Drummond* was in the trough, rolling her tophamper adrift and filling her decks, so that her bulwarks started to go.

Captain Quinn hoisted this Canadian ensign at the mizzen truck, in the hope of attracting assistance, either a tug to get the *Drummond* to Toronto, or someone to get the windlass in working order, and bring food for his too-numerous crew.

They could see the signal in Oakville, eight miles away, but in Toronto, ten miles off, lay the only tug then in commission on the north shore of Lake Ontario.

"Nipper" Quinn, Captain Jim's youngest brother, and Allan Kemp, the Oakville harbourmaster, drove down to the credit to implore the Credit men to help Jim. They did not know how badly off the *Drummond* might be. Capt. A.E. Hare, who had taken off the *Augusta* crew, needed no urging, only a boat. The *Grace Darling*, Sons of England lifeboat, lay in the Credit Harbour, where she had been left after her attempt the day before, her three men going back to Toronto. He first appealed to the crowded bar of the Port Credit Hotel to man her, for he thought the Port Credit boys deserved a rest.

The mate of the *Augusta* explained that his captain had left him in charge of the wreck while he was away trying to arrange for her salvage, "You've brought her to an anchor in the lee of the stove," said Al in scorn, and filled the *Grace Darling* from outside the hotel.

His only difficulty was in keeping her from being overloaded with volunteers. "Nipper" Quinn and Allan Kemp had to be taken, of course, and Albert Block and Steve Peer, who had been in the *Augusta* rescue, and Billy Hicks from the *Humber*. He had plenty to take the *Grace Darling* out under sail, and that was the way he was going to handle her, but a young market gardener from the Lake Shore Road, Billy Trenwith – he still has a garage near Lorne Park – begged and pleaded to be allowed to come.

"Never been in a boat," he admitted, "but I am strong, and I can bail, and I won't be scared so long as I can see you."

"I might be too busy to look after you if we got into trouble," urged Al. "It's too big a risk for you. Can't take you."

But when the *Grace Darling* shoved off there was Billy Trenwith crouched under the lug foresail, hidden from Al Hare's sight. The *Grace Darling* had two stumpy masts and three storm sails, a jib, lug foresail, loose footed and standing lug mainsail, with a little boom on the foot of it, to clear the coxswain's head.

She steered with a rudder.

They got out to the *Drummond* in no time, having wind astern, and Al Hare swung aboard. A worn-out yachtsman said: "There are five of us here, and we'd like you to take us ashore. Our own boat there astern is full of water."

"Have to ask your captain first," said Al comfortingly, "Captain Jim, what do you want me to do?"

"Well I want a tug, and I want to get my windlass castings fixed by a blacksmith. Can I get that done in the Credit?"

"Sure," said Al. "How about these men that want to get ashore?"

"Take 'em," said Captain Quinn. "I'll take the casting to the blacksmith shop myself when you go. Possum Mercer here and the rest of my crowd'll keep ship while I'm away."

"All aboard," said Al. "Ship the oars, for we'll need 'em going back."

So shorewards the *Grace Darling* sped, more slowly now for she was full of men, and the wind was ahead instead of astern. The big seas were still roaring up the lake, unsmoothed by the offshore wind, and rolling in on the wreck of the *Augusta*, and the beach at the river mouth, in long breakers from which the crests were blown back smoking like the tossing manes of wild horses.

"Keep her up to windward Al, keep her up!" everybody advised the coxswain.

Oars on both sides and all three sails pulling, the *Grace Darling* came directly for the squat white lighthouse on the end of the east pier. The spray was going over the lantern. Three monster seas piled up in one mountain and burst at the critical moment.

"Aft, everybody!" shouted Al. "My rudder's out of the water and she won't pay off for me!"

For one second it seemed as though she would shoot over the lighthouse. Then the explosion of the triple sea tossed her across the hundred-foot harbour mouth and she looked to be going to destruction on the opposite pier. Al kept his helm up, and she cleared that and the sailed crashed over like a three-gun salute as she lurched her other side in and was almost filled with the bursting foam. Three oars were broken, those who had been pulling them were head over heels in the water between the thwarts, and she seemed to have a cargo of chaos.

"Beach her, Al, beach her to loo'ard of the pier!" yelled Jim Quinn.

"And have her roll over on top of us?" answered Al. "Not on your life! She's going out in the lake again."

"Your mainboom's snapped, she'll never make it!"

"Shift over them good oars to the lee side and she will," Al answered back.

And they did.

And she did.

Foot by foot, fathom by fathom, helped by the hard offshore wind and the three oars, pulled double-banked on the lee side, the *Grace Darling* waded out through the breakers, settled down to steady going in the deeper water, gained an offing on the lighthouse, and swung around again for another try.

This time Al got a spare oar over the stern to steer in the rough water, held her back till the biggest fellows had broken, and then drove her hard for the entrance.

Once more it was touch and go. She lapped the lighthouse when the next breaker-burst came. On that she flew like a stone out of a sling. There was no directing her, with oar, or sail, or rudder. She was a chip on a torrent of water roaring through the funnel of the piers at train speed.

She just grazed one pier, at the inner end. But that graze stove in two planks like a cannon shot. Al gave a Herculean sweep with his oar and ran her on the mud in Goose Bay the tiny cove inside the harbour, beyond the west pier. She was full of water, and of wet men. But safe.

Then Al for the first time saw Billy Trenwith. He was jammed in a corner of the bulkhead and the foremast-thwart so tight he could not get out. But even so, he was bailing manfully, as he had done throughout the trip. And he was still afraid Al would be cross because he had stowed away.

"Were you scared, Billy, at the pierhead?" asked Al.

"No," said Billy, "I could see you wasn't."

Captain Quinn got his castings forged, and out to the *Drummond* again as the water smoothed. With Allen Kemp and Nipper and Possum Mercer and his whole crew helping he hove in on his cables and found he had parted the one for the little anchor, and lost that hook and had been riding to the big one all the time. They hove that one up and made all sail, even to the fly-by-night and the bluedevil that went to the fore-topmast head – except the main gafftopsail which had flogged itself to ribbons and stranded the main topmast shrouds.

On November 27, with the help of the late running island ferry *Ada Alice*, Capt. Joe Goodwin, to dock her, the *Jessie Drummond* ploughed through the mud of the Princess Street slip with 550 tons of hard coal for P. Burns & Co. – the last schooner coal for this city in that century.

One of the many adventures of one the many Credit worthies, Capt. A.E. Hare, stone-hookerman, baker, and boat livery keeper and evergreen at 82.

December 9, 1944
Chasing a *Lithophone*

Ever hear of a lithophone? Al Hare of Port Credit, caught the only one on record in April 1899.

Up in Bronte there used to be two Bob Joyces, Fisherman Bob and Organ Bob. They were both good sailors, but not related. Being, as one might say, inclined to the water, Organ Bob played the organ in the Baptist Church, and so got his name. He was a good hand at ship carpentry, and designed and built two very fast stonehookers on the scow model. They were about 55 feet long, 17-foot beam, and not more than 4 feet deep in the hold.

They were shoal, shapely and smart, but not strong, for they carried their weighty cargoes on deck. This made them easy to load and unload, but hard to hold together. The bottom of one of them, the *Olympia*, was concave up towards her deck with the pressure. The other one bowed so under her burdens that she had to be trussed togeth-er like a bucksaw frame, by wire cables tightened with turnbuckles over her centreboard box. Her lines were neat and clean, and her name was interesting – *Lithophone*. She was launched about the time Graham Bell amazed the world by the telephone. The same classic influence which had named her sister *Olympia* may have reasoned if the new telephone carried sound far and fast, stone would be carried farther and faster by the new *Lithophone*.

Forty-and-a-few years ago the spring freshet took the *Lithophone* out of the river.

Walter Hare had sold her to Walter Naish the fall before and Naish cut a hole in the river ice and plopped the anchor through it, with a good scope of chain. The rest of the chain was on board, with turns around the windlass barrel.

When the March-mad Credit broke up and hurried lakeward in pans and sheets of sand-stained ice, it parted mooring lines and took the *Lithophone* away from her anchor without delay, for the dog had been knocked off the paulpost and the windlass barrel revolved like a spool of thread, till all the turns were unwound. The barrel kept on turning, and the bitter-end of the chain having been made fast to nothing, the last of the cable quickly plopped overboard through the lake as fast as the icecakes themselves.

Wal Naish shouted for Wal Hare, and Hare hailed Jack Cummings and Jack Cummings got Newman and among them they dragged the *Lithophone*'s four lower sails in a Goderich-model fishboat. Walter's brother, Al Hare, came along and they importuned him to lend a hand, for it looked like a blow from the northwest.

"You'll never catch her in that little thing," said Al to his brother. "If you wait twenty minutes the river'll be clear enough of ice for us to get Bill Newman's big boat out and then we can do something."

The *Hecla* was a big mackinaw fishboat with two masts and three sails and could make three feet to the smaller boat's one. But they argued that the little boat could get out to the *Lithophone* in the twenty minutes the ice was clearing, and meantime the *Lithophone* was blowing ashore fast.

So Al jumped in and took the tiller, and two of the boys rowed. Going out of the channel they were almost swamped, and Al said they had better turn back while they could, but they were half way to the *Lithophone* now, and it was harder to pull back than go on, so all settled down to the chase.

She was light and high out of the water, having been stripped of everything for the winter, and her centreboard was up, so she blew off like a barrel. The more it blew the faster she went. But the poor little skiff, loaded deep with four men, four sails, four hundredweight of gear, and forty gallons of lake water, waddled slowly, even with the wind's assistance. By the time they had got the first lot of water out more was coming in, for the waves were running higher and higher.

Sweating like firehorses, they got to within a hundred yards of the *Lithophone*, but closer they couldn't come. They had to keep bailing and began to lose ground. So, none too soon, they tried to pull back.

Photograph by Anthony Adamson, courtesy of Lorne Joyce

The *Lithophone*, as she was in 1916.

Then they saw a cheering sight. The *Hecla*, under reefed sails, was tearing out from the river. Dan Sharp, the harbourmaster, was at the stick. He had sized up the situation and got her out as the ice drifted clear. But the *Hecla*, all eyes for the *Lithophone*, passed the little skiff without noticing her. In vain the boys yelled and waved after she had gone; no one saw or heard them as their low craft wallowed in the sea.

They pulled in to the ice of the old pier at Long Branch. That was the nearest they could fetch the land. They were four miles from home, and no way of getting back but by shank's mare.

They saw the *Hecla* sail around the *Lithophone* twice. But the knew she could do nothing, for the *Lithophone* was far too big for them to take in tow, and they had her sails and gear in their boat. The *Hecla* began to beat back for home. On one tack she headed right in for Long Branch, and hope revived. They began shouting and waving when she was a mile out, and kept it up. She stood in quite close, and then tacked out again, and again without seeing them. In the spring darkness they ploughed homeward through the Lake Shore Road mud, sometimes taking to the fields, sometimes to the railway tracks for this was long before the concrete highway.

Saddest of all was Wal Naish, who had lost his anchor, chain, *Lithophone*, supper, and investment, and found his family waiting for the funeral as soon as his body could be found, for the four of them had been given up as lost when Dan Sharpe reported there was no trace of them, either on the lake or *Lithophone*.

A week later the old *Chicora*, on her first trip to Niagara reported the *Lithophone* afloat in the lake, with decks awash, on the south shore of Ontario.

Again a rescue corps was organized. Wal Hare begged to be excused on the ground that he had gone into the butcher business and had never been across the lake in his life; which was true, though he was a post-graduate of the stonehooker fleet.

The revised Argonauts included Jack Potter, Lew Naish of the *Newsboy*, bound to stand by his brother Walter, Bill Newman, George Hare, Harry Fowler, and Al Hare. Hare was, by mutual consent, the skipper again. They took out the *Hecla* again, and headed for Port Dalhousie; ran into light airs and thin ice at night and lowered their sails and rolled themselves up in them, and slept through the freezing dark to wake in more fog. The boat was not sheathed for ice work, and to move through the skim-ice would have sliced her at the waterline. Like all fishboats she was open to the sky.

With the breeze the fog lifted and the ice broke and they worked into Port Dalhousie. Al Hare caught a glimpse of two thin lines late in the afternoon, which must be the masts of the *Lithophone*. He enlisted the sympathy – and the steam pressure – of Billy Hand, of the tug *Nellie Bly*, and gave him the compass bearing and assumed distance, five miles, and got him to tow the *Hecla* that far.

Time up, nothing visible in the dusk. Wal Naish cast off in the *Hecla* with part of the explorers, and after a short time they were all heard shouting, and the *Lithophone* was found. She was level with the water, her two masts like trees growing in a swamp. All that showed below them was her box-like cabin trunk and her rail. Most of her bulwarks had been knocked out or washed away and the stern was just hanging on to her. Only the wood in her was floating her. Her hatchcomings were above water, but not her deck.

The *Nellie Bly* tried to tow the waterlogged hulk and the *Hecla* into Port Dalhousie, with the boys vainly bailing with buckets to clear her. But it blew up from the southward hard and they could make no headway. So some of them got back into the *Hecla* and three-reefed her sails, and cast off, and Al Hare stayed at the tiller of the *Lithophone* and steered, and the *Nellie Bly* sat on her own safety valve and snored. It was a tight race, and ended in a dead heat at the inner light in Port Dalhousie. Both had to hustle to get in ahead of the steamer *Lakeside*.

There was a new man in this vessel, and Al remarked to Bill, "He's coming fast!" "You watch the fun when he tries to set his lines out," said Bill. Fun there was. One of the deck hands got caught in the heaving-line, fell off the dock, and was dragged under the ship's stern.

"Steam over and see what we can do, Bill," suggested Al and Miss *Bly* at once crossed the creek. Al grabbed a pike pole and thrust along the heaving-line near the screw till he felt the body and moved it. But it couldn't be brought up.

"Let go of the end of the heaving line on board!" he called, and as soon as they did the drowned man came free. They had him out and aboard.

"Just seven minutes by my watch," said a doctor, "but I'm afraid it's too late."

"Let me try," said Al, squeezing the water out of the body in great gouts. He got the boys to work his arms high overhead and press his elbows to his sides in turn. No sign and again the doctor said "too late." Al and his acolytes kept up the work. Tiny bubbles burst from the mans nostrils. Then he commenced to roar in great heaves as his elbows squeezed his ribs. Soon he was breathing regularly. They carried him to the hotel. The doctor and the captain wanted to buy out the bar for Al and his boys. But all he asked was to have his name kept out of the paper.

The *Lithophone* was towed home by the *Nellie Bly*. She continued her stony avocation for some years, and may be at it yet, in spirit, for she was beached and filled with stones to form a private wharf east of the port.

Snider Mysteries

Throughout the twenty-five years that "Schooner Days" appeared as a weekly column in the Toronto Evening Telegram, Snider, the consummate marine researcher, would frequently conduct an investigation into the identity of a wreck, and in the process describe some of the schooners that had sailed that particular area before coming to a conclusion.

In November 1941, he ran such a series on a wreck found at the base of the Scarborough Bluffs, which he had always called Scarborough Highlands.

November 15, 1941
At the Foot of the Highlands

East of Toronto, well east, the land heaves up in the Highlands of Scarborough. They are not the glens and mountains of Scotland, but a series of clay folds, increasing to the great Hog's Back, three hundred feet high under the cross of St. Augustine, and subsiding in widening ripples as they spread eastward. Mounting them, inland, the clear, clean air proclaims elevation, but the impression of simply rolling plains may persist until you come their most southern verge. Then, parting the sumac bushes, you are faced with the soft blue scarf of Lake Ontario, spread for thirty miles to a horizon vanishing in a bluer sky. The lacelike fringes a hundred yards under your feet are breakers creaming silently because they are so far below.

Seen from the water or the shingly shore the Highlands are utterly different. The friendly earth ends with savage abruptness in a ragged wall, perpendicular here, there overhanging and cut by spouting springs, elsewhere bastioned by pinnacles and isolated promontories accessible only to wings, yet capped with a few square yards of turf or a starved apple tree. It may have grown from a seed dropped by a bird, or be the survivor of a pioneer's orchard which has slipped into the lake with a century of erosion. In another place battalions of birches, aspens, sumacs, and evergreens may storm the heights, with auxiliary troops of castaway hollyhocks and iris from the gardens above, mingling with parachute corps of the great willow herb in uniforms of bright mauve. In another, the scars of the cliff may be sealed with tons of scrap metals – stove pipes, car bodies bath tubs, wrecked safes. In still another, the clay has been hewn into the shapes of gabled or hip-roofed barns. Like cast clouts of giants waiting to wade out, the wastage of the cliffs lies in layers at their feet and spreads in slow folds over the bed of the lake. Sometimes it forms a beach, sometimes a shoal.

Buried in one of these folds ten miles east of the city high above the high water and seeming to disappear into the face of the two hundred-foot cliff behind it, lies the skeleton of a wooden ship. A large ship for her time, today she's a pygmy compared to the 10,000-ton steel bulk freighters whose smoke stains the horizon fifteen miles out as they pass in midlake. The wooden ship may have been built a hundred years ago; may, indeed, have been a wreck for that long. The timbers and planking, much decayed, and the iron spikes and fastenings, heavily corroded, have been large enough for a schooner of 150 tons. This was quite a large vessel for Lake Ontario in 1840.

This wreck is towards the eastern end of the Highlands, where they fade in the valleys of the Highland Creek, the Rouge, and the Petticoat. Sailors used to fix the east limit of the Highlands at Centre Point, a decaying headland a quarter of a mile west of the mouth of Highland Creek. What it is or was the centre of, who knows? It is midway between Toronto and Whitby, by water. The wreck is a few furlongs west of Centre Point; half a mile west of the creek mouth. There is another wreck, or part of the same one, a mile or more farther west. Centreboard skiffs sailing along the shore nave noticed its weed-grown timbers under water. The wreckage, high at the cliff-foot, could be a side torn from this submerged wreck and washed along like a raft by strong southwest gales.

The wreckage is either the side or the bottom of a craft around one hundred feet long. Seven or eight of the old ribs can be traced in the sand and gravel. They have apparently been centred twelve inches apart. Although they are so much decayed as to be almost shapeless, from the fragments which are still around the ribs appear to have measured six inches by eight and in some instances eight by ten. The spaces between are irregular, indicating that some have been torn away by the waves or burned in bonfires. Others have rotted away completely. The sand, darkened by the decayed wood is full of loose spikes and bolts. All the timber of this wreck uncovered is oak – white oak. Some of it, sound enough to stand the axe, is stained blue as indigo with the acid of the iron fastenings a characteristic of white oak. And after all the years, no one knows how many, the white oak preserves its sharp sour smell when again cut.

Spadework below the timbers uncovers planking, which cross the ribs at right angles. The planks are rotting like the ribs, but, having been covered with sand, their measure has been preserved, and they measure from eight to nine inches in width and two inches in thickness. Allowing for attrition and decay, they have probably been 2 1/2-inch strakes.

Side planking of such thickness, spiked to six-by-eight frames doubled, is consistent with the supposition that this was a vessel of 150 tons burden. The fact that the ribs are not closely spaced and the planks are not wide, rather indicates that the wreckage is part of the ship's side. Were it the bottom one would find "floors" between the frames or ribs, making the transverse construction almost continuous or contiguous; the planks would be wider and there would be some trace of a keel and keelson.

A day's work with pick and shovel would reveal much more than meets the eye, but the wreckage has been so mutilated by picnic bonfires and summer campers and the tooth of time, that no amount of excavation would recover enough of the vessel to enable one to do more than guess at her original shape and tonnage.

She lies on this highest shelf of beach at an angle of forty-five degrees to the line of the cliffs, as though she had run blindly into the bank on an inshore tack, piking her bowsprit fifty feet into the clay. That, of course, is not probable, even in the blackest night or the thickest snowstorm. One doesn't run to the Highlands of Scarborough like bumping into someone coming around the corner. If the Highlands are completely invisible the roar of the surf at their feet give warning. Moreover, the water is too shallow for any vessel of burden to sail right up to them; she would ground in the breakers, some hundreds of yards out.

There is evidence that the water was higher at the foot of the Highlands long ago, but this wreckage is so high above the present lake level, and so far in from the present shore, that the ship was wrecked farther out, possibly some considerable distance away, and broke up.

Many vessels have been lost in the vicinity of the Highlands; in this century the schooners *Zebra*, *Defiance*, and *Rapid City*, the barges *Erie Belle* and *P.B. Lock*, and the steamer *Alexandria*, and the steam barge *City of New York*, and the scow-built steam barge *Arctic*.

Earlier than that were the *William Cawthrie*, and the *William Wallace*, which left Darlington one morning in October 1857, and was never heard of afterwards. It blew hard from the east that night and next morning some of the Wallace's cabin furniture was washed on the beach near the lighthouse on Gibraltar Point, Toronto. She was a Toronto vessel and William McCabe was her captain. Fishermen thought they found her hull in deep water, a mile off the Point but could not identify it. She had cordwood in the hold and stone on deck, a dangerous combination, brought about by some disarrangement which will never be explained. Some thought she rolled over and sank off the Highlands, where the sea was high and hollow.

None of these ran ashore or foundered on Centre Point, although their wreckage could conceivably be carried there were the water high enough.

November 22, 1941
The *Marysburgh*

Does the *Marysburgh* wreck lie at the foot of the Highlands?

We began the puzzle of which wreck lies mouldering at the foot of the Highlands of Scarborough a mile or more east of the Guild of All Arts and something west of Centre Point and Highland Creek. We got as far as guessing, from the eight-inch spikes and the dimensions of the surviving timber, that it was a vessel of around 150 tons register, and we weeded out almost a dozen vessels lost during this century, on the grounds that the size did not fit, or their lake grave was known to be elsewhere, or they were too recently wrecked to be so far gone. This threw us back into the last century, and the memories of older readers.

Photo by Rowley Murphy courtesy of Lorne Joyce

The *Defiance* of Oakville on the west bank opposite Oakville Club Landing. Astern is Rowley Murphy's small yawl.

One of the schooners lost near the Highlands in the 1800s was a two-master named the *Marysburgh*, and it has been suggested that the wreckage might be hers.

The *Marysburgh* was built in the ancient and vanished "Port of Cramaha" of the earliest Dominion registers, otherwise Colborne, Lakeport, Keeler's Creek, and Cat Hollow, some eighty miles east of Toronto, George Ault, a Kingston builder, was her master carpenter.

The date of her building was 1854, in the wheat boom of the Crimean war and she was then christened *James Leslie*. Her first recorded measurements are 99 feet length, 22 beam, 9 feet depth of hold, and 125 tons register. James Burke was one of her early masters. Later she was reported as 157 tons; still later 150. This last figure was after she had been rebuilt in South Bay, Marysburgh township, Prince Edward, in 1870 for Capt. James Collier, and renamed *Marysburgh*, as the name was then spelled. He sold her to Capt. John Allen of Oshawa by 1873; and she was lost soon afterwards.

Confederation was new when the *James Leslie* had her face lifted and when she emerged from master builder Jack Tait's beauty parlor with the permanent smile of *Marysburgh* all over her countenance. The beaver was more honoured as the national emblem then than it is now, and to distinguish her as a Canadian among the hundreds of American schooners then trading on Lake Ontario, she had a big flag at the foretruck featuring a brown beaver on a white background, with a broad blue border. Of course, in addition she had the new Red Ensign with it's "patch-work-quilt" escutcheon of the newly confederated provinces, which has since been simplified, if not improved. But the *James Leslie* had been an industrious schooner, and it was intended that the *Marysburgh* should be also, and the beaver was emphasized as her houseflag.

She was a green-painted schooner, green from the bulwark rail to the waterline, as an old picture in Picton shows, and she came to her death through the green light. Frenchman's Bay, in the old days, was the only port on the lake distinguished by a green lantern in its lighthouse – it was a "private" harbour, the piers having been built by a harbour company in 1843. The *Marysburgh* bound for Frenchman's Bay, was standing inshore one dirty night, sighted a green light, and next moment found herself pounding on boulders where no boulders should have been. Morning showed that she had missed Frenchman's Bay by five miles and come in to the eastward of Highland Creek.

The green light blamed for her undoing was claimed to be a railway semaphore light and there was talk of suing the Grand Trunk, which was a popular sport in the last century. The railway comes close to the water here, so close that for years a line of cribwork filled with stone was employed to protect the tracks between Highland Creek and Port Union where thirsty locomotives still need water for the wrestle with the Scarborough grade. The railway replied, with considerable emphasis, that there was no green semaphore light visible from the lake in this vicinity, and never had been. It might be possible, however, to see a green light on a train watering at Port Union, one mile or more east of the creek, but it would take good eyes to pick one out from the lake on a thick night. The *Marysburgh* got no damages from the railway – but total damages from the beach. She broke up.

The exact spot of the *Marysburgh*'s destruction has never been charted, for it was not in any normal navigation course, but it must have been east of Centre Point, where the boulders once bedded in the clay of the promontory strew the bed of the devouring lake. Ironwork of her wreckage, chainplates, wire rigging, and deadeyes, were raked up from under her remains by stonehookers in 1900, and planks and timbers in the marsh in the mouth of Highland creek, inside the railway bridge, were said to be the *Marysburgh*'s. Saying so was not convincing, for there have been more stories than one to account for old timbers in the Highland Creek marsh.

But the *Marysburgh* must have come in east of Centre Point, and this wreckage at the foot of the Highlands is west of that.

Ten to one this is not the wreckage of the *Marysburgh*, because forty years ago half of her – some of the port bilge and most of the starboard side, – was on the beach east of the mouth of the Highland Creek, opposite the fill which carries the railway across the Highland Creek marsh. This apparently was where the *Marysburgh* struck. Her wreck may be there yet, but is not visible. May have been sanded in. Some of it may have been carried into the creek mouth.

The creek outlet is now very small, sometimes six feet wide and a foot deep, sometimes completely choked within a gravel bar. The marsh behind it, once the estuary of the Highland Creek and now its delta, could hold the remains of all schooners of Lake Ontario.

It would take an ice shove of vaster proportions than Lake Ontario has seen to carry the remainder half a mile around Centre Point and land it in a birch grove at the foot of the cliffs where this other wreckage is now mouldering away.

November 29, 1941
Perhaps This Solves the Highlands' Secret

One dark night eighty-odd years ago, when the roar of the surf at the foot of the Highlands of Scarborough mingled with the sighing of the pines and oaks and elms on their crest in a great anthem of the elements, a small group of men staggered up the gulley. Here the Highlands were at their highest, towering three hundred feet sheer above the boiling lake. Then as now the gully was a gash in their face, a slanted sabre scar in the eternal warfare of land and lake, with a side slash from the lake's ally, the rain. Ages before, a tear of rainwater, reinforced by a hidden spring, had begun to furrow the stern cheek of the cliff. It had grown into a great wound, cleaving back into the forest, and giving the only passage upward from the lake for any unequipped with wings.

Lake water squelched in the seaboots of the climbing men and drained from their clothing, from their sou'westers downwards. They were shipwrecked sailors, seeking aid. As they staggered towards the heights they saw a light, a dim tallow candle all alone in the dark. Steering for it as the ground permitted they came to a farm clearing and in the clearing a pioneer cabin of squared logs It was from the cabin the light shone. They pounded on the door.

"We're from the *Jessie Woods* – she's pounding to pieces at the foot of the cliff – get us help!" they gasped.

To say "the *Jessie Woods*" was like mentioning the *Dalhousie City* or the *Chippewa* in these times. Everybody in the lakefront townships knew the *Jessie Woods*, the Niagara boat, one of three sisters built by the Niagara Harbour and Dock Company at Newark or Niagara-on-the-Lake, in the seven-year period between 1832 and 1839.

Niagara was then a shipping centre quite as important as Toronto, and the *Jessie Woods* had been the pride of the Niagara sailing fleet. Steamers had not entirely supplanted the schooners, even as passenger packets, and the *Jessie Woods* had "superior accommodations," as they were then advertised, for ladies and gentlemen crossing the lake. Governor Simcoe and his lady voyaged by sail between Toronto and Niagara, and the best people did so for long afterwards, although steamers had begun to cut heavily into the passenger traffic before the *Jessie Woods* was launched.

William Humphrey's first question was "Any passengers? Anybody left on board?" He was told all had got ashore. But the vessel had a valuable cargo and the captain had hopes that it could be salvaged and perhaps even the vessel herself could be hauled off once she had been lightened of her load. He had come to the right spot, for old William Cornwell, or Cornell, was a sailor and shipowner and his farm was near that of the Humphreys. He had built a schooner at Rosebank, at the mouth of the Rouge, when the bluff was called Billy's Point, and she had been confiscated at Ogdensburg by the American embargo which preceded the War of 1812. His sons, with Willy Humphrey's help, roused the neighbours and hurried down the the gully with lanterns, ropes, and anything they thought would be of service. Others set off for Toronto for further assistance. By daylight, with the sea going down, the salvage corps was in operation.

The schooner had first struck at some distance out, being a deep-draught vessel with a standing keel, but the pounding of the breakers had driven her in close to the tiny shelf of beach somewhere near what is now the Guild of All Arts. She was close to the cliffs, and it was easy to get aboard her. Proceeding systematically, her perishable cargo was hoisted out first – cases of Young Hyson and Bohea tea, barrels of sugar, boxes of shoes, groceries, cutlery, hardware, and drygoods. The lake schooners were the express service of the first half of the nineteenth century, before the railways came through, and wagon trains met them at the wharves or even at creek mouths, to carry their cargoes inland. The whole countryside, for miles back in the bush as far as the forest roads ran, was served by schooner. It was certainly not intended that the *Jessie Woods* should land her cargo at the foot of the Highlands of Scarborough, for that was a most inconvenient spot, but she had often before landed it on the beach and wagons had completed delivery.

As the hold emptied the narrow beach took on the appearance of the midway of a fair, for the goods were piled up wherever they would be above the water, and hundreds of helpers – and others – engaged in the slow and labourious task of dragging the cases up the gully, or the next gap, farther east, or in the ferrying the boxes away by rowboat.

They were not all helpers, and the worn out crew of the *Jessie Woods* spent as much time chasing away pilferers as they did in salvaging the cargo. The Humphrey boys and the Cornells were appointed night watchmen to keep thieves away in the dark. To keep themselves awake they brewed a kettle of tea. It was green and the resultant liquid, pale in colour. To add strength they heaped the leaves in until the brew was richer in hue and so potent it would have floated the *Jessie Woods* could it have been squirted under her. Willy Humphrey and Willy Cornell were so dizzy with the dish that for a time they could not tell which was the top and which was the bottom of the Highlands.

Underneath the case goods the *Jessie* was laden with slab of fine marble. The marble was excellent ballast, but it held the *Jessie Woods* down all to well. Even after some of it had been got ashore or thrown overboard she failed to float, for she was full of water. Reluctantly, her captain gave orders to strip her completely, so as to save her gear, sails and spars, and while this was in process another storm arose, and the poor schooner, held on the bottom by the remaining marble, broke up.

This ancient disaster is recounted in the effort to identify the wreckage at the foot of the Highlands near Centre Point, which has been forming a topic for the end-of-the-season discussion. The eight or ten white oak ribs and the few strakes of narrow eight-inch planking worn to two inches thickness which the *Telegram* writer uncovered there recently, far above the present lake level, may be the side of a vessel wrecked elsewhere and thrown up into its present position by a very high sea or very extensive ice pack.

As said in earlier articles, these timbers and their adhering spikes and other fastenings would be suitable for a vessel of 150 tons register; and 150 tons was the recorded measurement of the *Jessie Woods*. So a tentative identification of the wreckage is that of the *Jessie Woods*; not dogmatically, but in the hope that if it is incorrect, the disproof of it will lead to the proper identification.

It is admitted that there is nothing, in the eighty- or ninety-year-old story of the loss of the *Jessie Woods*, to prove that she was lost at the exact spot where this wreckage has been uncovered. All the evidence suggests that she was wrecked a mile or a mile and a half farther west, and it is believed that her keel and parts of her bottom are still embedded where she struck. The wreckage over which dinghies were sailing this summer is said to be close to the gully, to the westward, and it is also said that slabs of marble have been seen in the lake in this vicinity, and have been dived for often by campers. If marble remains in this wreck under the water it would be pretty good proof that this was the *Jessie Woods*.

But that would not prove that the other wreckage a mile away, was not hers also. When she broke up, her bulwarks, decks and sides were torn off, and floated ashore, either piecemeal, plank by plank, or in large sections. It can be said with certainty that this wreckage now found at the foot of the Highlands high and dry inland above the water lever, is in a position where part of the *Jessie Woods* might be expected to be found after strong southwest gales.

The marble cargo of the *Jessie Woods* follow her like the trail of a paper chase. There is the green shimmer of the stone in the water which canoes and dinghies have reported from time to time. There are marble fragments found in the scanty sand of the beach. There are the marble slabs built into Scarborough's fine memorial cross. There are marble slabs used as well-covers, milk coolers, window-stoppers, and plant stands in Scarborough homes.

At a garden party in Scarborough six years ago, Mr. James G. Cornell, whose ancestral home is on the Kingston Road considerably north of the wreck, showed one of the marble slabs, marked with nine circles where geranium pots have been stood for generations for watering. He also showed an octagonal Waterbury clock which had hung in the *Jessie Woods*' cabin – part, probably of the "superior accommodations." These things had been rewards from the captain for valiant efforts as salvager and night watchman. The clock came to Mr. Cornell from the Humphrey family.

Albert S. Humphrey, 78, also of Scarborough, has a marble slab which has been used as a well cover for many years; a matter of pride with the Humphrey family, for William Humphrey, Albert's father, carried it up the Highland on his back. No chore for less than a giant, for it weighs two hundred pounds, and even up the gully, or down east where the wreckage had been uncovered, the path is very steep.

The marble was given to William Humphrey. Also some chains which have been called the anchor cables of the *Jessie Woods*, but are more probably her bowsprit shrouds or other headgear. They are light for chain cable, but they are very strong, and when they were used in logging operations on the Humphrey farm the strongest horses could not break them. Mr. Humphrey also has a crowbar, which is thought to have come from the *Jessie Woods*, or perhaps, more accurately was used in the salvage operations. A well-preserved grandson of the pioneers, Mr. Humphrey can still use the bar vigorously.

That the *Jessie Woods* was considered a particularly fine packet ship in her time is proved by the pains an artist named A.C. Currie took to depict her in 1836. His picture showing her flag-decked like an excursion steamer, dropping down the river past the American lighthouse, is preserved in the Niagara Historical Society's collection in the Niagara Museum. The decorations of the quarter-badges and cabin windows for the passenger accommodation under the raised quarter deck are emphasized, although it is not quite clear how the cabin was divided. The vessel was white hulled, with a fine figurehead, probably modeled from Miss Jessie herself, the daughter of one of the Niagara Dock Co. directors. The schooner rig of 1836 would be a decided antique today; sails loose-footed instead of being laced to the booms, a square topsail with reefbands, a topgallant sail above it, and on the mainmast a square-headed gafftopsail laced to a yard, like a lug sail, the like of which no living lake sailor has seen. The *Jessie Woods* probably had the same rig when she was lost; it would necessitate a crew of six or eight men, double the number that had to make good in the fore-and-aft schooner of fifty years later.

The year the *Jessie Woods* was lost is not known. There is a record of her on the old Port Whitby Harbour Co. books in 1855. She was probably lost that year, for Mr. Humphrey is certain she was gone before his father was married, and that was in 1856.

The log cabin where the sailors sought aid is still standing near the head of the gulley.

Written in 1951, this is the story of the Loretta Rooney, *the schooner that Snider had crewed upon fifty-five years before, about 1896. He knew her well, and it may have been one the vessels whose forecastle was described in the episode entitled "Watchamacallit."*

December 29, 1951
Little Lady of Fifty-five Years Ago

"Do you recall" asked R.W. Johnson, of St. Thomas, a while back "a trim fore-and-after called *Loretta Rooney*?

His question was prompted by mention of the recent death in Toronto of Miss Loretta Rooney, a beloved teacher in Loretto College, a near relative of James H. Rooney, MP for St. Pauls. The answer, although long delayed, is an emphatic "Indeed I do!"

The *Loretta Rooney* of Kingston was a white two-masted schooner with green trim at rail and covering board, a red beading in her bulwarks and lead colour paint below her load water line.

She was, as Mr. Johnson says, a trim fore-and-after, but she was trimmed pretty close. She was on the old canal model, blunt and straight sided. This enabled her to carry a big load on light draught for her inches, but her inches were few. She measured 156 tons and was 91 feet 7 inches from stem to sternpost, 23 feet 7 inches beam, 8 feet 3 inches depth of hold.

We got three hundred tons of soft coal for Garden Island into her by piling two heaps of it on deck over the hatches. This put her down half a foot by the head that is, six inches out of the horizontal plane, so that she rooted or steered like a truck with a flat tire.

We didn't know how much a truck would steer, in 1898, when I joined her, for rubber-tired self-propelling trucks were then in the future, but we got a good preview. Nevertheless we sailed her to Kingston and Garden Island and took her to Oswego afterwards without hitting either side of the lake, or, indeed using a tug. Eighteen ninety-six was an economy year on the lakes. Not that I ever knew any other kind.

This voyage was memorable because it unrolled for me the great scenic beauty of Ontario sailing. I had sailed before between city ports, but this introduced the charm of the islands and the rivers. We sailed up the Genesee for three miles to the loading trestles. My heart was in my mouth with the beauty of the river gorge and the terror of getting her around the bends without spearing the railroad bridge or the melon patches. It was my trick at the wheel. The Genesee had some fine falls hidden behind factories in Rochester, N.Y., if you know where to look for them.

Another great delight was viewing the Upper Gap and the islands studding the bosom of Lake Ontario between the Bay of Quinte and the St. Lawrence River – the outliers, indeed, of the Thousand Islands.

We came in between the False Ducks and Timber Island, with the Main Ducks and Galloos looming mysteriously in the enchanted air, and Amhurst Island, Simcoe Island, Wolfe Island, the Brothers, Salmon, Snake, Whiskey, Cedar and so forth sparkling in green and gold.

All were then plumy with trees, even Salmon, which is now as bare as a gnawed bone. Our destination also introduced me to Garden Island, the great rafting centre, the suzerainty of Hiram Calvin MP, then known as the King of the Island, as had been his father before him. The great man came down to the wharf and kindly invited us to divine service in the community church which served his colony of French and Irish timber men, ship carpenters, drogher crews and tugmen and their families.

The *Loretta Rooney* had been built in Kingston in 1866, thirty years before this voyage. She was christened the *Mary Taylor* and became the property of Capt. George Sherwood of Brighton. Some time after 1880 she passed into the hands of the Rooneys of Cobourg. They piled great loads of lumber on her for the box factory at Oswego, N.Y. Once she had so much that her stern was pressed down her rudder and locked it fast so that she could not be steered. Leaking like a sieve under the strain she floated and drifted across the lake, held up by the buoyancy of the cargo within her. The wind being fair, she drifted within sight of her destination, Oswego, and was towed in by the harbour tug. Unloaded, her rudder again functioned and she steered home for Cobourg.

Here she was so thoroughly overhauled and rebuilt that she was entitled to a new name, and *Loretta Rooney* was the name given, after pretty little Miss Loretta, who had arrived not long before.

The renamed vessel was later bought by Deseronto lumber shippers. She was damaged by fire the year after I was in her and became a tow barge.

All the Rooney schooners are gone now. Captain Hugh and Capt. "Big" Dan, in one generation, followed by Capt. "Little" Dan in the next, had among them the three-masters *Jessie Drummond*, *Sophia Minch* and *Annandale*, *Picton*, *Annie Falconer*, the *Loretta Rooney*, the *Wilfred Plunkett*, and the steam barge *Frank Campbell*. Capt. "Little" Dan Rooney, praise the powers, still flourished in the Senate at the town hall and in his Perry Street home above the lake, in Corktown, in Cobourg, of which he may well be proud. He cast his vote in the municipal elections of this month – and he will be 90 next Monday, the last day of old 1951.

A fair wind and smooth water to him, and to R.W. Johnson, who prompted such pleasant recollections, and to all other sailors, for 1952, and many Happy New Years.

Highland Creek and Rouge River

Just to the west of the old Port Union lies the mouth of Highland Creek. It is fourteen miles west of Toronto proper, but is only noticeable when passing over it on the Via or GO trains.

The creek is only a step across at its bar mouth now, but it must have been of impressive dimensions long ago, before the CNR bridge was built.

The creek mouth was a bay before the railway was built, probably ten or twelve feet deep inside the shoreline, with a bar outside where the silt of the river water met the lake waves and settled to the bottom.

When the railway line was built, a large fill was projected along this bar, leaving an opening where the west bank of the creek rose steeply for the ancient Centre Point, midway between Toronto and Whitby. This opening was bridged across. The railway built a long line of cribbing eastward, almost to Port Union, to protect the shore from erosion by rain and waves before the line was built, and to clear to the edge of the bank. Half of the stone filling these cribs disappeared by night back into the hold of the stonehookers who had earlier filled the cribs by day. The fill chocked the mouth of the creek and it became the swamp north of the railway line that it is now.

Before the railway came – or Port Union was built – the mouth of the Highland creek was a harbour of sorts, affording shelter for large rowed boats and small schooners.

A mile or so east of Port Union is the Rouge River. It was a favourite landing spot of the Highland Rangers, a number of small craft and small schooners that made their living taking small cargoes to and from the small ports and harbours east of Toronto, to Toronto. They date from a long way back.

There is a record of a handsome schooner called the *Duke of York* built by a Captain Hadley in 1820 at the mouth of the Rouge River. The next vessel known to have been built at the mouth of the Rouge was the *Wood Duck*, a small schooner of twenty-five tons which was owned and sailed by Moses Niblock of Port Credit forty years after her launching.

The steamer *Canada*, of 250 tons, one of the earliest steamers on Lake Ontario, was also built in the Rouge mouth in the winter of 1825-26 and towed up to York to receive her engines. She went into commission in 1827. Some time later Capt. William Quick, a staunch Loyalist, came to Rosebank – or the Rouge mouth – and spent a season building the schooner later christened *Charlotte of Pickering*.

There is a story that the *Charlotte* was frozen in the river when the winter of 1837 set in, and some of the Patriots, terrified by the fiasco of Montgomery's Tavern and the rebel leader Mackenzie's flight to safety in the United States, conceived the idea of following him in the *Charlotte*. There is a rumour that Captain Quick took them out to the lake, then turned to west by night, and turned them in to the militia at Toronto.

The *Northerner*, a fine three-masted schooner of moderate burden, 120 tons, valued at the high figure of $12,000 in 1856, had been built in the mouth of the Rouge, just before the Grand Trunk Railway closed the entrance to all but rowboats and canoes, with its bridge. She must have been the last vessel built there.

Both Highland Creek and the Rouge were navigable for sailing vessels of less than one hundred tons burden, for perhaps a mile in from the lake until the bridges for the railway were built in 1855 or 1856.

Hardwood ashes and potash (from the forest clearings) were carried in schooners from the mouths of the Rouge River and Highland Creek, and return cargoes of salt, flour and furniture were brought in. The hollows and ravines of the cliffs were hiding places of contraband goods. Large quantities of tea, leather (for harnesses) and general merchandise were landed night after night at the mouth of "Gates Gully" as recently as 1833 to avoid the import tax of "1 & 3" (£1, 3p.) and for other necessities of the early settler, including tobacco, which was nearly double the price of those in the United States.

Like so many other long lost ports of the northern shore of Lake Ontario, there is a story of the secret of buried treasure amongst the bulrushes of Highland Creek.

There was a big smuggling trade in the river mouths of the Humber, Rouge, and Highland Creek or the gullies of Scarborough Heights (now Scarborough Bluffs). Anywhere tracks could be made by farm wagons. Smugglers would send their illicit cargoes to shore at night by yawlboat after receiving a whistle signal in the dark from shore. There were always farmers, peddlers, or bagmen waiting, cash in hand.

The vessel would wait offshore with sail hoisted, and anchor ready for hoisting and slipping at the sound of a warning shot. Whole cargoes would be dumped or abandoned if something went amiss, as the penalty for smuggling could involve hanging.

The story of buried treasure in the marsh at Highland Creek is thought by some to have started when a smuggler had to quickly unload a cargo of tableware when its delivery to local farmers was unloaded.

The mouth of the Rouge River is now a Metropolitan Toronto park, and its boating activities is restricted to the very active Canoe Club.

Port Union

Its heyday as a port was before the steam railway was built between Toronto and Belleville. But a busy port it was.

In the early 1840s the farmers of the adjacent townships of Scarborough and Pickering (the old Edinburgh Township), separated by the townline between York and Ontario counties, joined forces with farmers and merchants back in Markham and formed the Scarborough, Markham, and Pickering Wharf Company, a favourite form of pioneer enterprise.

They had no natural harbour to develop, but they had enough business for one. They had to import their livestock, farm implements, nursery stock, hardware, sugar, salt, and drygoods, by way of either Toronto or Whitby, and this meant a heavy haul from either centre to the farms along the lake shore or back in the bush.

It was a long day's drive to town with their grain, potash, pearlash, logs, lumber, cordwood, shingles, tanbark, and other products of the soil which they wished to sell, and another long day's drive back with what they had to buy. So they picked a spot roughly half way between Whitby and Toronto, near the mouth of the Rouge River, built a wharf, and in effect said "Bring what we want here, and we will bring you what you want there."

It was sort of a lakeside market, and it worked.

They built square cribs from the two hundred-foot pine trees growing on the shore. They built the first one at the very edge of the water, and filled it with stone. The next they hauled out till the water was "up to the horses bellies" and anchored it with poles and sank it by filling it with more beach stone. The next they had to pole into position and anchor and fill, and so on, until they had a series of long stone-filled boxes projecting into the lake in a line about fifty yards long. When the outermost crib was sunk the water was not more than twelve feet deep. They decked this like a bridge and built a storehouse at the lake end and another on the shore. The lake bank, which has since receded seventy-five feet or more, at this time dropped gently down to a beach of sand and gravel.

The wharf which gave the port a name – and existence – ran from the end of the town line (now called Port Union Road) in a southeasterly direction so that the entire wharf was in Pickering Township, as was the village and the railway station.

The storehouse at the shore end of the pier was so constructed that farmers could shovel their grain into its bins from the level of the foot of the highway at the top of the bank. There are old recorded memories of the well-fed teams standing for hours, switching away the flies, on the highway or townline, all the way down from the Kingston Road, while wagon after waggon backed up to the open doors of the granary, and men below ran vessels trying to load at the wharf while the wind permitted. The storehouse on the outer end of the pier was for apples, of which there was a large export, or for perishable goods arriving.

Thomas Adams, an "American Dutchman" carpenter and mariner, came to Port Union about the time of the War of 1812 and built a schooner in the mouth of Highland Creek in partnership with one John Allen. She was called the *Mary Ann*. Records of 1851 indicate that the schooner *Caledonia*, ninety-five tons, was built at Port Union in 1851 by Helliwell and Heatherington (There is a record of the *Caledonia* making shipments from Port Whitby to Kingston and Montreal in 1853 and 1854).

Port Union was not, of course, a port of registry but it did boast of a fleet known as the Highland Rangers. These were small craft built on the beach or in the creekmouth, and plying a thrifty trade in farm produce, ashes, cordwood, stone sand, gravel and other freight as could be picked up along the shores of the Highlands of Scarborough. Wood at one time sold as high as $7.50 per cord because of its quality. This price was brought down to $4.50 by 1896 with the competition from coal, but not before a million dollars worth of wood was cut from farmers bushes in Scarborough and Pickering. The Highland Rangers of Port Union carried a large share of this cut.

The railway was built in 1856, and it would appear that Port Union was an original stop (because of the Scarborough grade, the engines needed water, and a water tower was built at Port Union, which became a landmark from the lake). In 1857, *Lovel's Directory* lists "Port Union, Canada West," as a small place with a population of "about 30." When the schooner *Lillian* was lost at centre point, just above Port Union, in 1899 or 1900, that place was described as having "a water tank, six houses, a hotel and a pumping station."

Port Union was not always a popular port with ships captains and ships owners because of its poor anchorage and lack of shelter. The schooner *Ayr* (Captain Muir of Port Dalhousie was the skipper) ran ashore at Port Union about the end of November one year. It cost $2,000 to get her off.

Port Union was at its peak in the early 1870s. It had two hotels in 1871 – Joseph Moon's, which may have been called Heatherston's or Herrington's originally, and a hotel owned by Thomas J. Laskay, built in 1860 by a man named Stoner.

There was still an in-and-out trade from the wharf: small vessels calling for apples, flour, grain, or tanbark; or to land farm animals or young fruit trees from across the lake long after the arrival of the locomotives. There are records of steamers calling to take farmers on excursions to Toronto or Hamilton, and moonlight dancing with a band. Great quantities of cordwood were delivered at Port Union to fuel the locomotives, and there was a yard for single-cutting the logs and storing the wood for shipment to Toronto. Many schooners had a part of this trade up until the 1880s and later.

By 1895 the wharf had washed away, the storehouses had fallen down, and the flow from the farms to the cities had begun.

All that remains of a once thriving metropolis is Laskay's old hotel, much changed, unrecognizable as to its original purpose. Gone is the two-storey verandah with four pillars, a panelled timber front and clapboarded sides and front, ballroom and fancy dining room. It was until recent fire a private residence, standing alone, lost behind the Johns-Manville Plant and the recently demolished General Electric factory, and only visible from the passing trains. The nearby GO Transit station is now called Rouge Hill. The name Port Union remains only as the name of the roadway leading to the dead end at the train tracks.

Frenchman's Bay

In 1843 William Edwards and William Henderson of the village of Dunbarton, in the then-named township of Edinborough (now Pickering), cut a channel through from the lake which turned Frenchman's Bay, five miles east of Port Union, into the port of Pickering Harbour. They used what was described as "sort of elevator worked by Horsepower" for the dredging. Schooners were then able to come up to a stone bridge at the head of the bay – now a culvert under the railway tracks – where a wharf and warehouse were built.

Neither the bay, nor the name, appear on early maps, even one dated 1813 which was based on Governor Simcoe's surveys.

The bar from Duffin's Creek, which now encloses the bay, may not have been in existence when the survey was made. When the sandbar stretched across the high shore near Petticoat Creek, to the west of the present harbour, Frenchman's Bay became a landlocked pond. The water from the other creek at Dunbarton to the north trickled through the sandbar, but apparently there was no navigable entrance from the lake until the above men with their crude elevator worked by horsepower scooped away the channel, and cribbed it to keep it from filling up again. For this reason, Frenchman's Bay was, and is, one of the very

Photo courtesy of Lorne Joyce

At left the *Wood Duck II*, at right the *Lillian*. The *Wooduck II*, a former yacht converted to a stone-hooker, was owned and worked as a stonehooker out of Port Credit by Snider and his brother Roy.

few private harbours in the country. A harbour that was an afterthought of nature, developed by pioneers' enterprise, and has ever since been treated as an orphan by politicians. Even the coal oil for the green harbour light had to be paid for by harbour dues, which the harbourmaster had great difficulty in collecting.

The original warehouse at Dunbarton was removed about 1853, ten years after it was built, and the wharfage rapidly fell into decay. This wharf was replaced by one near the east side of the entrance, serviced by a plank road along the beach to the lower end of the sideroad just east of the village of Dunbarton. This wharf was replaced, by a another wharf on the east side of the bay.

Because of the shifting sands in the harbour, ships entering from the lake had to steer straight north, past the piers, then break off sharply to avoid the sandspit, then head eastward to a timber crib in the middle of the bay, and then over to the big red elevator, coal sheds, and ice houses on the east side of the bay which provided the wharfage of the port from the 1870s onward.

As business in the harbour deteriorated, the red elevators and the ice house was torn down, and a new warehouse was built to serve as a storehouse for the stone, sand, and gravel business which dominated the area in the early 1900s.

There used to be ten feet of water at the harbour entrance, and vessels drawing more than that were hove out of the harbour by kedge and windlass and capstan to the three-fathom line, just outside the piers.

There were many regular schooners in and out of the harbour, including the *Highland Chief* and the *Lillian* the *Island Queen* the *Madeline* and even the *Sir C.T. Van Straubenzie*. Excursion steamers including the *Argyle*, the *Garden City*, and the *Chippewa* were frequent callers, taking passengers to Niagara. The passengers were ferried from the pier to the large steamers by Mr. Sparks fishing boat. Many stonehookers frequented the bay in later years.

The *Belle of Dunbarton* was built at the mouth of Duffins's Creek, (not in Frenchman's Bay). Some of the old schooners were no doubt built within the harbour.

In the olden times, when there was ten feet of water in the channel, some larger sailing yachts of the day entered the harbour. The Churchill brothers *Medora*, and Commodore Gooderham's *Vivia 1*, a deep forty-foot cutter, are recorded as entering the harbour. However, when W.G. Gooderham's *Aileen*, which drew over ten feet, tried to enter in a storm she bumped hard on the bottom in the heaving seas of the entrance, and had to lighten ballast before they could exit the harbour and sail her home again when the storm died down.

Perhaps the last "big vessel" to enter Frenchman's Bay was Capt. Dan Rooney's three-master *Charlie Marshall*, which rode out a gale in the piers in 1913, the time the steamer *Alexandria* was lost. Or maybe George Atkinson's old *Guido* was the last three-and-after to enter Frenchman's Bay, although there is a suggestion that she was wrecked near Grafton before 1913.

November 18, 1944
A "Hesperus" out of Frenchman's Bay

In 1864, with the American Civil War drawing to a close, William Bellchambers built a little schooner in Frenchman's Bay. He named her the *Anna Bellchambers* after his wife or daughter. The vessel was called "Anna Bell" for short, so her name has become confused with that of Annabel Chambers, in narration, but *Anna Bellchambers* it was, and so it stands on the first Dominion register after Confederation.

This gives the vessel's dimensions as 52 feet long on deck, 13 feet 6 inches beam, 5 feet depth of hold and 31 tons register. She was a narrow version of one of the many stonehookers which used to crowd the bridge at Port Credit or Westmarket street slip in Toronto. She was not a stonehooker, but a wood carrier, one of the fleet which supplied the growing Queen City with fuel for its homes and factories, steamboats and locomotives. There were no internal combustion engines, coal was a novelty, and everybody used cordwood – hard or soft. Woodwharves, which stretched from George to Yonge Street, were piled with cordwood like the coal mountains of today at the east end of the harbour.

Snider Collection, Archives of Ontario

The *Madeline*, Bronte built, entering Toronto harbour after she had been converted to a stonehooker, towing her scow.

Photo of a sketch by Snider

The *Sir C.T. Van Straubenzie* of St. Catharines, clearing Toronto, 1895. This vessel was owned by Capt. John Williams of Kew Beach.

Towards the end of October the *Anna Bellchambers* loaded fifteen or twenty cords of green wood on the shore half a mile west of Frenchman's Bay, ferrying the sticks from the beach. It blew hard from the northwest, but she lay in the lee, and when the wind lulled, ventured out for the wood market in Toronto. Her captain was William Edwards, maybe the very man of that name who cut the channel into Frenchman's Bay. Captain Edwards had two men in his crew. Peter Young of Dunbarton, an old saltwater man, and another named Mansfield, and he also took along his son, Joseph Henry, a lad of fourteen. The schooner had been named after his mother, who had died four years before.

A man and a boy could handle the small schooner, but she leaked with the heavy deckloads, and an extra crewman was required to keep her pumped and to pile out the wood at the wharf. While the wood was in her she was sure to float, but in the two preceding autumns she had waterlogged whiled trying to get into Toronto, and lifesavers had taken her crew off and helped pump her out when the lake calmed down.

Capt. Jack Marks of the RCYC steamer *Kwasind* used to tell of seeing his boyhood chum, Joe Edwards, going aboard the *Anna Bellchambers* that morning, all eager for the trip to the big city, his pockets bulging with red snow apples, his eyes dancing with expectation.

It took hours for the laden schooner to beat up the meridian of the Eastern Gap. This was then a half-mile stretch of shallow water across the long neck of the peninsula which started at Scarborough Bluffs and hooked around towards the Garrison and Queen's Wharf at the far west-end of Toronto. There was a narrow winding channel through it – marked by two buoys – but no lighthouses and no piers.

When Captain Edwards got this far he anchored and sent one of his men ahead in the schooner's little scow to hang lanterns on the buoys. It was dusk, and the wind was going around so that the schooner had to zig zag to get through. He did this with some misgivings for it was just in the same position that the *Anna Bellchambers* had waterlogged twice before; and she was already leaking more than enough.

The man either missed the buoys or lost the lanterns, and sculled on across to the city. When he got what he wanted there it was blowing too hard for him to get back. The wind had gone around to the east and was freshening to a gale.

The *Anna Bellchambers* reared and plunged at her anchor, with all on board watching anxiously for a lantern's beam and a hail from the returning scow. They pumped and pumped, but the water gained on them.

The Port Credit scow *Samson*, or the *Olive Branch* – they couldn't be sure which – drove past in the early night under a squatted foresail. They could just make her out in the dark. They talked of her big race with the *Catherine Hayes* and the *Hunter* ten years before, when Bob Collins wrung the *Samson*'s mainmast's head off, carrying the sail. Billy Hutchinson was sailing with more caution this time.

They climbed up on the drenched deckload, for the "Annabels's" deckload began to wash away. Before it was all gone the weight of it, water-soaked, rolled the little vessel over on her side. Poor Peter Young was swept off and drowned, although Captain Edwards caught him once. He could not hold on in the fore rigging. Captain Edwards scrambled up the main rigging and lashed himself to the crosstrees, with young Joe buttoned inside his overcoat to keep him warm. The only friend they had left was the tall, stone lighthouse on Gibraltar Point, two miles away. Its regular flash through the darkness beamed encouragement.

"Bear up, Joey," said the father. "They'll see us as soon daylight comes, and take us off. They did that the last time before. It'll soon be light! It'll soon be light!"

"Don't be scared to die, Pa, I ain't," whispered Joey through numbed lips. "I can hear music sounding on the shore."

But the only earthly music was the tramp of the surf and the howl of the increasing wind. It got darker after midnight, and thick, smothering snow began to fall. Even the faint glow of the city gaslamps on the clouds vanished. The light on the point shut out, hidden in snow whirls. Billy Hutchinson, homing for Port Credit, missed this stern range, and could see nothing of the Credit light ahead. In the dark he tried to round the point of Toronto Island and gain shelter at the Queen's wharf, but the hooker swamped in the trough of the sea and drifted before the bursting billows until she struck on the Dutchman's Bar, and was dashed on to that shaly headland on the far side of Humber Bay known variously as Pig Iron, Two-Tree, Booten's, and Van Every's Point. And there she was found next day, her masts gone, decks stove in, everything covered with snow and ice and Billy Hutchinson and his mate dead in the breakers.

William Ward, a hardy fisherman whose name survives in Ward's Island, had to dig his way out of his island cottage in the morning. The cottage stood a thousand feet south of the present island breakwall, and three fathoms of water now washes over its hearthstone. The first thing he saw on the shore was cordwood.

"Don't tell me the "Annabel" has waterlogged again!" cried he. He fired a gun and roused Bob Berry, a big oarsman, and they ran a fishing skiff down the snowbank to look for the wreck. By this time it was light enough to distinguish a sort of iceberg rising and falling to the eastward, but moving in with the seas. They pulled to it, through a wide wake of floating cordwood and planking, which crystallized into a small schooner on her beam ends. There was a blob at the main crosstrees which they took to be an unstowed topsail. William Ward hacked with his clasp knife at the frozen lashing and cut loose the captain and his son in one mass.

The frozen bundle fell into the boat. The rescuers dragged the mass into the Ward cottage and sent across to the city for three doctors. For seven hours, till darkness fell on that short November day, they worked ceaselessly on the man and the boy. When the lighted the coal oil lamp on the kitchen table William Edwards began to murmur; "Light! Light! They'll see us soon, and come for us Joey! It's getting light now!"

But for Joey the light that shone was from the place where there is neither sorrow nor crying, and there is no night there, for the Lord God giveth them light. He had passed hours before into the arms of our heavenly Father.

The *Anna Bellchambers* parted her cables as the day wore on, and drove up the lake. Her broken hull washed in on the beach under the tall lighthouse whose far off ray the night before, sole comfort of the perishing, had been smothered by the November snow while four poor fellows died.

Such was the wreck of the Lake Ontario Hesperus in the midnight and snow of 1873. The facts are as given by Capt. Jack Marks, Capt. William Ward, and Mrs. Edith Southgate, Toronto, who had them from her mother, a sister of Captain Edwards, who survived the wreck. Captain Edwards married twice, and had a second son, Joseph, who has been very kind to "Schooner Days." The date of this was October 30, 1873.

October 13, 1945
A Credit to the *Maple Leaf*

The Maple Leaf man is no more. Referring not to Alexander Muir, creator of the gallant song, but to Capt. Richard Goldring, for thirty-one years master of the comeliest little schooner on Lake Ontario, the *Maple Leaf* of Toronto.

He brought his good ship up from babyhood, for she was newly built when his father bought her and put him in charge of her, a proud young skipper, just out of his teens. As such he brought her safely through the Great Gale of 1880, and he brought her back to life from the Great Esplanade Fire of 1885, in which she burned and sank with a half dozen other craft for which there was no comeback.

With his own hands – and Bronte master carpenter Lem Dorland's assistance – he hewed out the new chestnut frames and fine arching clipper stem which transformed her from a spoon-bow to a yachtlike profile. With these same capable hands, and his younger

Capt. Richard Goldring, of Port Whitby, at the wheel of the *Maple Leaf*. Behind him is the yawlboat on the davits.

brother Charlie's staunch help, he lifted a hundred thousand tons of stone from the bed of Lake Ontario and brought it in the *Maple Leaf* for Toronto's pavement and buildings, from foundations to gravel roofing, for the city's harbour cribs, piers, and entrance works.

A hundred thousand tons is a lot for two pairs of hands to lift into and out of a one hundred ton schooner, but "Little Dick" Goldring and all his brothers belonged to a generation of Canadians who did not shrug off hard work upon the despised and envied "foreigners" who reap its rewards.

Canada satisfied "Little Dick" Goldring. The rewards of his useful life were: a large, well brought up family, every boy and girl occupying an honoured place in the country; a Royal Humane Society Medal for saving lives with the *Maple Leaf* off the Eastern Gap; a comfortable, substantial home, built with his own hands, in Port Whitby, surrounded by an orchard, flower beds, and vegetable garden of his own planting, his own vine and fig tree. This very year, at 87, he dug, sorted, and basketed the winter supply of potatoes which he himself had planted in the spring. He was at work in his garden four days before he died.

He had outgrown his beloved *Maple Leaf* twenty-five years ago. When he sold her she died soon after, broken-backed and broken-hearted. He established a yard in the little port where he had been glad to bring coal cargoes for others in intervals between stone raking and carrying YMCA boys on summer cruises to the Thousand Islands. The *Maple Leaf* was never idle while "Little Dick" Goldring had her.

Snider Collection, Archives of Ontario

The *Maple Leaf*, towing a stonehooking scow, as she sailed out of Port Whitby.

"See these stones?" said the old man with pride one evening in Port Whitby last month. "I got them when I took the family on a holiday to the Bay of Quinte in the *Maple Leaf*. It was just a pleasure cruise. So I threw in a load of stone before we started back and unloaded them for the foundations of this house I had planned for here. In my mind's eye I already had my anchors down in Port Whitby. Have you noticed them?"

Yes they had attracted attention to the house before knowing who lived there. In each corner of the walk leading in under the shade of the maple trees was a neatly designed anchor in the concrete – laid out as a sailor would for good holding, splayed, not tandem or parallel.

He told us of how he came through the Great Gale of 1880; not heroically, just sensibly. Newly installed in the original *Maple Leaf*, he had taken her down to Prince Edward County for a bit at the barley trade – 1 1\2¢ a bushel, from bay ports to Oswego, $60 freight for perhaps a week's work and waiting. They wanted him to load at Wellington, on the dangerous open, harbourless, west face of the county. But he wouldn't be tempted. Instead he beat into South Bay and up behind Waupoos and then into Black Creek and up till he came to the roller bridge that was pulled back and forth by oxen. Somewhere above it and near the village of Milford was the loading place. The barley was carried aboard the *Maple Leaf* in bushel boxes with a handle at each end. Four thousand times the box had to be emptied to make up the load.

Then to get her down the creek they had to heave her out with the windlass, dragging her bodily through a shoal of yielding sawdust formed by fifty years of dumping from a Milford Mill. However, they got her out and through the roller bridge and down to the big bluff at the mouth of the creek, below where Goldhunter and the Hibernia were built. Beyond that the open water of South Bay; beyond that the open lake.

"Little Dick" was in haste to reach Oswego and cash his freight but did not like the look of the sky. It was muggy and fitful, that November 6. Capt. John Walters spoon-bowed scow *Sea Bird* was lying loaded at anchor between the Black Creek Bluff and Waupoos. He wouldn't go out either. "Little Dick" moored the *Maple Leaf* right in the river mouth, making her lines fat on the biggest trees on the shore.

At midnight it blew a hurricane. Turning out to see that his lines were holding, Captain Goldring was almost blown overboard by the gusts sweeping down the creek. But there was no scope for the sea to make up between the banks and the *Maple Leaf* never surged, though the wind pressure on her bare poles listed her and torn-off branches filled her deck. Uprooted trees came hurling down from the bluff above but missed her. With morning light he looked for the *Sea Bird*. She had dragged both anchors and gone ashore and bilged on the point, even in the shelter of South Bay, but the crew was safe.

On the lake, five vessels had been totally wrecked, twenty had been damaged, and thirty sailors had been drowned. Groping through a fog some time afterwards, a near-calm off Bald Head Island, Captain Goldring saw a square post projecting from the water. He put down the *Maple Leaf*'s yawl boat and sculled over to it. It was a schooner's paulpost, the great timber forward of the windlass, into which the heel of the bowsprit fits. Like every paulpost on the lakes then, it had a horseshoe nailed on it for luck. Captain Goldring recognized the horseshoe.

The paulpost was the solitary memorial, the oaken tombstone, of the schooner *Belle Sheridan* of Toronto, which had been wrecked on that November 7, 1880, drowning Capt. James McSherry, with three of his sons and all of the crew save one.

Originally published in 1935, this is the true story of a little girl on the lakes about 1865, and describes schooner traffic into the lost port of Dundas Ontario and some of the problems encountered by Canadian schooners in American ports during the American Civil War.

November 24, 1935

Six-Men Lassie

When Mrs. Covell of Toronto was a little girl, her name was Amanda Quick, and she lived at Presqu'ile Bay.

Her father, Capt. William Quick, built a beautiful new schooner on the bay shore, and called her the *Amanda*, after her. The *Amanda* measured 118 tons register. She could carry one hundred thousand feet of lumber. She was white with green trimmings and red petticoats, and she had a half-clipper bow.

Captain Quick often took his little daughter sailing with him. Even though she had to stretch to reach the kingspoke of the wheel, she was a good helmsman. Many a time she steered her namesake around the old stone lighthouse on Toronto Point and into the harbour past the little wooden lighthouse now standing on Fleet Street with automobiles whizzing past it.

Fleet Street was all deep water then, a quarter-mile from the shore, and the wooden lighthouse wasn't where it is now, but out on the end of the Queen's Wharf, about where one lone willow tree stands behind the Rogers Majestic plant.

They used to trade to Dundas, she and her father and a crew of five or six men, loading lumber there for Charlotte on the south shore of Lake Ontario. The only maritime trade anyone would dream of attempting with Dundas in these days or this century would be by prairie schooner. To us, Dundas – seven miles west of Hamilton – seems as inland as Orangeville. We connect it inseparably with truck traffic and the great motor highway.

But Dundas was not ever thus. Schooners were built there – the *James Coleman* for one, and the *Great Western* for another. James Coleman and Co. were vessel owners in Dundas. One of their ships was the *Three Seas*, renamed the *Lochniel*.

The *Amanda* would sometimes make two trips a week between Dundas and Charlotte, with $900 freight per trip. Fine returns for a little vessel rated at an insurable value of $4,000 in 1862. The "Dundas Highway" she followed was paved with gold – American gold, for the Civil War was on, and careful skippers insisted on payments in the States, and came home with pickle-jars full of American eagles and half-eagles, the proceeds of a season's work when banks were little used.

To reach Dundas the *Amanda* used to sail through the Burlington piers, cross Burlington Bay, and nose into Desjardins Canal, through the railway drawbridge, scene of the still famous disaster of 1857. There was no tow path on either side of the canal. It was just a shallow cutting through the marsh, sometimes with nine feet of water in it, with piling here and there to keep the marsh silt from flowing back. You may still discern some of this old piling as you whizz over the cut-off on Highway No. 2.

In the days of the two *Amanda*s the only way of getting through the canal without a tug – then rare – was to pole the schooner along, men walking from bow to stern, pushing with poles against the muddy bottom, pulling them out with a weary suck when the walk was ended, and towing them forward to start all over again. The poles made a great splashing among the fleets of geese which almost paved Burlington Bay and the canal with shining whiteness. Sometimes a stray goose made good eating.

The alternative to poling was running lines from post to post and heaving the vessel along with the windlass or capstans. Sometimes, when the wind was strong ahead, this was the easier way.

One day in the 1860s the *Amanda* piled her decks high with another load of Dundas lumber, and trotted back to Charlotte with it, steering in through the old wooden piers, guided by the stone lighthouse, all overgrown with vines now and dark for decades, but still standing on the hill on the west bank of the Genesee. The first morning, when they came to unload, Tom was missing from the crew. Next day Dick and Harry had gone. So had Hank and Jim. Next day, when the last of the lumber was out of her, even the mate had disappeared.

Bounty-jumping was one of the Canadian sports or industries at this Civil War time. Uncle Sam needed soldiers to march through Georgia and other parts. Voluntary enlistment petered out. They tried the "draught," which was just conscription, and bounties or rewards for volunteers. Thousands of Canadians served in the Union armies, from devotion to principle or need of pelf, shouting the "Battle Cry of Freedom." And hundreds of others, little to their credit, took the bounty money, or hired themselves as substitutes for Americans who had been draughted, and deserted at the first opportunity, and hired themselves over again or took the bounty whenever they could get it. Some were deservedly shot and some were killed jumping from trains, and some got deservedly rich spoiling the Egyptians.

The *Amanda*'s crew were parading in Rochester in forage caps and blue uniforms, along with the crews of a dozen or more Canadian schooners which lay idle in the Genesee. Nothing could be done about getting Tom, Dick, Harry, and the rest back. Other captains decided to wait, in the hope that some of the bounty-takers would succeed in deserting, and come crawling aboard in the dark, but Captain Quick said, philosophically, "Well, I still have two Amandas," and the others good-naturedly fell-to and helped him hoist the big sails which required a full crew. One of these captains was old Captain George, of Brighton, whose crew had stayed with him.

Captain George threw off their lines for them and, with a fair wind out of the river, and little Amanda at big *Amanda*'s wheel, Captain Quick sailed for Presqu'ile and home with $900 freight money in the cabin and a winter's work in shipbuilding on his mind.

So much confidence had he in the two ladies of the same name that he set both gafftopsails and the jibtopsail as the schooner dropped out of the piers. They had a nice quiet run across, all the way, fifty miles. They were all day and all night crossing.

In mid-lake they sighted a large, square, stick of oak, lost overboard from the deck-load of some vessel. There was a great trade in square timber at this time. Captain Quick had his eye open for material for a third schooner, to be built during the following winter. He had built one for Sarah Jane, his elder daughter, and this one for Amanda, and hoped to build one for her little brother, William John. So he ran his fore-gafftopsail down and rounded the *Amanda* to alongside the flotsam. After a lot of heaving, they at last swung the big twelve-inch stick on deck.

"It'll make a grand keel" cried Captain Quick, hoisting up the gafftopsail again and letting the *Amanda* fill away for the north shore.

The wind held light. Sometimes Captain Quick stretched out for a sleep while Amanda steered and sometimes he steered while she lay down, or got their food ready. They were all night in the lake. When the sun rose next morning no land was to be seen, but lake gulls came to them through the haze and after a while the tall light on Presqu'ile Point showed up.

They sailed into Presqu'ile Bay while the day was still young. Old Captain Leslie, the customs officer, father of R.Y. Leslie, of Brighton, sauntered down to receive Captain Quick's arrival report.

"Any American cargo?" asked he, as a matter of form.

"No," said Captain Quick, equally formal, "nothing but a cargo of timber, loaded in Canadian waters."

"Humph," laughed Captain Leslie, "where are your crew?"

"That little lass there," said Captain Quick, "is all six of them."

February 23, 1935

Gunboat Times on the Great Lakes

That square stick of timber Capt. William Quick and his little daughter picked up in mid-lake when they were bringing the *Amanda* home alone, did make a grand keel for the new schooner Captain Quick had planned to build at Brighton the following winter.

This was the *William John* called after Captain Quick's second son. William John became a captain like his father. The schooner named after him had a successful career, until one night she struck the water works pier at Kingston. And that was the end of her.

Orin Quick, William John's elder brother, never had a family schooner named for him, but he did better than that. He became a master mariner out of Presqu'ile and then crossed the lake to Wilson, N.Y., and established a shipyard there. He continued to sail vessels as well as build them.

Capt. William Quick's sailor daughter Amanda, who helped him salvage the *William John*'s future keel, became a sailor's bride. She married the late Capt. John Covell, of Brighton. One of her treasures is a large framed model of a Great Lakes barquentine, the *Jessie Bell*, which her husband made sixty years ago. Captain Covell sailed a small schooner called the *Jessie Bell*, liked the name, and he called this big dream ship, represented by the barquentine model, after the actual craft. He was a well-known lake mariner. One of his early commands was the Brighton schooner *Primrose*, of sixty-one tons register, built at Oswego. She drowned crew after crew until he got her, and then she behaved herself. He later commanded the excursion steamer *Flower City*, plying from Rochester, and still later took charge of the American tug *Blazer*, which towed the great dredges engaged in keeping the Maumee River clear at Toledo.

Mrs. Covell now lives with her grandson, Mr. O.A. Marshall. She was born at Presqu'ile Bay, ninety miles east of Toronto. Not at the Cove, around which the present summer colony clusters, but away up the bay on the west shore, north and west of Brighton Wharf. Her father had his shipyard and wharf and warehouse on the west shore. There was a considerable settlement at the head of the bay at this time, and grain, lumber, and cordwood used to be shipped from the wharves. Farmers used to line up for half a mile back on the roads, teaming grain to the long wharf in the bay.

This was a generation before the Murray Canal was cut through into the Bay of Quinte. Cargoes for Quinte had to be unloaded at the Carrying Place docks and run across on the wooden railway. Where the canal was cut through was Weese's Creek, usually filled with vessels crowding in to load cordwood. Cordwood was the domestic fuel for the province, and cordwood fed every locomotive and every furnace and every firehold. Sometimes as many as fifty vessels would be in Presqu'ile Bay. Capt. Dolph Corson, the elder, sailed the schooner *Wanderer* out of Presqu'ile at this time. Old Capt. George Sherwood was another of the bay traders. He would never sail on Sunday; but little Amanda Quick noted and remembered the comment that it always turned out that at the end of season he had made as many trips anyone else. His son still lives Brighton.

Captain Quick built vessels in between seasons and sold them or sailed them himself. First he bought the American schooner Kentucky at Sackett's Harbour, took her to Presqu'ile and used her bottom and outfit to build a larger schooner which he called the *Sarah Jane*, after his first daughter. This was in 1843.

He sailed the *Sarah Jane* for eleven years or more. There is an entry in the old books of the Port Whitby Harbour Co. in 1853, of the schooner *Sarah Jane*, William

Quick master, loading 5,440 bushels of wheat there at 3 1\2¢ a bushel freight, for Kingston, and carrying lumber from Port Whitby in 1854.

In 1862 he built the *Amanda*, in which he and little Amanda had their good times together, carrying lumber out of Dundas at $900 a freight sometimes, and making generally well while the sun of the Reciprocity Treaty and the American Civil War shone on the Great Lakes. The *Sarah Jane* worked until she rotted and was dismantled. The *Amanda* continued in the lake trade until she waterlogged off Port Hope one night with a cargo of cordwood. Captain Quick and his crew escaped with their lives when the schooner was lost.

The ten years between 1855 and 1865 were prosperous in Canada, from the high prices for natural products beginning with the Crimean War, and the disturbances which followed when John Brown's body lay a-mouldering in the grave.

It was exciting, too, sailing the lakes, when they began to sprout gunboats, homemade ones like the *Rescue, Hercules, Royal, Prince Alfred, Magnet*, and the *W.T. Robb, Cherub* and the *Britomarte*, and the *Heron*, following the "Trent affair" and the Fenian Raid of 1866. Captain McMaster formed his Volunteer Naval Brigade and trained them to be "ready-ay-ready" in the schooner *Eureka*, out of Toronto. The *Robb* was a Toronto timber tug, which carried troops to Ridgeway in 1866. Her bones have been a bulwark for Victoria Park for forty years. The other "homemade" gunboats were tugs and passenger steamers pressed into service.

Scares were many among the lake shipping during the American Civil War and Fenian Raids.

Frank Guy was telling the other day of how the rising mist one morning revealed a schooner in the marsh where the creek came into the lake at Oshawa. Apparently small vessels could get in there seventy years ago. Someone spotted a "redcoat" on board, and the rumour ran that the Fenians were landing, disguised in the uniforms of the British regulars. The soldiers who held Mr. Daniel Conant's residence as a picket point, rushed down to the beach only to discover that the "redcoat" was the red and black checked flannel shirt of a deck hand who was altogether amazed at his own sudden importance.

About the same time word reached Whitby that the schooners *Trade Wind* and *Enterprise* had left Charlotte with armed men on board. Supposition was that the Fenians captured them in the Genesee river and were making another raid. Citizens besought the harbourmaster to stretch chains across the harbour mouth. This was vetoed, because the chains might wreck any vessel attempting to enter the harbour in the dark. Next day the *Trade Wind* and the *Enterprise* appeared manned by their usual crews.

"Where are your arms?" some of the relieved burgesses demanded jokingly trying to cover their scare.

"Behind our fists!" shouted back the sailors, not at all pleased at being taken for Fenians. "How d'ye think we'd get them sails aloft if we kept 'em folded like you town dudes?"

Black eyes and bloody noses given and taken behind the old International Hotel on Port Whitby Road restored harmony in the community.

The narrator of this next story is Magistrate J.J. O'Conner. This is a story as told to Snider and retold many years later, as only Snider could retell it, in his eighteenth "Schooner Days" column. Magistrate O'Connor came from Oshawa, and as a youth had sailed, and in later years was captain, of many schooners sailing out of Whitby Harbour.

This story concerns the schooner Magdala, *built by McKay and Sons of Quebec in 1870. She was described as being "beamy, fine lines fore and aft, with lofty top-masts and a long jib boom." At the time J.J. O'Connor shipped on her she was commanded and owned by Capt. George Farewell of Oshawa.*

May 30, 1931

The Hickory Jib Boom

I had some lively times on the *Magdala*, not the least of which was when we towed out of Port Hope, after discharging a cargo of coal, bound for Whitby. It was blowing a living gale from the eastward with a heavy sea. When the tug let go we set the fore-sail and a squatted foresail, making the run of thirty-six miles in two hours and twenty minutes. We entered the Whitby piers at a terrific pace. In lowering the foresail, it jammed – bless those heavy man-killing halliard blocks – and would not come down.

We let go both anchors. They fouled.

With the piece of the foresail on her and two anchors tumbling over another on the bottom instead of taking hold, she would neither steer nor stop.

Her long jib boom striking out ahead of her like a lance, was a beautiful tapering spar of hickory. According to forecastle lore at the time, this was agin' the law, although I have never been able to find anything about it in the statue books. The idea was, I suppose, that such a stout stick was a deadly weapon in the collision, where a spruce or pine spar would snap off easily. The *Magdala*'s nosepole certainly made a wicked gash: for as we swung slowly to the wind she poked it into the side of the Watson elevator – since demolished – and ripped open a bin of barley. The gushing grain made a splash of dull yellow in the settling dusk. Then, stopped by the solidity, the force of the wind at length caught us and caused us to drift back from the wharf until the anchors held her in the harbour.

Archives of Ontario

Aerial view of Port Whitby taken in 1919.

When things were snugged down for the night the skipper asked me to take the boat, go ashore and wander around the old International Hotel which then flourished in Port Whitby, and note the comments on our entry.

In those days the International Hotel in Port Whitby was a sort of Royal York, St. Lawrence Market, Albany Club, Board of Trade, and Union Station rolled into one very compact hall. Port Whitby is now about as dead as Mount Pleasant so far as shipping goes, but at this time it had big sailing vessel trade in grain and lumber, and steamers called regularly.

Travellers drove to Port Whitby and put up at the International to await the boat for Kingston and Montreal, or Toronto and Hamilton or, crossing the lake to Oswego and Ogdensburg. Farmers stayed there when they came in with their oats and wheat and barley or to buy their winter's coal which the vessels brought in.

The whole country used to be supplied by vessel, and not only bulk cargoes, like salt and plaster, but groceries, furniture, hardware, and drygoods were unloaded on those long since deserted wharfs. The International Hotel was the scene of many a deal and dicker, from the hiring of foremast hands to the sale of a season's corn or a winter's lumbering.

The bar glowed warmly against the night and the sobbing east wind as I passed its windows and lounged in through the ever-creaking door. It was thick inside with the smell of pine tar and coal oil lamps: pungent with spilled beer, cigars, whisky, and the reek of spittoons, blue, of course, with tobacco smoke.

City fellows were there, in wide-checked suits and low crowned "christy-stiffs" buying barley or selling horse rakes. The two red-nosed hostlers had come in from the big driving shed with an "I-don't-mind-if-I-do" ready to drop from their arid mouths. Swanky farmers in long boots with copper toes and red or blue tops and broad brimmed felt "knockabouts," blue or black with the crowns ringed instead of creased, were elbowing sailors in fur caps with ear-flaps or dinted derbies. A couple of side-bearded men in stove-pipes, and clothes more solemnly black than any undertaker dares put on nowadays, were store keepers. They were outward bound on a buying tour to Oswego.

Everybody wore black when dressed up then. I remember the first Sunday the *Annie McInnes* which Captain McAllan had just bought, passed Whitby. She tacked in abreast of the lighthouse, hoisted all her colours, burgee, pilot, jack, ensign, and fly, then came grandly around, and stood up the lake ablaze with bunting. So were the other vessels of the McAllan fleet then "dressed" and lying in the harbour.

Captain McAllan himself, jolly sailor, father of sailor sons, good citizen and pillar of the community, strode up and down the wharf as was his Sabbath wont, also "dressed," but oh so differently from his glorious ships. In funeral black from top to toe. Not that he was gloomy. Not at all. He was respectable.

Upstairs, while christy-stiff and knockabout and stove-pipe and earflap hobnobbed down below, a harmonium assisted lady guests to assert that:

"Of all the things that I love best
And fill me with delight,
It is to take a ramble
Upon a starry night."

I backed up against the wainscotting to listen to an "inquest." It was, as I expected, in full swing. But like some other inquests, its evidence left much to be desired and the verdict more. It ran something like this:

"Thet there barley was wuth a good fifty dollars, cash money."

"Yes an' how much of it was lost? I'm tellin' ye not more'n two bushels was spilled after they'd run it back through the fannin' mill."

"Well who's to pay for the fannin' *and* the two bushels that was lost?"

"Tret-'n'-tare. Never see that in yer bill?"

"What I says ta that any farmer e'd stop a stoneboat handier than thet there feller did that there schooner."

"The feller that was wheelin' her oughta been wheelin' a wheat bar."

"If her jib boom hadn't a stopped her she might-a knocked the hull elevator over. Good thing it was wuz hick'ry."

"Minds me o' the time the old *British Lion* appeared the little lighthouse on the end of the pier at Gravelly Bay and went sailin' on with it on the end of her horn and the light still burnin'."

"And her Old Man bust his lungs yellin' 'Hard up, hard up, the hellum! No! Hard down, hard down the hellum! Never mind what the hellum, but git her past that damn light somehow!' Yeh, I mind thet well."

"Nothin' but two steamboats backin' on her coulda stopped thet *Magdala* when she rounded up and anchors fouled. It wuz a naxdent, pewure naxdent."

"Betcha they wuz some langwidge."

"Well, what I says ... "

I listened till the ladies upstairs had gone on the seventeenth mile of their starry-nighted ramble but really got no nearer to a conclusion for Captain Farewell.

I have always found that it is easier to handle a vessel when on the wharf than when on the quarter deck or bridge, with all the responsibility.

Captain Farewell, his mate or his crew were in no way to blame for the happening. It was one of those unfortunate things that come as part of the day's work in the life of a lake sailor. Responsible opinion evidently realized that. There was no action for damages and the whole incident, like the spilled barley itself, went out into the night of things forgotten.

Port Oshawa

Oshawa had it beginnings when the cluster of stores and houses on the Kingston Road was still called Skea's Corners, and the port, two miles south, was sketchily known as Sydenham Harbour.

It was in 1842 that Edward Skea got his postmaster's license for his black and white chequered store. The Sydenham Harbour Company had already been formed. There was no real harbour, just a wharf and shipyard in the bay between Bluff Point on the east, and what is now Guy's Head to the west. There was an argument as to what to call the soon-to-be bustling town and harbour which had an important trade with the Chippewa Indians. "Name of here?" was asked of the Indians. "Oshawa" was the reply.

"Why?"

"Where stream is crossed," came the reply, referring to the Salmon River, then quite a river, but is now called Oshawa Creek, which meanders through the marsh.

So as a compromise, the new post office was called Oshawa. But the harbour was still called Sydenham in the Canada Directory of 1857. As Lord Sydenham of Kent and Toronto, Governor General of Upper and Lower Canada, was long dead, the harbour quietly became Port Oshawa, and the company that operated it, the Oshawa Harbour Company.

Thomas Conant, in his book *Upper Canada Sketches* relates that "freights were so high in the fall of 1837 that carrying salt from Sodus N.Y. to Whitby, the next port to Oshawa, brought one dollar a barrel and the same freight was earned on flour out of Oshawa and Whitby for Kingston."

Oshawa was a great grain shipping port in the early days, although it never had a harbour until 1930 when all of the sailing vessels had departed. In their time they loaded at a pier, and had to scurry out for Whitby, (then a major commercial harbour) Port Hope or Toronto if the wind came up strong from the east or west and brought with it much sea.

The last commercial schooner to enter, or nearly enter, Port Oshawa was the stonehooker *Helen* which was wrecked there in 1922. Thirty years before, the very famous lake schooner *Oliver Mowat* was ashore close to the same spot. She was got off, by good luck and good management, after her crew had been taken off by volunteer lifesavers.

Other wrecks off Oshawa include the *Caledonia* in 1881 and the *Magdala* a short time later.

The ancient shipyard was at the foot of the hill – or rise – east of the modern concrete harbour. Old folk interviewed in the l930s told of how there used to be oaken skidways here for launching, with a buoyed anchor bedded in the lake for hauling off, and a big wooden capstan on the shore for hauling vessels up the ways for repairs. The timbers of the ways became the sills for Elder Henry's barn.

The first vessel to have been built in Oshawa harbour may have been the *Lord Durham* built by Capt. Joseph T. Moore, whose house is still standing in Old Port Oshawa, and is on record as paying tolls in Port Whitby harbour in 1844, and again as late as 1849.

Port Darlington

Situated on what was originally called Barber's Creek, (Augustus Barber had land on it) Port Darlington has been for over 150 years an important port of call on Lake Ontario.

It was a long, hard, haul to get the wood, barley, pork, whisky, and ashes to Oshawa or Port Hope over the heavy roads of Durham and Ontario Counties, and to bring back the salt, fruit trees, implements, and other goods imported from the United States for farm use. The creek mouth south of the village of Bowmanville was a natural harbour, so in 1837, a very prodigious year for new harbours on Lake Ontario, the Port Darlington Harbour Company was formed with James McClellan as Harbourmaster or Wharfinger.

Their enterprise was an immediate success. They built piers and a storehouse where sails were stored in the winter and up to six thousand tons of coal (ten big schooner loads) and other goods in the appropriate seasons, and, most important, a lighthouse. The harbour company had spent $88,000 on improvements by 1878. The port not only served the local township residents, but was a regular port of call for many of the large schooners and steamers of the day. By the turn of the century it was fast becoming a resort area catering to cottagers from Toronto.

In the year 1850, 29,113 barrels of flour, 27,818 bushels of wheat, 910 barrels of oatmeal, 700,000 ft. of lumber, 5,830 bushels of potatoes, 188 barrels of whisky (which sold for 5¢ a glass, 185 kegs of butter, 100 tons of bran, 1,000 cords of firewood, 80 barrels of pork, 23 barrels of ashes and 300 bushels of barley were shipped through the port. After the end of the Crimean war in 1855, and the beginning of the Reciprocity Bill with the United States, trade boomed, and the harbour grew even faster. The McKinley Bill of 1891, which protected American barley growers, cut down on the then lucrative barley trade in the harbour; but excursion boats, such as the *Garden City*, which left Newcastle at 7.00 a.m., stopping at Port Darlington, and arriving in Toronto at 11.00 a.m., and the *Erindale*, which ran 25 cent excursions to Toronto with music both ways, made the port ever popular.

Belden's Atlas of 1871 describes the port as "the port of Entry for Bowmanville and is 40 miles N.E. by E, 1\4 E. of Toronto and 26 miles W. 1\2 S of Cobourg. There are two piers at Darlington which run N. & S. The west pier is 325 feet in length and extends 50 feet further south than the East pier, thereby breaking the roll of the lake from the southwest. The distance between the piers is 150 feet. The depth of water at the outer end is 12 feet.

"Darlington is a good place to take with westerly winds, but when the wind is Easterly and vessels coming into this harbour, they require to keep up their after canvas and keep the east pier close aboard. An east wind causes a heavy sea at the entrance but none with a westerly wind.

"The lighthouse was burned down in the fall if 1870, but was immediately rebuilt the same year. The lighthouse is 54 feet high and shows from the south a red light, and approaching from the east and west a bright light."

The arrangement of the harbour light made it most useful for seaman to enter the harbour at night, straight ahead with the red light which showed you were south of the harbour and the piers were in line, a flash of white showing when you were off course to the east or the west.

The piers and lighthouse are no more. Commercial vessels, even the commercial fishing boats, no longer use the harbour. A large marina and hotel complex revived the harbour, and with an active boat building establishment close by, the harbour is still active for pleasure craft, despite silting problems.

Twenty-two ships and five centuries are enshrined in the "Schooner Days'" Desk. The desk is now part of a display at the Marine Museum of Upper Canada, Toronto.

April 14, 1934
Where "Schooner Days" Come From

Fraught with five centuries of ship lore, there stands in a High Park home, a desk and series of book shelves which form a "last harbour" for remnants of two and twenty vessels of renown.

It is from this haven that "Schooner Days" put forth, week, by week, for the 150,000 readers of the *Telegram*, and the other 150,000 readers of Canadian and American papers which copy them so extensively.

The desk is the product of a forty years' study and gathering of material, in journeying covering thousands of miles; and two years of painstaking and sympathetic craftsmanship by Mr. Louis W. Mackenzie, of Toronto, who built it for the owner from the latter's design.

"Schooner Days" ought to transmit some of the romance and adventure of sail, coming from such a shipyard!

The tapping of the typewriter raises ghostly echoes of far-off cannonading, of thundering canvas and creaking timbers, of surf pounding through the ribs of wrecks for centuries. Here plank and wale-strakes and treenails and keelsons and foothooks, and metal fastenings of more than a score of vessels of widely differing time and type, have been skilfully wrought into one memorial of the ships and their stories. It is the hope of "Schooner Days" to build up another such memorial on paper.

To date the collection commences with two fragments of the sixteenth-century pinnace of the *Delight*, of Sir Humphrey Gilbert's expedition to Newfoundland in 1583. How this wood was recovered at Bonavista, in Newfoundland, four years ago, and how it was identified, is itself one of the twenty-two romances of the desk. Between the pieces of the rib is shown a small metal plaque, reproducing, in an enlargement, a tiny copper token found in the ancient wreck. This has the Gilbert letter "G," the Gilbert's cognizance, a double-headed eagle; the crescent and star, the heraldry proclaiming the younger son which Sir Humphrey was, and a small escutcheon with a sitting squirrel, which was the crest of Sir Walter Raleigh, Gilbert's kinsman, and which gave the name to the little vessel in which Sir Humphrey perished.

Poor Gilbert, after losing the *Delight*, was lost himself in the *Squirrel* – but not before he called across the raging billows to his shipmates in the *Golden Hind*, and down the ages to all men: "Be of good cheer, my masters, for we are as nigh heaven by sea as by land."

The seventeenth century is represented by timber and ironwork from the supposed wreck of La Salle's *Griffon*, built in 1679, the first vessel to ply the Great Lakes west of Ontario. The hand-wrought iron ring which decorates a panel proves, on analysis, to be identical with the seventeenth-century Swedish iron wrought in France; and the oak is exactly the same as the oak from HMS *Tecumseh*, built within a few miles of where the *Griffin* was built on the Niagara River.

From the eighteenth century the collection has several reminders. A small lectern on the desk is oak from the *Royal George*, in which Admiral Kempenfelt went down, "with twice four hundred men," in 1782. It was given to the present owner by Lady Windle, as a keepsake from his friend the late Sir Bertram Windle, FRS, her husband, who used it for many years.,

There is oak, too, from Nelson's *Victory*, built in 1765, and more from "Old Ironsides," the USS *Constitution*, built in 1794; and a large amount from the wreck of the French man-of-war *Iroquoise*, the last built on Lake Ontario by the French, which was sunk in 1760 after a long battle against the British. Her remains were examined by Captain Van Cleve in 1820, and discovered by the compiler of "Schooner Days" in 1916 by following Captain Van Cleve's directions.

Another possible eighteenth century bit is oak from the supposed wreck of the *Toronto Yacht*, the government vessel for the conveyance of early Governors and their suites, built at the mouth of the Humber in 1799, and wrecked on Toronto Point in 1817.

The War of 1812 has furnished many pieces. Belonging to this period is the famous *Nancy*, although from the date of her launching, 1789, she is eighteenth century. The desk has some wood from her, and a very fine half model of her, mirror mounted, so as to show the whole ship. It was a gift from Mr. J.P. Weagant, Owen Sound, who has since completed a beautiful full model of this heroine of 1812.

Other eighteen-twelvers enshrined are Commodore Perry's two flagships in the Battle of Lake Erie, the *Lawrence*, of which he was beaten, and the *Niagara*, with which he retrieved his fortunes; Two more of his fleet, the *Porcupine*, which escaped the British cutting-out expedition at Fort Erie, and the *Tigress*, captured by the *Nancy*'s crew after she had taken part in destroying the *Nancy*.

One shelf is faced with fir from the USS *Chesapeake* and an accompanying picture, showing five stages of her battle with Captain Broke's "gallant ship the *Shannon*," is divided by splinters from the captured American.

An alligator with gaping jaws reproduces the figurehead of the famous American privateer *Young Teazer*. It is carved from oak from the keelson of that terror of the Nova Scotian coast. The *Young Teazer* was blown up at Chester, N.S., in 1813, by her lieutenant, frantic from fear of capture. This wood was recovered there in 1926.

One timber used shows the oarlock in the rail of HMS *Navash*, a sister ship of the *Tecumseh*. Like the *Young Teazer* on salt water, this British man-of-war on Lake

Huron was propelled by sweeps in calms, for it was in the pre-propeller days that she was launched. The top of the desk is made from the planking of the first steam man-of-war on Lake Ontario, HMS *Cherokee* of 1843. She was a side-wheeler, built at Kingston. Later, as a sailing vessel, she crossed the Atlantic.

Four large panels of the desk are formed from maple and white oak taken from the super-dreadnought of her time, HMS *St. Lawrence*, of 112 guns, the mightiest warship fresh water ever floated. She "won the war without firing a shot," for upon her launching, the American fleet of sixteen men-of-war ran into Sackett's Harbour and pulled the harbour in after them. They remained there, blockaded, until the War of 1812 ended. The remains of the U.S. brig-of-war *Jefferson*, one of the fleet which the advent of the St. Lawrence anaesthetized, furnished frames for the glazed doors of the upper third of the book case. The owner obtained the cross-grained oak from her hull on a voyage to Sackett's Harbour, twenty years ago.

The ribs of the *St. Lawrence* of 1814 were oak timbers running to sixteen inches in diameter and weighing tons each. In contrast with them, ribs of the British airship *R-100* of 1930, have supplied hinge straps for the bookcase doors. The little cris-cross braces which built up the webbed girders of duralumin in the *R-100*'s frame, weigh an ounce apiece; yet the *R-100* was almost four times as long as the *St. Lawrence*, and

Photo by Lorne Joyce of a painting by Charles Gibbons

Two boys sitting on the remains of the eighteen-twelver HMS *St. Lawrence*.

in fifty-seven hours crossed the Atlantic from Montreal to Cardington, a voyage for which the *St. Lawrence* would have required almost a month.

One other twentieth century piece of furniture on this desk is an inkwell from brass taken from the hulk of the German battle cruiser *Von Moltke*, part of the great fleet ingloriously surrendered and scuttled at Scapa Flow in 1918. Like all wood and metal used in this piece of furniture, this brasswork from the *Moltke* was "personally recovered." The owner was at the raising of the battleship ten years after the scuttling, when she was brought to the surface bottom upwards and towed in that condition six hundred miles around the coasts of Britain, until she reached the breaker's yards in the Firth of Forth.

It is curious that the timber of so many ships, all identified as "white oak," should vary so greatly in hue and appearance. The "white oak" of the *Delight*'s pinnacle is black as bog-oak and fine and curly in the grain; so is that of the *Nancy*, but straight-grained. Others samples of "white oak" are bright buff in colour, or a deep brown, or greenish brown.

None of the woods in the desk has been filled or finished with anything but plain linseed oil. But of all the samples, only the *Griffin*'s and the *Tecumseh*'s are alike; and the *Jefferson*'s and the *Belle Sheridan*'s.

The *Jefferson* and the *Belle Sheridan* were built forty years apart in time, but within forty miles of one another in place – one at Sackett's Harbour and the other at Oswego. Both used the native oak of that part of New York State. Only last year, the owner of the desk brought home to Toronto the remains of this ship, which started out with a fair wind from Charlotte for this port fifty-three years before. The wood was retrieved through the kindness of Mr. John Townson, mature specialist of the *Globe* staff.

Teak from HMS *Ganges*, last sailing frigate built in the British navy, form bookends. A massive chair from timbers of Nelson's flagship in the Mediterranean, the *Foudroyant*, stamped with memories of Lady Hamilton and of the great running fight in which the *Guillaume Tell* was captured, is part of the collection.

Port Britain

In 1783 Capt. Johnathan Walton was sent with a government vessel, probably the schooner *Onondaga*, to locate settlers at Smith's Creek, in the Township of Hope. Other members of the Walton Family (who came from Pennsylvania when it was still British), eventually settled at Marsh's Creek, which is three miles west of Smith's Creek. The settlement was called Port Britain.

To assist in your orientation, Smith's Creek is now called Port Hope. Port Britain has remained as a very small hamlet.

The Canada Directory, 1857 describes this port as follows: "Port Britain – a small but important village on Lake Ontario in the township of Hope and the

County of Durham. An extensive harbour of refuge and wharves are being erected at this village. Within the breakwater there will be an area of 14 acres with 14 feet depth of water. The Grand Trunk Railway has a station on the harbour. The village has a trade in shipbuilding. Distance from Port Hope 4 miles and from Toronto 59 miles. Mail daily. Population, 350."

Port Britain was actually founded by one William Marsh, one of a long line of settlers by that name, who had obtained large grants of Crown Land in Prince Edward County, near Carrying Place, and in Durham County, east of what is now Port Hope. Marsh developed and was responsible for much of the settlement of Hope Township.

The origin of Port Britain was based on the pond, now dried up, where he floated his logs for rafting. Here he built his ships and from here he shipped his forest products – tar, tanbark, potash, pearlash, lumber, shingles, staves, and timber. The Canada Directory of 1857 describes him, among the three hundred and fifty inhabitants of Port Britain, as "William S. Marsh, lumber merchant and shipbuilder."

It was he who built the launching ways, at the foot of the sideroad west of Lot Twenty-two, west of the mouth of Marsh's Creek, and east of the present Willow Beach. The shipyard in which Marsh built seven vessels, was here, and he seems to have launched his ships directly into the lake, heaving them off to kedge anchors rooted in the blue clay bar opposite.

Port Britain was a stop on the new railway, and was the place that the first locomotives for the old Grand Trunk were landed – at the mouth of Marsh's Creek.

Obviously there was evidence of a once busy harbour port as early as 1843, and by 1853, by posts in the marshy creek, where rails and rolling stock for the first railway in Upper Canada were unloaded, and grain, flour, lumber, and timber may have been shipped to Quebec. Where a dynasty rooted in British connection rose, flourished, built its family seats, furnished them with pianos built by its own imported workmen, launched fleets of schooners and sent them to sea, and then faded, leaving to the lonesome lake gulls the remnants of an old wharf and the dim traditions of the greatness of Marsh's Creek and Port Britain.

In "Millhaven and the Oliver Mowat," *Snider tells about a cruise in 1936 aboard the luxury yacht* Kingarvie, *which many years later he was able to purchase and use for extensive cruising on the lakes, and about the three-masted* Oliver Mowat, *the first big schooner in which he served as crew.*

April 12, 1936

Millhaven and the *Oliver Mowat*

One of the pleasantest sails I have ever had was in the ketch *Kingarvie* last Labour Day, when we were edging back for moorings in Collins Bay. The *Kingarvie* is in the "preferred class," but not in the sense that Collins Bay suggests. Her owner, G. Herrick Duggan, of Montreal, keeps her there during the summer, between cruises, and lays her up in Toronto in the fall.

On this occasion we had spent the night in Prenyer's Cove, on the south side of the Bay of Quinte, above the Upper Gap from Lake Ontario, and in the morning we weighed and stood across the bay in a faint trickle of air. Usually one has to give the Quinte shores a good berth, unless you can float in a dewfall, but on this occasion we fairly scraped the bank. The wind was light and hauled enough to the southward to just allow us to edge along on the starboard tack. The water was smooth, and at this part of the north shore it was deep enough to allow us to sail within the proverbial biscuit toss of the limestone edge of the bay.

Thus it came that we almost sailed down the main street of Millhaven. The walls of the old limestone building that gave the place its name were still there, and so was the little mill stream gurgling over its limestone bed into a basin just the right size for sailing toy boats. But silence had long settled over the old mill wheel. Among the acacia trees we could see two houses, and the outline of a service station on the old Bath Road, where had probably been the old village blacksmith shop.

And this, lying very still in the September sunshine, was the whole of the lakeport which saw Lake Ontario's first steamer launched and had built its own sailing ships, filled them with grain and flour, and sent them across to the United States or down the river, Europewards.

I do not know of any schooner ever sailing directly for England from this two-house town. Our overseas cargoes, in schooner days, were seldom loaded in one port. Grain and lumber were picked up sometimes in a dozen places before the hatches were finally battened down in Montreal for the sea voyage. But I do know that thousands of bushels were shipped out of Millhaven, and at least one three-masted schooner was built there. And while we floated past we could almost read, through the glasses, the inscription on the obelisk marking the spot on the shore whence she was

Snider Collection, Archives of Ontario

The *Oliver Mowat*, 1894, the year Snider sailed as crew. A three-and-after schooner, she was built at Millhaven, Ont., 1873, and lost off Main Duck Island 1922 after a collision with a steamer.

launched, 129 years ago, Upper Canada's first steamship, the *Frontenac*. There is nothing else now to mark that a shipyard had ever been there, but a spit of limestone intimates where the ways probably reached deep water.

The large schooner mentioned was built in Millhaven by master carpenter E. Beaupre in 1873. His granddaughter, a Mrs. O'Brien living in Highland park, Mich., has a half model, made in lifts of light and dark wood, of this vessel and of two other built by her grandfather, presumably at the same place. Beaupre built other lake schooners at Napanee and Belleville.

This Millhaven vessel of his was the first "three-'n'-after" I sailed in, the *Oliver Mowat* of Port Hope. She got her name before Sir Oliver Mowat got his title, and she hailed from Port Hope when I was in her because she was registered there after being rebuilt in 1892.

Her forecastle, airy, bright, clean, and well-painted received me in 1896. Capt. Jim Peacock of Port Hope was sailing her then – still going strong, though now 82. "Young Bill Peacock" was then mate; long since risen to master papers, and portliness. In fact he was commander of the last three-master on Lake Ontario, the *Julia B. Merrill*, burned at Sunnyside to make a hot dog harvest. Tom Paddington of Port Hope was in the forecastle with me, and a redheaded high school boy, whose name I have forgotten, and Tommy Slight and Johnny Bowerman, two grizzled old chums who always sailed together – and drowned together in the *Emerald* seven years later. Mrs. Paddington was cook, and I still smack my lips over the buttered biscuits and spiced apple sauce she used to set out for the lunch when the watch was changed at midnight.

This *Oliver Mowat*, built in Millhaven, was no pygmy. She registered 295 tons and could carry 700 tons of coal or 21,000 bushels of grain. She was 131 feet long, 26 feet beam and 10 feet 8 inches deep in the hold: very good proportions for a Bay of Quinte grain carrier, where you have to watch your water all the time. She was fast too, especially in light airs, in comparison with other schooners. She had a squaresail yard and rafee, and was always painted white above, with a particularly pleasing blue shade of lead-colour below. Sailors never willingly paint a dark blue because the colour is unlucky. The only really blue you see is in yachts, and yachtsmen, of course, don't know any better.

The *Oliver Mowat* was always white with blue grey, with pretty combinations of buff and chocolate for her gaffs and booms and white mastheads – always but once. That was the year Capt. Dolph Corson had her, and he painted her black. The Corsons seemingly always went for black, in the *W.J. Suffel* and the *Straubenzee*, and the *Starling*, and the *Erie Belle*, but while it may have suited these vessels it made the *Mowat* look like a hearse. McClelland and Galbraith of Darlington, who for many years owned shares in the schooner in partnership with her captains, put her back in white next year, and white she remained for the rest of her life.

Captain Peacock sailed the *Mowat* for seventeen years, and was succeeded by his son. My own next association with this schooner was on November 26, 1905, when she was in the breakers off Bluff Point, east of Oshawa, with her yawlboat gone and the crew sending messages ashore in bottles. Major Douglas Hallam and I started down the lake in the tug *Skylark* to rescue them, but off the Highlands the tug skipper got cold feet and turned back. His pedal temperature was affected by the fact the seas were filling us from rail to rail and lifting his engine house off the deck.

By the time Hallam and I got straightened away again on the rescue job, some Whitby boys had pulled out of that harbour, four miles against a big sea, in the laid-up lifeboat of the steamer *City of Owen Sound* and by the time they got there a gallant gang from Port Hope had brought a fishboat up on the old Grand Trunk, stopped the train, and dumped her off opposite the wreck, dragged her across Farewell's frozen marsh, and pulled out and got the crew. All the rest of us got out of it was the exercise and a laugh.

But I got one thing more: the lasting memory of Capt. George Robinson's wife. He was sailing the *Mowat* then, with a broken ankle, and Mrs. Robinson was cook. She is alive still in Port Hope, 84, and sometimes needs glasses to read! It was pitiful to see poor George hobbling around on one foot, leaning his weight on the capstan bars, when they went to heave the *Mowat* off, after the gale died down. Mrs. Robinson, brown-eyed, bright faced, ordered two hundred tons of coal to be jettisoned, had other anchors run out astern, and got the schooner off the boulders without much damage. But she did all the bossing by the mildest of suggestions: and when I asked her if she despaired before the lifeboat came she said, "Well, no, you see I kept on praying, and I knew the Lord would take care of us."

My last sight of the *Mowat* was in the Bay of Quinte one bright morning in 1916, some miles above her birthplace, Millhaven. She had come in through the Upper Gap, bound for Picton or Belleville with coal, while I was working down with the *Blue Peter*, bound for Carleton Island in search of an old French man-o-war sunk at he time of the conquest of Canada (I found her too). Capt. William Savage was by this time master and owner of the *Mowat* and gave me a friendly hail. He had bought her in 1914 and sailed her for seven years. Then Capt. Thomas Vandusen of Picton bought her. Soon afterwards – on September 1, 1921 – the schooner was run down at night off the Ducks, by a steamer, and Captain Vandusen, his mate, Jacob Corely, and his cook, Mrs. McGregory, were drowned. They were all in the after part of the vessel. George Keegan and John Minaker, sailors who were forward, were picked up. Of course, the schooner was not murdered nor the afterguard drowned of malice aforethought, but the captain and mate of the steamer were very properly sent to jail for keeping such a poor lookout.

Nosey O'Brien

Some of the "characters" used by Snider in stories about "Schooner Days," particularly on the Toronto Waterfront, were seldom identified by their full names, but they were real persons. "Slabsy," "Panface" and "Nosey O'Brien" were three of those characters.

Thomas "Nosey" O'Brien, an old schooner sailor and mate, who served aboard the Albatross when Snider served aboard her in the forecastle, was one of his major characters, and one he quoted often, i.e.:

1935: The late Nosey O'Brien, so named because half his jib boom was shorn away by the teeth of an opponent in a waterfront brawl, told me thirty years ago ...

Nosey was of great age when he so deposed at the close of the last century. He, Nosey, had known and survived the Brooks Bush Gang out of which young Brown was hanged for the murder of Thomas Sheridan Hogan, MP, in the old covered bridge across the Don. He, Nosey, had fought in every forecastle and waterfront bar between Montreal and Michigan. That was where he left most of his figurehead and won his name.

Snider Collection, Archives of Ontario

The *Julia B. Merrill*. Typical of the large lumber, grain, and coal carriers on the lakes. In her later years she carried coal from Cleveland to Toronto. She was burned at Sunnyside Beach, Toronto, as a crowd-attracting spectacle.

The following story is probably one of the stories told by "Nosey," and typical of what actually occurred in "Schooner Days."

February 24, 1940
New Wine in an Old Bottle

With the weariness of forty years' hard service in her bones, she leaned against the worn piling of the old Adamson elevator at the foot of West Market Street, amid patients which overflowed there from "the Hospital," the adjoining Jarvis Street slip, where sewer slush used to staunch the leaking seams of the stonehooker scows unloading there.

"She" was the *Garibaldi* of Port Hope, last of four schooners to bear the great name of the great deliverer of Italy. Revolutionary ideas were at work within her.

"Ye see," explained Capt. John Breen of Port Hope to the assembly sniffing newly baked apple pies from the *Garibaldi*'s galley, "it's like this, this here vessel don't class high enough for grain, maybe because she's old. That's why I've got her carrying stone. But she's good as the wheat, and here's the chance to go to Charlotte for a jag

Archives of Ontario

Stern of the *Julia B. Merrill*, a grain and lumber carrier in the upper lakes, before coming to Lake Ontario.

of soft slack for the Toronto Electric Light Co. at 20¢ a ton. I know she oughta get 25¢ like the other vessels, but that's what they offer. This here vessel registers 123 tons, you can see it in her papers and she can carry three-hundred" – "With her name board underwater," interpolated Nosey O'Brien.

"That's just because she's a mite dropped by the stern," said Captain Breen hastily. "But she really loads by the head. But say we take only two hundred and fifty, for a fast trip. That's $50 freight. Take half for the vessel, to cover maybe a tug bill and the groceries, and half for the crew, share and share alike. I don't want any more for myself than anybody else gets. Watcha say?"

This was rank sedition on the waterfront, where wages ran $1 a day or $30 a month in summer to $2 a day in the fall, or sometimes $25 a trip in the last of the season.

"Ain't that socialism?" demanded Panface Harry suspiciously.

"Nah, that's being sociable, different thing," contributed Slabsy McGuire, catching sight through the galley door of Mrs. Breen's pies being divided into six luscious wedges.

Three little Garibaldis, nephews or nieces whom Mrs. Breen was treating to a trip, forthwith emerged from the cabin armed with fragrant triangles.

"Like a piece of pie, Mr. Slabsy?"

"Have a piece of pie, Mr. Panface?"

"Auntie says ..."

"I'll go to Charlotte with you Cap," said Slabsy between mouthfuls.

"An'me," chorused Panface.

Tommy O'Brien, old enough to be both their grandfathers, snorted through all that was left of a proboscis that had been battered in every waterfront brawl since he began.

"'Tis a fine lot of Latter-day Saints yer making of these early Christians, Jack Breen. It's eighty miles to Braddock's Point and twelve more to Charlotte, as you well know. I've seen us take a month to get up from Charlotte in better vessels than the Old *Garry* was when she was new. I'll come with ye, if it's only for the sake of yer poor wife and these childher, but mind ye, I'll do none of the pumping."

"All right," said Captain Breen "You're the mate, Nosey, single up your lines and cast off."

Out floated the ancient one from her berth, pushed by a gentle north-wester that made a tug needless and did not put too much strain even on the gosh-awful, black, bepatched square-headed mainsail that threatened to leave her with every zephyr. The same breeze blew her into Charlotte next morning, and she sailed through the swing bridge and well up the river towards the trestles before it left her. The sociable socialists had to tack her up the creek for the last mile, by running lines from bank to bank, which they didn't enjoy, but Captain Breen said it was a pity to waste money on a tug when there was a fair wind, and pointed out that there would be nothing to do for all the rest of the day, while they were being loaded, which was true. The longshoremen's union saw to that.

So by night the *Garry* was loaded with her nameboard under and floating down the river again with one anchor at the cathead, ready to let go, and a kedge at her taffrail to bring her up short. The railway bridge obligingly stayed swung open till she angled through, carried by the current. Then the socialites groaningly gave her the muslin, and a faint trickle from the eastward wafted her out into the lake.

The easterly held, without much force, and the *Garibaldi* was able to sail in through the Eastern Gap and enrich J.J. Wright at the Electric Light Co., with 278 tons of slack, forty-eight hours after she had left Toronto. Wonderful luck.

"Five for you Panface, five for you, Slabsy. Five for you, Nosey, and don't tell me you've ever made more in two days since you've been sailing. Five for the missus, because she was cook, and five for me, like the rest of you. Everybody satisfied?"

"Then why not you?" commented the Venerable Beak. "I'm not grudging the $35 the Breens make out of it and pay nothing but the groceries. But ye should praise the Man above and not cast aspirations on her betters. I made $25 in two days, the time Alex Ure went from Hamilton to Oswego and back with the *Undine* and her underwater most of the time going and coming. We shipped at $2 a day or $25 for the trip and I chose the trip. But the next year I picked $2 a day and drew $42 on the three-weeks trip the old *St. Louis* made over the same water. Ye never know yer luck."

"And is $5 all we'd get if we'd been three weeks on this trip?" pondered Panface, whose mental processes were slow motion.

"Yes, and it's more than ye'd a been worth," answered Slabsy.

The co-operative experiment continued to be the great scandal of the waterfront. Sometimes it paid dividends. It always paid for the groceries.

Temptation ever waits on success. With $100 clear (including his good wife's hard earnings, cooking three meals a day for a family of five and three hungry, hired men) Captain Breen encountered old Dick Fugler. Fugler was Mr. George Gooderham's sailing master for the yacht *Oriole II*, the flyer that won the great match at Mackinac against the *Idler* of Chicago.

"Er – you wouldn't be having anything better than that to give away now, would you?" said Captain Breen indicating his misfit mainsail, so often condemned. He knew that used sails were the sailing master's perquisite in Mr. Gooderhams generous economy.

"Well now," meditated Fugler, "there's our spare old mainsail, never been out of the bag since we got the new outfit two years ago. Mr. Gooderham's getting a new suit from Ratsey's, in fact it's in the customs in Montreal. I might be able to get you the old one reasonable."

"But," objected Breen, "It peeks too high for the *Garry*." Her worn-out sail was notoriously low-headed.

"That'll save you carrying a gafftopsail," retorted Fugler. Captain Breen remembered that the gafftopsail was in even worse repair than the worn-out mainsail.

They started out at $200 and they compromised at $85, and Fugler to have the *Garibaldi*'s unneeded topsail.

Captain Fugler knew where he could sell the gafftopsail for a boat cover, but he did not say anything about that. And Captain Breen knew that he could get $15 for his old mainsail for junk up at the big yard on William Street. So the big deal was completed.

In December Captain Breen got a load of sawdust in Toronto for the ice-houses at Port Hope. The freight was only $25 but he was glad to take anything that would get him and the *Garry* home for the winter. The social club which had voyaged to Charlotte so prosperously were willing to make the trip to Port Hope on the old terms, "half the freight" all except Nosey O'Brien, who calculated that half of $25 split five ways would hardly pay his fare back to Toronto. So the *Garibaldi* sailed without a mate. But she had a new mainsail that looked like a cup challenger's, and made her feel as comfortable as her skipper would have been sailing in a silk hat. And did she step.

They sailed out of the Eastern Gap at ten o'clock that wintry morning, and when Mrs. Breen rang the bell for dinner they were opening up Frenchman's Bay. An hour later they were off Whitby. The next hour they did well, but not so well. She seemed loggy. They pumped the *Garry* every watch as a matter of routine "whether she needed it or not," but as she always needed it they seldom bothered about sounding the well. This time they did and the eighteen-inch sounding rod came up all wet with sawdust sticking to it. So they rubbed the galley poker with ashes and put it down and it showed she had two feet of water in her. They then pumped in earnest and kept on pumping.

"It's that new mainsail!" gasped Panface between strokes, "She was used to the old one and it was easy on her and stretched before stretching her, but now she's racking to pieces. Why don't you lower away Cap?"

"Because I don't want to get my ears wet out here on the lake," shouted Captain Breen from the opposite pump brake. "You and Slabsy go forward now and fill those old spud sacks with sawdust. Sling them over the bows with enough drift for them to be in the water. Then our new mainsail will bring her through – perhaps."

Mrs. Breen had the wheel and was steering a chalkline course. It was blowing pretty fresh, so fresh the old mainsail would have gone out of her of its own accord, but the wind was off the land and the water smooth. Panface and Slasby hastily crammed sawdust into the sacks which had carried the seasons' supply of potatoes, and soon two bags were dangling under each hawse-pipe, churning up and down against the planking in the bow-wash. The ragged sacks were neither waterproof nor sawdust-tight, and the Garibaldi went snoring along through and over a track of sawdust. Much of it went to waste in her wake, but before it got there it had to pass around her and under her, and some of it was sucked or pushed into the opening seams of the ancient planking.

When the boys came back to spell the captain he sounded the well again. The water had only gained two inches. When he spelled them they had gained an inch back. The seams were "taking up" the floating sawdust, and by steady pumping the water was at least held to its first discovered level.

Six hours after leaving Toronto, the *Garry* had reached Port Hope piers, completing the fastest passage ever clocked between Port Hope and Toronto – or so her worn out pumpers believed. Without much difficulty they kept her afloat long enough to get the soggy remains of the sawdust cargo out of her hold and into the icehouse, for she leaked less with her sails lowered. They could see the grains sticking in her seams as she came up, plank after plank as her light load grew lighter still. Next day, having berthed his family ashore for the winter, Captain Breen stripped the *Garibaldi* and let her drift over to a shoal part of the west harbour.

There she found a soft spot, and there she stayed. For keeps. Her sailing days were done. She settled on the bottom and froze in. All of her that protruded above water disappeared for firewood in the course of succeeding winters and what there was left of her was buried under a new coal dock.

"She was a good vessel," said Captain Breen long afterwards, "but she couldn't keep up to modern progress. We've all got to go sometimes."

In 1930 he himself followed.

In "The Pickled Prince," a very apt title, Snider relates the history of one, (or is it two?) vessels. A story whose basis came at first from his own vague recollection, (as told to him many years before by Nosey O'Brien – who was never wrong), and developed by searching records and seeking out and then questioning some of the ancient mariners who had a personal recollection of the vessel, and then telling the story as developed in a nautically accurate way. The sail to the lakehead is over a route that Snider himself had sailed and knew well.

December 30, 1944

The Pickled Prince

When Adamson's Elevator, at the foot of West Market Street, fell down thirty years ago, with its bins filled with crushed stone instead of the wheat and barley which had filled it thirty years earlier, it dropped on a grimy tow barge which was lying in the slip alongside like an old cow ruminating upon the greenness of the pastures she had known as a calf. Workmen pried loose the torn strips of galvanized iron and the dusty planks and timbers which then completely hid the barge from view, and a dipper dug into the heaped-up stone pile until the battered old hero came up for air. She had been pressed to the bottom of the slip – which wasn't far – with the thousand-ton weight on her, but her timbers had stood the strain without cracking and she was ready to bring in another elevator ready to unload and store it.

"And why shouldn't she?" demanded old Nosey O'Brien, the Nestor of the waterfront. "She went across the Atlantic Ocean without leaking a drop so why should she fall apart in a market slip for a few thousand ton of stone? And her heir to the crown of England, too, mind ye."

The name in blistered paint on her stern was *Sligo* of St. Catharines. She was looked up in the Dominion Register and sure enough a three-masted schooner of that name was found recorded as built in St. Catharines in 1874. It was not difficult to trace in this battered tow barge the lineaments of an "Old Canal size three-and-after." But all the inquiries from that day to this failed to find any record of the schooner *Sligo* crossing the Atlantic or having royal blood in her veins, though there were enough Norrises and Conlons and Battles and Neelons among the Celtic kings of the Welland Canal zone to justify the choice of the name "*Sligo* port below" for any St. Catharines schooner. And there was the interesting record of the *Sligo* having carried the first grain out of Fort William – 17,000 bushels in 1883, "trundled aboard in wheelbarrows pushed along planks over her rail." And another interesting record of how she got to Lake Superior, neither schooner nor crew ever having been there before.

Regarding this last exploit, it seems that in 1878, John Ross, of Montreal, railway contractor, chartered her after she had been in the timber trade for years, to carry machinery of all sorts to Prince Arthur's Landing, as the later Port Arthur was known, for the building of a hundred-mile section of the Canadian Pacific Railway west from Nipigon.

Capt. J.J. Daley, Mate Pat Deasey and a St. Catharines crew worthy of the name *Sligo* brought the schooner to Toronto. At Sylvester Bros. wharf, at the foot of Church Street, which was the biggest derrick on Lake Ontario, they loaded an old Intercolonial donkey engine on deck and in the hold put 250 tons of iron rails and black powder, picks, shovels, hexagon steel bars for drills, wheelbarrows, sledges, hay, oats, and cattle feed for the horses and horned beasts then being imported into Algoma. Lake Superior was then not much better known than the Sahara Desert, but off they sailed for the Sault River. They had no tug and no pilot and never been up there before, but up they went by way of Lake George, with the kedge a-cockbill, the lead going all the time and Mack Daley growling "port" or "starboard" to the man at the wheel as Pat Deasey hailed less or more water. So they got as far as Sugar Island, where you have to turn to the westward, and here they anchored. As soon as they got an east wind they hove up and went on as before and sailed right up the river to the old wooden lock at the American Soo.

This lifted the ship up twenty feet, and, still unaided by a tug, she sailed out of the canal into the river again, past Gros Cap, and into Whiskey Bay, where the *Sligo* began to taste the "wine of the country," viz., Superior's 40°F waves.

Off Cariboo Island came rain, then snow from the northeast. And this well on in June! Double reefing her all round they stood by, and had four days of snow, wind, fog, and vapour from the water.

"On the fifth day," said Capt. W. D. Graham of St. Catharines (the captain made this voyage in the *Sligo* in his twenties) "we lay becalmed, fog thick as hair on a dog, the booms hanging in amidships, not a breath of wind. The hash hammer (cook's bell) sounded for breakfast. We gulped it down and came on deck to see Thunder Cape coming out from the fog about four miles to starboard of us, Pie Island, ahead and Isle Royale astern, with Mount McKay rising strong to the westward."

What a sight for these lower lake men who had never sampled Superior's grandeur before! They reached Prince Arthur's Landing in the afternoon. Tom Marks had a general store there, and he and the few whites and all the Indians and husky dogs turned out in mass formation. The only wharf was three sunken cribs covered with corduroy logs.

Here the *Sligo* discharged her perilous and ponderous cargo in safety, none of the powder getting wet or going off, and the donkey engine away on her own rails. The schooner carried 22,000 bushels of oats to Collingwood from Chicago in October 1878, and corn in 1879, and came to Lake Superior again in within five years for the CPR construction work which crept along the north shore year after year. Capt. Mike Kerwin had succeeded to her command.

Like many another tall schooner, the *Sligo* was turned into a tow barge because it was cheaper to buy coal to tow her than to pay sailors to sail her. She jogged along for some time after the elevator fell on her, and might have been jogging yet, for she seemed to be as miraculously preserved from decay as the famous "one-hoss" shay. But to facilitate the loading and unloading of the crushed stone they widened her hatches from covering-board to covering-board, and that was like cutting her backbone through. She wriggled in a seaway like a rattlesnake with the colic, and drowned off Sunnyside, with a load of stone in deep water in about 1913, and there she lies.

All this casts no light on Nosey O'Brien's cryptic remark that she was the heir to the crown of England and had been across the Atlantic, but the old man was never wrong.

The same Captain Graham already quoted solves the mystery. We had noticed in the old St. Catharines and Port Dalhousie register that a barque named the *Prince of Wales* was entered as "Broken up" in 1874, and asked him why. Quoth he:

"The barque *Prince of Wales* was built for Capt. J.C. Graham, her master and owner, by Louis Shickluna in St. Catharines in 1860. The late King Edward VII, when eighteen years old, was visiting Canada that year. He was staying at the Queen's Hotel at Niagara-on-the-Lake at the time and came to St. Catharines for the launching. He christened the vessel with the usual champagne, for she was named *Prince of Wales* in his honour.

"She was really a fine product of Ontario shipbuilding. She had two complete suits of sails and was built about five feet deeper than the ordinary canal-sized vessel of her time. On her foremast she crossed three yards for square sails. Her mainmast and mizzen were fore-and-aft rigged. She was a true barquentine. On the lakes we called them barques. Her standing rigging was hemp. Wire rigging and double topsails were coming in, but she had a single topsail with three reefs in it, and all her rigging was rope. She had five thick rope shrouds on either side of her foremast, besides rope backstays and headstays, all tarred to protect them from the weather.

"Having a charter to carry a cargo of coal oil in barrels from Cleveland, Ohio, to Liverpool across the ocean, she loaded all she could carry on a nine-foot draught down the St. Lawrence canals, and on reaching Montreal, loaded several hundred barrels more which had been shipped by rail.

"Clearing the St. Lawrence, off Newfoundland, she made good weather of rough going, but the heavy sea and the angle of heel put so much pressure on the lower tiers of barrels in her hold that they were crushed flat. She did not take any water aboard, and none through her bottom, but on sounding the pumps oil was found in the limbers and the crew pumped oil all that trip.

"There was an oil slick across the ocean from Newfoundland to Liverpool in the wake of the Prince of Wales, and she ran dry as a carpet slipper all the way. Arriving at Liverpool when the top two-thirds of her cargo were discharged there was nothing left below but crushed barrel staves and a reek of petroleum that would wake the dead. She was oil from stem to stern, she had been swimming in it, and days of sanding and scrubbing made no difference to the smell.

"The only return cargo she could get was iron rails for the Great Western Railway. In Toronto, at the foot of Yonge Street, when she came back, Captain Graham said he had made the round trip and never lost a ropeyarn, on lake or ocean."

'Tween-decks, taking the weight off the upper tiers, would have prevented the crushing of the lower ones, but this would unfit her for bulk cargoes, so shortly after her return from overseas she was cut down to Welland Canal draught. Her new registered dimensions were 138 feet on deck, 23 feet on beam and 11 feet 8 inches depth of hold; 335 tons register. Before being cut down she registered 509 tons and could carry a thousand.

Her rig was changed to a "three-and-aft" schooner, the barquentine foremast, which was in three sections, being replaced by a schooner's lowermast and topmast. Possibly a new ceiling qualified her for the grain trade. The drenching with coal oil would certainly make her none the worse for the timber trade, in which she was engaged for years. Her timbers being soaked with coal oil to a depth of three or four feet was the secret of her longevity.

October 12, 1946
Toronto's Timbermen

The timber drougher was a picturesque figure in lake life for almost a century, especially at her peak in the 1870s and 1880s. She began, as we all do, "in a small way." The first droughers, in the 1830s, were little wooden schooners of less than one hundred feet long, finding employment in carrying squared timber cut on Ontario farms and intended for rafting down the St. Lawrence for export. The drougher loaded her timber from where it was cut on the shore, and got it to some convenient rafting place like Garden Island at the head of the St. Lawrence, or Carleton Island farther down the river.

Some of the old men-of-war of 1812 made good droughers, notably the American brig *Oneida*, for these were straight-sheered and stoutly built. On deck, they carried heavy cargoes where they used to carry cannon, and could stand pounding on the bottom. Often the drougher, getting as close as possible to the shelterless beach from which the timber was floated out to her, was caught on a lee shore and had to bump there until a change of wind and rise in the water enabled her to kedge off. Some, like the *W.Y. Emery*, were double-floored and framed for this reason. The *Emery*, built at Port Burwell in Lake Erie, was so strengthened for such purposes. She was too small for the timber trade when she was launched, and she was not provided with the hinged sternports of a typical drougher. She was later owned in Toronto, but never carried timber from this port.

By 1850 the type was crystallizing into longish, wall-sided vessels, almost flat on the bottom, full in the bows, and square in the stern with moulded runs. In the stern she would have four hinged doors or ports – two above the deck and two below. These latter would be irregular in form, being cut and carved to fit the shape of the ship's run.

In the bow she might have similar ports, and on each side small, square staveports for loading barrelstaves and lumber. The hold would then be filled through these bow, stern, and staveports, until the portsills were down almost to the water's edge. Then the doors would be closed and caulked all around, with battens or strips of canvas nailed over the caulking. The remainder of the cargo would be loaded through the deck hatches, and a deck load of the lighter wood preferably would be run in through the upper ports in the transom or hoisted over the rail. Whatever came in had to be hoisted out again at the destination.

Toronto had her timber droughers once upon a time, although no record of a timber drougher being launched here is to be had. This port's timber shipping began with the logs floating down the Humber and was stimulated by the Midland, Toronto Grey and Bruce, Great Northwestern, Canadian Pacific, and other railways bringing down the season's cuts of square timber from Georgian Bay district. The flat cars would reach the old Esplanade in the area between John and Bathurst streets just below the spar-strewn Prince of Wales Walk, or Front street escarpment, overlooked by the Greenland Fishery and Duke of Cambridge waterfront taverns.

These were the places that rang with chanties like the "Cruise of the *Bigler*," when the Calvin fleet would be in from Garden Island, or the *Straubenzie, Fulton, Albacore* or *Emerald* were fitting out for Georgian Bay trade. The *Bigler* was another drougher, an American – "the timber drougher Big-a-ler belonging to Deetrite."

The flat cars would dump their sticks into the slips between the grain elevators of the old "Norther docks" area, which was a lumberyard the year round, and a timber cove in spring. Frenchman's from "below," Garden Island at the foot of Lake Ontario, or maybe even the Quebec timber coves, would sort out the floating sticks into rafts for towing down to Garden Island or Collins Bay, where they would be turned into "drams" for running the river. Personal memories do not go back to the times when Capt. W.B. Hall had the Fenian Raid tug *W.T. Robb*'s towing rafts out of Toronto for the St. Lawrence. But in the 1890s we saw probably the last raft weaving through the newly cribbed Gap, which it blocked for most of the afternoon. The *Robb* also towed the schooners *John Bently* and the *Marquis*, but these were lumber carriers rather than timber droughers. The difference was that the lumber carrier piled more on deck, for quicker dispatch.

The droughers around Toronto surviving into this century were the Calvin fleet from Garden Island, which made annual visits and the *Sir C.T. Van Straubenzie*, three-masted schooner, when Capt. Johnny Williams took her over in 1892. She was built for a drougher in 1877 or 1878, a mate of the *St. Louis* and experienced Lake Superior's buffets during the CPR construction. Straubenzee Reef and Straubenzee Bay on the chart are testimonials of her service. She spent one winter in the ice. She was a stout, strongly built vessel, and when taken over by Captain Williams went nine seasons without needing caulking. After some years in the coal trade, with sideline grain and lumber carrying, he put her back in the last flickerings of the timber trade, towards the end of the century.

He had never worked timber before, but nothing ever daunted Captain Johnny by its novelty. He was fortunate in getting a mate who was a good timber man, and had a profitable season carrying square timber from the south shore of Lake Superior for the Collins Bay Rafting and Forwarding Company. Being in tow of a congenial steamer, he put tremendous loads into her, over 32,000 cubic feet of oak, which would weigh 770 tons, a whopping burden for an old Canaller. When he was "on his own hook," under sail, he modified the load to 21,000 cubic feet, which was still a whopping burden. He went to Georgian Bay ports the second season.

His success spurred the two-masted *Albatross* and the *E.A. Fulton*, ex-*A. Boody*, which had been droughers, to try the timber trade again, and possibly the *Emerald*, which was lost in Lake Ontario a few years afterwards. They only traded to Collins

Bay the one season. The *Fulton* was waterlogged in Georgian Bay and never came back to Toronto. The *Albacore* was lost at Oswego in 1900, but not in the timber trade. She had gone back to coal.

The Calvin fleet came from Garden Island, but in the 1890s and 1900s was almost a Toronto institution, from the regularity of its spring calls for the accumulated winter cut. Old timers will remember them, steamers like the *D.D. Calving* and *Armenis*, bulbous bowed and painted green and white and the barges and schooners they towed painted black and lead colour, like the *Norway* and *Valencia*, or all black, with perhaps a bright yellow beading like the three-masted *Ceylon*, which had topmasts. The black *Augusta* had none.

The Calvin firm began as Calvin, Cook and Counter in 1828, and became Calvin, Cook & Co., Calvin and Cook, Calvin and Breck, Calvin and Son, and finally the Calvin Co., Limited, ending with the lake timbers' disappearance in 1914.

Garden Island was laid out in three blocks of lots, in seventy-six one-acre plots. Between the blocks, a wide "East Passage" and "West Passage" ran north and south. Water Street, Second Street, Third Street and Glebe Street crossed the town, east and west, each being the standard sixty-six feet wide. Glebe Street cut off a ten-acre block labelled "Clergy's 7th for the Town." There was a five-acre plot too for the "Parson" south of the East Passage. North of the East Passage was the Market Square, which continued to the harbour shore south of the inner range light. Hospital Street was the east boundary of the Town with four acres reserved from the government between the street and the water for a hospital. Across town to the west was Grave Street, with a four-acre burying ground.

Grafton Harbour

Ten miles east of Cobourg, and some two miles inland from the North shore of Lake Ontario, is the quiet, rural village of Grafton. Things were not always so peaceful. Not in the early to mid-1800s, when the local distiller produced whiskey "you could skate on (or thought you could) all night, and so genially potent that if you fell down in the process you got up next morning with the smile of a baby," and a head as clear as an income tax return. Whiskey was a shilling a pail, at first, then went up to 5¢ a glass.

But the lifeblood of the small community was Grafton Harbour which had a history starting in 1837 when it was first incorporated as a harbour. Here during the nineteenth century were mills and wharves, warehouses, industries, homes, and happiness. It boasted a customs house and wharf in front of it which projected two hundred feet into water, ten feet deep, doing a prosperous business landing and discharging hundreds of sailing vessels, and steamers, feeding a thousand homes in high-rising Northumberland County, the families, firms and individuals who built up Ontario before it became a province as well as a lake.

Two steamers called at Grafton as regular as clockwork up until 1878, and later. They were the *Corinthian* and the *Rochester*, stopping for passengers, cargo and mail, promptly at eight o'clock, one on each side of the pier. There were many other regular callers at the harbour, shipping out the fish, flour, lumber, whiskey (before the McKinley Act in the U.S.A.), apples, grain and livestock, and importing machinery, sugar, salt, tea, household furniture and the stock of the general stores at the crossroads, which is not that sleepy little village.

The government, ever niggardly in developing lake ports never got around to giving Grafton Harbour a lighthouse.

The sidewheel passenger liner *Corinthian* got ashore there one night. It had always been supposed that it had mistaken the fisher's flare for the lantern which was usually hung out when a vessel was expected.

Tugs and lighters got the passengers off without mishap.

In September 1942, Snider received a letter from T.M. Kirkwood of Toronto, former head of the Kirkwood Line:

"I was aboard this steamer that night and I wish to give you more data.

"We were going west, and left Kingston at 5 p.m. When we got abreast of Grafton there was a freight train's head light standing still on the tracks ashore, half a mile inland. The first mate, on watch, turned in to the head light thinking he was at Cobourg. When the train started going west, he discovered the mistake and stopped the *Corinthian*'s headway, but it was too late. We grounded, but we backed her off, and we got away for several hundred yards when the steampipe burst, and we drifted ashore again, for an all-night bad time.

"The high sea from the south would lift her and drive her ashore, so much so that in the morning we could walk ashore in three feet of water.

"In due time, Captain Howard, who was the manager of the Richelieu and Ontario Navigation Company, sent two powerful steamers, the *Hiram A. Calvin* and the *Chieftain*, with steam pumps, in charge of Captain Donnelly and his son from Garden Island. They pumped her dry, and lightened her more by dismantling the paddle wheels, draining the boilers and putting the freight and furniture ashore. Then they made a rope fast to a stick of cordwood through a porthole in the forecastle, with the result that both steamers backed up as close as possible and made a run.

"This tore a hole in her iron hull without moving her. Next they made the rope fast to a long fender inside of the hull, and both vessels kept pulling her off, little by little.

"When afloat they took her to Cobourg, and a diver went under her and found a large boulder fastened to her bottom, which could not be removed.

"Captain Howard gave orders to tow us to Montreal with a tow boat on each side of the *Corinthian*, but as a storm blew up again the tow boats made matchwood of our guards and he made them let go and tow ahead.

"All hands went aboard of the tow boats with the exception of Captain Howard, Captain Donnelly and his son, and myself. At that time I was in my teens and made up my mind that I would rather stay on the *Corinthian* than aboard the tow boats. As she was lightened she got tossed like a cord until we reached Kingston.

"May I say that I crossed the Atlantic forty-four times and did not get tossed as bad as going down the lake on the *Corinthian* that night."

The schooner *Parthenon*, which became the *Robert McDonald* and later a steamer, got aground at Grafton in seven feet of water in the height of the barley export rush when the McKinley tariff was clamping down in 1891. They got her off by jettisoning some of her cargo, and she afterwards made three trips to Oswego, towing all the way behind a tug and getting towed back, to make up for lost time. It paid to do so, for the barley trade was about to vanish.

The schooner *Ocean Wave* loaded 5,800 bushels of barley at Grafton Harbour for Oswego in November 1871. She loaded many cargoes there, but was lost in 1890 with her two owners, Capts. Tom Brokenshire and Billy Martin, carrying a very heavy load of headings, barrel staves, and lumber from Trenton for Oswego. Perhaps the lumber got wet and swelled and burst her, for when the wreck was found south of the False Ducks in Lake Ontario, the stern was out of her and all her crew gone.

They overloaded vessels unmercifully in the lumber trade, probably because they relied upon the cargo to keep them afloat. Capt. Dan Rooney, shipped as a boy in the schooner *Mary Taylor*, which was later rebuilt in Cobourg by an uncle of his and renamed after a member of the family, who is alive, although the schooner has been gone these forty years.

This time when he shipped in her in Trenton she was loaded so deep with lumber that it was piled above and over her cabin top. When she reached the lake through the Upper Gap, the lake seas shoved this huge deckload aft until it put so much weight upon her ancient tail feathers that the transom settled down upon her rudder stock and jammed the rudder. She was leaking like a basket and could not be steered. They kept her before the wind by taking off her after canvas, and sometimes she headed east and sometimes she headed west and sometimes north. But whether she was going backwards, sideways or ahead she was all the time blowing nearer to Oswego to the accompaniment of much profanity on board, and much jeering from passing vessels.

They had no sympathy for her as long as she was in no danger of sinking. When she sashayed into Oswego, though, the jesters came around and helped her exhausted crew unload her and pump her out. Relieved of her load, her transom released the rudder stock, and her helm could again be turned. So they put 250 tons of coal into her to pay freight for a return passage, and brought her home to Cobourg, where she was rebuilt and emerged as the *Loretta Rooney*. Both as the *Mary Taylor* and as the *Loretta Rooney*, the bluff-bowed, straight-stemmed, slab-sided two-master, built on the lines of a half-size Welland canaller, was a caller at Grafton Harbour up to 1890.

"Out of Cat Hollow"

"Out of Cat Hollow" at one time was a familiar call amongst schooner sailors in the 1800s. They were referring to those famous schooners that sailed out of the harbour of Port of Cramaha, which was more commonly called Cat Hollow.

"Where is Cat Hollow?" you ask. Well at one time all the sailors on Lake Ontario, and in fact the entire Great Lakes system, knew where it was.

The Port of Cramaha appears in the earliest Dominion registers of Canadian shipping, and then vanishes like the many schooners once therefrom. But Cat Hollow and the Port of Cramaha were very real.

"A mile and a half southwest of Colborne, and eight miles from Presqu'ile Point" is its geographical location. Two hundred and sixty-five souls lived in Cat Hollow – men, women, and children. Each spring forty-two masters, mates, sailors, and cooks packed their bags and joined their vessels. Cat Hollow was an uncomfortable place to moor at any time, and almost impossible for "laying up" through the winter, yet the port had its docks, its shipyard, its grain elevators, it warehouses, and its scales.

The name "Port of Cramaha" probably never had any real existence, except in the mind of the registrar of shipping. It was the registrar's translation of the area in what natives of Northumberland County called "Crammy," south of the inland town of Colborne, and embracing Lead Creek and Keeler's Creek – and they were in existence long ago – Cole's Dock and Keeler's Dock, and Campbells's Dock and McCallum's Dock, part of which was in the Township of Cramahe and part in the adjoining Township of Haldimand.

They finally got a good big pier, the remains of which were still in existence in 1936, but there was no natural protection from the east, west or south. The docks were just landing places for loading cordwood, tanbark, lumber, grain, flour or apples, or unloading coal, but they gave no shelter.

Cat Hollow's earliest recorded launching, the *Trade Wind*, was built at Keeler's Creek in 1853, followed by the *Alice Grover*, a brigantine, the *Mary Grover*, a schooner, and the *Jane Armstrong*, another schooner, all three built by or for J.M. Grover at Cole's Dock which projected into the lake east of Keeler's Creek. Many other commercial schooners were built at this famous "port."

In all, sixteen vessels belonged in Cat Hollow in the old days, one of them, the *Trade Wind*, was purchased and sailed by a very famous schooner sailor, Capt. John Allan of Whitby.

Weller's Bay

Weller's Bay is a natural harbour near the northeast angle of Lake Ontario formed by Prince Edward County and the Northumberland shore at Presqu'ile Bay. It was frequented from the early part of the last century, when fishnets landed so many fish at Weller's Beach that they were salted and shipped in barrels from the shore. Weller's Bay was then a small lake, big enough for an island or two, and cut off by a mile of sandy beach from Lake Ontario.

"Ashore at Weller's Bay" was a common call in the 1800s for a very good reason. It was, and still is, a bad place to be on Lake Ontario during a gale or storm. Fortunately many of the victims got off the bar because, if the vessel did not break up in the gale that blew her ashore, the soft sandy bottom afforded no real holding power, usually allowing her to get off with the right wind and sea conditions.

In the 1850s, it is on record, Lake Ontario broke through, as that great lake had probably done before. By 1855 the channel was ten feet deep and the steamer *Chief Justice Robinson* of Toronto, and a big one for her time, took the Sons of Temperance in across the bar and down to Consecon, on their way from Brighton to a big Fourth of July celebration in Oswego.

The new channel gave access to a harbour of importance to Prince Edward County, particularly in the growing barley trade of the day. Loads were transferred at Consecon to the wooden railway for shipment to Carrying Place and the Bay of Quinte. It is said that cargoes of iron ore and feldspar or gypsum were shipped out of Weller's Bay for Oswego and Rochester, where there were blast furnaces.

In the mid-nineteenth century there were two grain storehouses in the thriving village of Consecon, with their docks for vessels to tie up and load barley. Vessels drawing up to eight or ten feet could then navigate the bay and anchor at the docks. The Prince Edward County Directory of 1865 states: "The largest lake vessels can safely ride at anchor during the most severe storms, being protected from the roughness of the lake by an extensive sandbank. The government has decided, we believe, upon enlarging the mouth of the creek and dredging the harbour which, when done, will add to the trade of the village of Consecon by including many vessels to take advantage of its superior accommodations (two hotels included) and winter there."

Its usefulness as a port was greatly lessened by the narrow, shifting, winding, unprotected channel, continually being attacked by the pounding of lake seas, and continually being scoured out in fresh groves by currents which play in-out like fish.

The Granddaddy of Great Lake storms may well have been the Great Storm of 1880, in which a number of schooners were lost, with much loss of life, and many more were severely damaged.

Snider reported on many of the victims of this storm over the years that his column appeared in the Toronto Evening Telegram. *Probably the most famous of the wrecks he reported was the loss of the* Belle Sheridan, *at Weller's Bay, Prince Edward County, Lake Ontario, as told in his column January 6, 1933.*

January 6, 1933
The *Belle Sheridan*

In old Albert Hall, on the east side of Yonge Street, between Queen and Shuter Streets, about where Scholes Hotel is now, the Longshoremen's Union used to gather for concerts and dances when the aforesaid hall was not packed with revival meetings or Paul Patullo's boxing bouts. A thing that always got a hand from the coalheavers "The Wreck of the *Belle Sheridan*" composed and recited by Mike Ryan, one of the boys. This rare inspiration of the native muse ran somewhat thus:

> In the year of eighteen-eighty,
> On a dreary November day,
> With coal bound for Toronto,
> They left old Charlotte Bay.
>
> They watched old Charlotte Harbour
> Till they were out of sight.
> They thought of dear old Scott Street slip
> Which was the boys' delight.
>
> They sailed along for many miles,
> While the crew stood on her deck
> They little knew their ship would go
> All in that fearful wreck.
>
> The first mate John Hamilton
> A man who knew no fears,
> Had sailed the lake from time to time
> For over twenty years.

The second mate was Samuel Boyd
A powerful giant and true;
With the Captain and his four young sons
Comprised the entire crew.

They sailed along the stormy waves
And tossed a silvery spray
And watched the moon appearing
At the closing of the day.

The moon was bleared with anger,
The clouds were rolling by
The rain came down in torrents -
Oh! how dismal was the sky.

"There's a storm fast approaching!"
I heard the Captain say;
"I only wish we were back
Once more in Charlotte Bay"

"Hard aport! Hard aport!"
The first Mate then cried out.
"Lower down your canvas boys,
And let her come about!"

She ran before it all that night,
And anchored at break of day,
"She has struck aground," the Captain cried,
    "On the beach is Weller's Bay."

They shouted to the farmers
Who had gathered on the shore
To save their lives, the farmers tried
To save them o'er and o'er.

The Captain died while standing up
Where he was lashed to stay,
And in a moment after
The youngest passed away.

"There's the oldest and the youngest gone,"
The other brothers cried:
Then one secured a loosened plank
And for the lifeboat tried.

He was picked up by the lifeboat
And carried to the shore
Where for many hours unconscious
Inside the farmhouse door.

His three remaining brothers
With the first and second Mate
Saw their saddest hour approaching fast,
And death their only fate.

The ship then went to pieces
Three of the crew were found,
While the others sleep in Weller's Bay,
In the cold, cold ground.

Although it is fifty years since it happened, the wreck of the *Belle Sheridan* at Weller's Bay is still talked of in Prince Edward County farm houses on winter nights, when the oil lamps flicker and the storm whirls the snow down the chimney. The *Belle Sheridan* was one of the many victims of the Great Gale of 1880. Sixteen vessels were in sight of one another at dusk on Saturday night, November 6, "On the south shore of Lake Ontario" and by Sunday morning two were pounding to staves on Prince Edward County, one had capsized and drowned her crew, another had gone down with all hands, two were on the beach at Oswego and all the others were staggering into Kingston with sails in ribbons. Gaffs and booms and deck loads gone, and the bulwarks washed away. It was a hard time for the insurance companies – and for men afloat and women at home. The gale blew for a week. The death of Capt. James McSherry last Tuesday removed the only survivor of the *Belle Sheridan* in the storm, and recalled the pitiable fate of his father and brothers.

James McSherry came out from Ireland in 1840 in the packet ship *Margaret*. She made the remarkable voyage of sixteen days out from Ireland to Quebec with passengers and fourteen days home. James McSherry was not a passenger, but the ship's carpenter, and knew his trade thoroughly as an artisan, builder and rigger. How he came to reach Toronto is not known, but he soon established himself as a wagon maker, and had a little yard at the bayshore, first at the Don mouth, at Cherry Street.

Here, besides building prize-winning wagons for York County farmers, he turned out small vessels in the winters – the *Echo*, the *Clipper*, the *Swift*, the *Garibaldi*, the *Alabama*. He also reared a large family – Pat the eldest, and Johnny, Jimmy, Tommy, Eddy, and Henry were the boys, and there were girls too. The family grew up in the *Echo*, the first of the McSherry fleet, for those vessels Captain McSherry did not sell he sailed for himself, with the help of his growing sons. All summer, while the lake trade was good, the family would ply the blue waters, and in the winter the *Echo*, like her little ark, would come to rest on the Ararat-by-the-Don, and McSherry and his boys would go to work in his shipyard.

Here he rebuilt the schooner *Persia* and the old brigantine *New York*, and the *Montezuma*, and the schooner *West Wind*, he owned the scow *Sampson* and the *Clipper*, of his own building; little hookers in the stone and cordwood trade. Captain McSherry had become a substantial citizen by this time and owned several houses in addition to his vessel property.

The *West Wind* got ashore near Cobourg late one fall and had to be left on the beach until the ice melted. When Captain McSherry and his boys went down to salvage her with the first of spring they found the hospitable Cobourgites had cut her down to the level of the winter's ice for firewood.

That was a heavy setback, but, rallying all his resources, the gallant Irishman raised $3,600 and bought the *Belle Sheridan* which had been lying on the bottom at the foot of Church Street for the last year.

The *Belle Sheridan* was no spring chicken. She had been built in 1852 at Oswego and this was 1878. She had a rebuild of sorts five years before. Her decks were above water where she sank, and it was no trick to raise her. She merely needed pumping out. Captain McSherry towed her to the Don mouth and found her underbody sound. She was planked with three-inch white oak, with four-inch plank in the bilges, and her frames were six-inch oak, doubled. Her decks were of pine. These were done, Captain McSherry replaced them, gave her a thorough overhaul and slipped her back into the water "as good as new." So he believed. He had spent $3000 more in repairs. The marine insurance inspectors, less enthusiastic, classed her B-1 – good enough to carry grain.

At the end of October 1880, the *Belle Sheridan* loaded wheat at Adamson's elevator at the foot of West Market Street, finished at the Norther elevator at the foot of Brock Street, and cleared for Oswego. She made a good run of sixteen hours, unloaded, and came up the lake to Charlotte where she loaded 300 tons of coal for J.R. Bailey of Toronto. A good trip so far, with paying freights both ways. She would earn $500 or so for the voyage. Father and the boys were jubilant. Pat, having reached mans' estate, was not with them. He had been sailing vessels on his own for five years. He had taken command of the Echo at sixteen. Johny, now come to 21, Jimmy, 17, but sailing this particular schooner for the first time on this trip; Tommy, 17, and Eddie, 13, were on board with Captain McSherry. The mate was a Toronto man John

Hamilton. Sam Boyd, an old Toronto sailor, completed the crew. Seven were plenty to handle the vessel.

The southerly wind was light when the *Belle Sheridan* towed out from Charlotte Saturday morning. She hugged the south shore as vessels always did with the wind in that quarter, expecting to get broken off by a westerly shift after clearing Thirty-Mile Point, which is thirty miles from Niagara. A west wind would then let her lay a course for Toronto. By eleven o'clock at night, while the "Thirty" was blinking at her, the glass had fallen, and everything promised heavy weather. The green and red lights of the vessels in company were blotted out. Captain McSherry ordered the jibtopsail and gafftopsails furled, lowered the last reefband and double reefed it. The vessel was thus in good shape for the rough stuff the night might bring.

At midnight, just as the wheel was being relieved and one watch was getting ready to turn in, there came a fierce squall from the south west. It was so heavy that although, from the direction of the wind, she could have laid Toronto, the schooner was kept off before it, the outer jibs run down, the foresail and mainsail halliards let go by the run. She was scudding by the fore staysail only, until they got ten feet or so of the fore and mainsail peaks hoisted, to give her steerage way. She headed east by north, for the Canada shore, which was fatal.

By one o'clock the lights of Charlotte, which she had left in the morning were again in sight; but the schooner was ten or twelve miles out in the lake and in the hurricane that was blowing Captain McSherry could not take the chance of entering Charlotte's narrow piers. With black squall succeeding black squall, each fiercer than the last, and the seas mounting up so that the crew could not see their tops ahead or astern, the schooner scurried before the blow, like a hare hounded by beagles.

Off Charlotte the squatted mainsail bloated up like a circus tent and burst. Its fragments wrapped themselves around the gaff, boom, and both spars flailed about like cripples crutches and broke. The mainboom would burst over the stern of the *Belle Sheridan*, fill her up to the level of her rail and spill over on both sides. Every man and boy was drenched to the skin and numb with the bitter cold.

At two o'clock they thought they could see the lights of Bowmanville on the north shore. But there was no making that harbour. It was harder to get into than Charlotte. The first shelter would be Presqu'ile, in the corner where Prince Edward juts out into its great peninsula.

At three o'clock the maintopmast went out of her, snapped by a particularly heavy roll. It fell clear and they chopped away its entangled shrouds and halliards. Still they had hope; for morning would show them Presqu'ile and shelter.

They were abreast of Presqu'ile by six o'clock, while it was still dark, having run fifty-four miles down lake Ontario since midnight, almost under bare poles. To get into Presqu'ile the schooner would have to turn sharp to the north and west. But how could it be done, with her aftersail gone and mountains of water and wind of express train velocity pushing her eastward at nine miles per hour?

Captain McSherry steered for Presqu'ile light. To fetch it too close meant destruction on its rocky base. He gave it as narrow a berth as possible. The gathering of many seas into one, as they backed up from the pen into which the mad southwester was flogging them, hurled the schooner past the light for half a mile before she answered to her helm. She headed up almost to north-west, but without after sail she would not go ahead into Presqu'ile Harbour. She was driven sideways across the opening and the lee-shore of Prince Edward County came rushing out to meet her.

They let go the port anchor, gave her a big range of chain, and then let go the starboard one with every shot remaining in the locker. She rounded up. And there she lay, rolling wildly in the partial lee Presqu'ile Point gave, looking into the harbour she could not enter.

Bone wet, and bone weary, foodless and fireless all night long, the seven in the *Sheridan* greeted the wild sunrise of that November Sunday morning with trembling hope.

To leeward against the angry flames of morning, the breakers were spouting masthead high on the sandy shores of Prince Edward. To windward, three-quarters of a mile away, great seas rolling down Lake Ontario in water hills twenty feet high, burst on the Presqu'ile bar and spouted higher than the lighthouse top.

The harbour mouth was open wide but nothing but a powerful tug could get to them. There were no tugs in Presqu'ile. None nearer than Toronto, or Charlotte, or Oswego, and all impossible to summon through the storm.

The roadstead was a wild turmoil of broken water. All depended on the wind. If it shifted to the north of west the shore would begin to give shelter. November gales usually ride that way around the compass.

Dragging in the wake was the smashed yawl boat on the stern davits, a wave wrenched the wreck of it away.

The wind went from southwest to west-southwest, from west-southwest to west. There were even times when the wallowing schooners battered bowsprit pointed north of west.

"She's coming nor' west, and we're saved!" shouted Captain McSherry above the uproar.

As he spoke there was a sharp twang of the straining anchor chains. The port one parted, right at the hawespipe.

Would the starboard one hold her? When she reared from a plunge that chain straightened out ahead of her like a steel rail.

It held.

But the anchor dragged.

Foot by foot and fathom by fathom Presqu'ile lighthouse receded and the grim face of bald head on the Prince Edward shore drew near.

There was just one chance. Perhaps by cutting the cable and setting the remaining sail, the schooner could thread the narrow cut that gave entrance to Weller's Bay through the long sandbar where the breakers piled in endless fury.

Ere they could try this the chance toughened. The wind, as they had hoped so hard a few minutes before, coming out of the north west. The wind now bore north. There was no making it. Foot by foot, and fathom by fathom the schooner drove past this last slight hope of escape – dipping, lunging, rearing, plunging; ever facing the assaulting waves of the lake, ever losing ground to them.

It was ten o'clock when the cable parted. At noon she was in the breakers, having dragged five miles in two hours.

When she struck, she slewed around so that the bow was higher than the stern. Flooded out of the cabin by the seas that swept her, all hands crowded up into the narrow space in the forecastle head, between the paulpost and the windlass bitts and the hawespipes. Jim and Tom McSherry got some shelter by rolling themselves in the staysail. John and Jim, the oldest boys, took turns holding little Eddie in their arms, trying to warm him. He was crying from the bitter cold and the fear that he would never again see his mother.

The schooner was creaking and groaning in every timber, and each wave tore off another piece of rail or bulwarks. With a scream of drawing spikes the new pine planks of the deck started to go next.

The normal beach was only a hundred yards away, but far up its face the seething breakers thundered. Beyond their line a thousand people gathered from Consecon and Brighton. Farmers backed their wagons into the surf. All were helpless to save.

A fishboat was manned by five heroes – Walter Lossee, Stephen Clark, Frank Bonter, and two others whose names should be written high on the scroll of honour. Twenty times that boat was capsized in the breakers and rolled up on the beach, without even getting clear of the shore. Three times it got through the first rollers and neared the wreck only to be tossed away like a cork by an acre of water that burst and spread fan like, sweeping it half a mile down the beach.

Few were the words of the doomed crew as they waited for fate. John Hamilton, the mate, said if he got through he would never go sailing again.

"We're not through, we're done for," said Captain McSherry, quietly, and at one o'clock he died. His stiffened body frozen in the coils of the rope which bound him to one the timberheads. Then came a sea larger than the rest, and loosed his bonds, and washed him away.

Eddie's crying ceased.

Jim, looking into the face of his little brother, after another big sea had swept them all, saw that he too was dead; drowned or frozen, or both. His rigid body was hard to hold. The next big sea tore it from Jim's arms.

"Try the fore-rigging" shouted Johnny, bringing his head above water.

All edged their way along the rail to the fore-chains and started to climb the shrouds.

Jim saw the fishboat pulling through the surf again.

"I'm going to risk it," he shouted to the climbers.

"You might try it," called his brothers. They were so exhausted they could barely drag themselves up the ratlines. They could not unlock their legs from where they clung.

Jim McSherry worked his way along the rail to the main rigging, a black oil-skinned figure disappearing completely in the yeast of the breaking seas when they boarded. How he fared he thus told the *Telegram* four years ago.

"We could hear and feel the ship cracking to pieces as the water and wind tore at her.

"I started to go back to where the deck was breaking up. Three seas went over me, but I saw a chance and took it. Finally, holding by the rigging and dodging the seas, I got aft and seized a plank eight feet long, eight inches wide and three inches thick. Then I stood on the rail for a moment with my plank and then the crowd on the shore saw me and knew what the idea was. There were buggies and rigs there from all over, as the news had spread of the great storm, and that the *Belle Sheridan* was going to pieces with all on board her.

"I took the plank and the next wave swept me away. I had an oilskin suit over my heavy clothes and that protected me some from the cold. I was carried east, most of the time under water as it seemed, but I saw that the lifeboat was in the surf near the shore, racing along parallel to my direction. The boat could not make way to reach the schooner, but could live with the following seas. I got a sight of the lifeboat after I had travelled half a mile, and saw it was just opposite me and that I had gained one hundred yards onshore. Then I seemed to be submerged again in the waves and when I took another sight I had been carried a mile east, and I was another one hundred yards nearer the rescue boat.

"After the third plunge, I found I was right off the boat, so I grabbed her ringbolt and then my feet struck bottom for an instant. The men grabbed me and carried me in through the surf, where I was put in a buggy and bundled up in a buffalo robe. They put me in a fish shack, stripped me, and rubbed me with their rough coats. I was then driven further in, and into a farm kitchen.

"It was one of those old-fashion kitchens, as big as the modern home nowadays, and there was a high-backed stove in it, and a crowd of people that filled it. The fire was going and the people were steaming, and you can figure the heat. I smelled the heat, and saw the people, and then keeled over. I was unconscious four hours."

Once again, after rescuing Jimmy, the gallant fishboat put out. This time they got to within thirty feet of the schooner and looked up to the faces of the crew as they called to the four in the rigging to jump. Next moment the boat capsized and the five men were in the water themselves. They clung to their craft, and were all washed up in a heap together, a mile down the beach.

Dusk settled down. Before the lifesavers could get out again the *Belle Sheridan*'s main mast fell, striking the fore-rigging. Right afterwards the foremast began to totter. It went over the side with four men entangled in its network of shrouds, halliards and ratlines.

Bonfires blazed on the beach all night, but no one was washed ashore. Days afterwards little Eddie McSherry's body was found in the sand. And later on John Hamilton's, headless, as though the mainmast had decapitated him. And still later was found a human heart, silently eloquent of Lake Ontario's rage. The schooner herself was beaten into kindling wood, and the shores of Prince Edward were strewn with her debris, all the way from Weller's Bay to Wicked Point and from Soup Harbour to the Carrying Place.

And so, of all the *Belle Sheridan*'s crew, Jim McSherry alone came home, to be the support and comfort of his widowed mother. A fine fight he made of it. The girls grew up and married well. The remaining boys all became vessel's captains and steamship masters. Jim himself carried hundreds of thousands of passenger across Toronto Bay in the ferry service, and retired to an honoured position with the Toronto Transit Commission. He was in their employ when be died this week of pneumonia, at 71.

July 22, 1950
Vienna at Needle's Eye

Trenton, Ont., looks smart and modern with its brick and business streets, and clean concrete bridgework over the broad brown Trent, with the locks of the Trent Valley Canal and the white-walled airport beyond.

It was more picturesque in the old days. Then the big stone mill on the waterfront loomed amid a forest of masts like Chepstow Castle on the Wye, the wharves were piled high with fresh sawn lumber, and at night the stacks of the sawmills blazed like torches under their grated hoods as the day's accumulation of waste and sawdust was burned up to keep steam in the boilers. The most picturesque feature was the old red covered bridge which spanned the Trent, teeming then with rafts.

The bridge was long, and hopped from timber crib to trestle and trestle to timber crib. Some of these had twisted and settled or been lifted up by the ice and the spring fresnhets. The bridge was of wood, truss, span, floor, and railing. To prolong its life it was roofed over, as high as a hayload, and had side walls of sheeting laid lengthwise. Square ports were cut in these walls, high up under the roof eaves, to light the roadway, for the covered bridge was as dark inside as a sewerpipe. It was always hard getting through that hole, for the gap available when it was swung completely was not much more than twenty-five feet – the beam of a full-sized canaller. Sailing vessels had to be hove through by the capstan, as a rule. They had to go through exactly straight, for any weaving or angling meant she would jam on both sides. One touch might be a $1,000

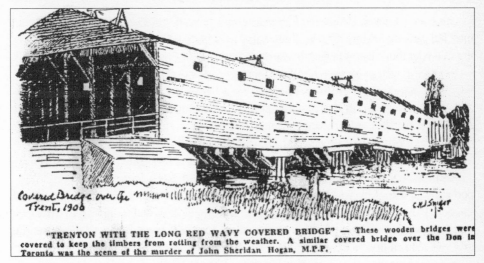

"TRENTON WITH THE LONG RED WAVY COVERED BRIDGE" — These wooden bridges were covered to keep the timbers from rotting from the weather. A similar covered bridge over the Don in Toronto was the scene of the murder of John Sheridan Hogan, M.P.P.

Snider's sketch of Trenton Bridge.

smash for the vessel or the bridge – and if you did any damage, or even held up traffic overlong, the county would promptly tie you up until you settled it.

The "Old Man" – or captain – of the schooner *Vienna* pondered these facts of life well as he walked the cabin top of that smart fore-and-after, newly brought to Lake Ontario from Port Burwell, her Lake Erie birthplace. She had passed through the Trenton bridge as the capstan-pauls measured her progress by inches, her midship fenders gently rubbing both sides. She was a beautifully modelled vessel, "all in one piece, not two ends and a middle," as sailors put it. That is, she curved like a seed instead of a cylinder. Her greatest beam was just aft the fore rigging. From there she narrowed in a gentle curve towards the stern, accentuated by the way her quarters were tucked in by the round of the tumblehome. Such a shape was easier to push through the water, and through a rectangular opening.

The skipper knew he could get out of where he got her in, but he saw what had happened to the *Nellie Hunter*, the vessel which had just wriggled through, outward bound. She had finished her loading when he still had four hours work to do. And she was only now heaving out to an anchorage in the bay, clear of the bridge, where she would get her snubs, warps and running lines disentangled after all the strenuous heaving, before beginning to make sail. There was a good breeze blowing, but that had made it all the harder to get through the bridge for not having steerage way the vessel had dragged heavily on the lee side and had hung on every obstruction above and below the water.

The *Vienna*'s captain thought she could beat the *Hunter* to Oswego on an even start, but not with a four-hour handicap.

"Boys," he said suddenly, "we're going to sail out."

"Sail her out?" said the mate encouragingly. "Well she's your vessel, now 'tenny rate. Maybe the county'll own her t'night. Er what's lefta her."

"Marsh," said the Old Man to Marshall Spafford of Point Traverse, the best wheelsman aboard: "Can you take her through that bridge under sail?"

"Yes," said Marsh, "if I'm left alone."

"We'll make sail then. Blow the horn for the bridge," said the skipper, giving his little gold earrings an extra shake to improve his eyesight.

They got everything on but the fore-gafftopsail, which, as you know, is better left clewed up if you have to do any tacking. They took a little hitch up the basin inside the bridge, to get way on her, and put the wheel hard down.

She was a smart vessel, the *Vienna*, and she came about in a quarter circle with no loss of headway, and looked the bridge in the eye. The widening black slit of the bridge covering showed the span was opening. They could hear the bell ding-donging to keep the buggies back.

"Keep her well to windward" injured the mate. "Don't let her drop down, er she'll smash the lee 'butment."

"I said I'd take her through if I was left alone," said Marsh, lining her for the opening.

"Don't let her fall to loo'ard," admonished the captain.

"You take the wheel then, and I'll go pack my bag" retorted Marsh.

"Aw, now, Marsh," begged the captain, "I didn't mean that." Then savagely: "Shut up, everybody! Didn't I tell ho to leave Marsh alone?"

"Meaning me?" glowered the mate.

"Yes you, if you think you are anybody."

Whoosh! she shot through that gap like a gull through a window. One glimpse of snorting horseheads and farmers whiskers to leeward, and to windward the bridgetenders eyes popping out of his head like peeled onions. The red humpbacked roller coaster seemed rushing up the river and then went under the stern of the *Nellie Hunter*, still getting her anchor. They were off for Oswego ahead of her.

"Give her the fore-gafftopsail!" shouted the captain. "Marsh, will you come with me as mate next month?"

"I'm quittin' right now." said the mate-to-be-deposed, "so ye kin gimme my time to the end of the month. Nobody ever fired me and nobody ain't never goin' to."

"Hold your horses, mister," said Marsh, "I don't want anybody's sight but my own. All I want's to be left alone when I've business to attend to."

The cook's bell broke in, and Marsh had his way. As was the custom in good weather, all went to dinner except the man at the wheel. They ate in the cabin, the captain at the head of the table, the mate at the foot. So for fifteen minutes Marsh was left alone in his glory.

The mate was the first man out from the full fast meal, and according to the same custom he relieved Marsh. As he did so he awkwardly tendered him an uncut plug of T & H.

"That," he remarked as to the fore-gafftopsail, "was the finest piece of wheelin' I ever seen."

Following his purchase of the Kingarvie, *Snider conducted extensive research into both the wrecks of schooners and of the people who sailed them during his regular summer cruises of the Great Lakes.*

Modern sailors would not consider the town of Napanee as a destination port on the Lake Ontario, but in 1944 Snider reported on "A by-product of a recent sail to the site of Upper Canada's earliest flour mills" where he met Stanley Babcock, an old schoonerman, and the source of some fascinating stories of schooners sailing out of that part of Lake Ontario.

July 29, 1944

Hunting Out a Hidden Port

Babby sat before his cottage door waiting for the cool of the evening to come. His arms were tattooed with anchors and other emblems of a sailor's calling. His eyes, blue and innocent as the Bay of Quinte itself, fell placidly upon a group of sunburned holidayers staggering under a thick steak, boxes of crimson raspberries, and bottles of milk – spoils of a foray on the local A & P store.

"Scuse me, boys," said Babby, politely, "would you know that fore-'n'-after I see laying down at the foot of the street? Would she be a Gooderham & Worts yacht, perhaps? We ain't seen anything else come in here under sail since the *Lyman Davis* was burned at Sunnyside."

"There are no more Gooderham & Worts yachts," answered the oldest of the yachtsmen with regret, "but the one you see is ours, and you're welcome to look her over."

Babby was on his sea legs instantly. "You're sure you wouldn't mind? I used to sail, and I hanker for anything that does."

He had sailed before the mast in the *Lyman Davis* with Capt. Jack McCullough, out of this very port of Napanee, though it is one hard to find, being uncharted, unlighted, and miles inland up a winding river.

He made a wonderful voyage with Captain McCullough late in the fall, when they were paying $15 for the trip. Not much better than $1 a day if the trip took two weeks, as they often did, but this one didn't. Sailed out one Saturday morning and got a cracking run over to Oswego. Hunky Scot in the harbour tug picked them up and berthed them smartly at the trestle, and lay right along side.

"They'll have you loaded in two or three hours, Jack," said he, "and you've got a fair wind home already, so I'll snake you out as soon as they've finished trimming."

So he did, and they got away by dark, and the good "soldiers wind" held, and pushing her 400 tons of coal through the water like a steamboat across the lake, the *Lyman Davis* galloped, fifty miles north by west, past the False Ducks and through the Upper Gap, and thirty miles more up the Bay of Quinte to Capt John's Island off Deseronto.

By this time it was morning and the marvellous wind came fair for the real trick of the voyage – the last six miles up the river to where Napanee lies hidden from the lake.

But a corkscrew tidal navigation confronted friend Babby and the *Lyman Davis* that Sunday morning in 1910 or so. And there were not twenty-one buoys at the time, but two. Capt. Jack McCullough, then very modern and enterprising, had a little kicker or gas engine in his yawlboat, capable of moving the *Davis* at a mile an hour once he got her started. But he also had a lot of luck, and it stood by him. The wind whipped into the north west, a "fair wind" up the river, and by four bells – or 10 a.m. – the *Davis* had wriggled through all the reaches her raffee sometimes spreading wide over the trees on both banks at once, and oozed in the coal wharf below the old soap factory, and the swing bridge, and the pretty little park and the mill wheels of the ancient and enterprising town of Napanee.

"Whadda ya come back fur?" demanded the dockwallopers who cast the *Davis'* line off twenty-four hours before.

"To unload our coal," said Captain McCullough.

"Thought you wuz full of water and sinking when we saw you comin' up the reach," said they. "Where'd you get your coal anyway?"

"Oh, it's some old Captain John sold us in Deseronto," said Captain McCullough.

"Jack you're a caution," was the reluctant acceptance of the joke, and the fact of his arrival coal-laden from Oswego, twenty-four hours after leaving Napanee. "If ennybuddy hadda told us this we'd a called him a damn liar."

"Mebbe I am," said Jack, but Babby knew different.

August 5, 1944
Sails Still Shimmer on Napanee River

Who of the thousands who rush through Napanee daily by train or automobile would guess that the place had ever been a port at all – or still is – tucked away seven miles from the seemingly nearest navigable water?

Napanee is one town in Canada with an attractive approach by train – old mills tree embowered, with their race dammed like the picturesque canal locks on the Thames above London. A gem of a public park brook, that here was a deepwater lake port – and on tidal water too – owing to the rhythmic inflow and outflow of the Napanee River as it reaches the Bay of Quinte in two hour respirations.

The Old Mill at Napanee Harbour.

Napanee has been a lake port for a century or more; perhaps ever since the Indians tried to say *"la farine"* or *"le pain"* for the bread flour which has been ground by its merry mills for a century and a half. The French are fond of offering this derivation of the name, but the evidence that they ever had flour to offer the Indians is slender. It was the English who grew the grain and built the mills in Upper Canada and who opened the continent to the world. Never forget that. The first mill was built at Napanee in 1785 by a Loyalist – twenty-five years after the French had lost their claim to Canada.

Earlier fore-and-afters trading to Napanee were the *Countess of Napanee* and the *Emblem of Napanee*, the latter built at Bronte and rebuilt after a collision and renamed *Olivia*; the *I.D. Bullock*, which became the Volunteer and batted her brains out on the Belleville Bridge, the little *Richmond*, built on Amherst Island and owned by E.D. Dickens.

But the one which will be longest remembered is the *Mary of Napanee*, sailed by "Young Andy" Baird, so called to distinguish him from his father, Capt. Andrew Baird, Sr. who sailed the *Lone Star*, *Snow Bird*, *W.T. Greenwood* and *W.Y Emery*. "Young Andy" succeeded him in the *Snow Bird* and graduated from her to the *Mary*, which he sailed so long that he became "Old Andy" to the memory of the surviving generations of lake sailors.

"Young Andy" Baird was a popular Napanee boy. Such was his passion for sailing that he sailed toy boats from the *Lone Star* when the family lived aboard her, and sailed iceboats on the frozen river. When he himself owned the *Mary*, he kept a lit-

135

Napanee Harbour.

tle sailboat for harbour sailing with his wife whenever he had any spare time. Every schooner he sailed had a maintopmast staysail, a "fly-by-night" or "fancy-kite," not generally used by our fore-and-afters, the mark of an active enterprising captain.

When he was master of the *Snow Bird*, his wife insisted on sailing with him all the time, for the *Bird* was then ageing, and if anything happened she wanted it to happen to both of them. But when he got the newer, larger, and stronger *Mary*, she allowed him to persuade her to stay ashore, and that's how he saved her life. She is still living in Western Canada, or was a few years ago.

"I'd shipped in the *Mary* as cabin boy, to take Mrs. Baird's place as far as I could, with the cooking," said Stanley Babcock of Napanee, the other day. "It was late in the fall, and Captain Andy wouldn't let her come for this trip, although she had often sailed with him. The other boys in the *Mary* were Ben Davey, Edward Markle, who sailed as mate, Al Humphrey, and Captain Andy himself. When the wind came fair from the eastward to get out of the river, Captain Andy cast off the lines, but my uncle on the dock wouldn't let me stay on board. He had a queer feeling that he shouldn't let me go, and he acted on it. They had a fair wind, and couldn't wait to get anyone else, so out they sailed and I trudged home, bitterly disappointed.

"They never came back, any of the them. The *Mary* got to Fairhaven and loaded her coal. She was last seen running before the gale off Oswego under bare poles, in a sea too high for the harbour tugs to take."

This was in November 1905. But the memory of the four who went out in the trim clipper-bowed *Mary*, white above, lead-coloured below, with green rail and red beading, and a jaunty maintopmast staysail between her gafftopsails, still haunts the waterfront of this hideaway of the lake ports.

March 21, 1936
Snow Bird

Thirty years ago Albert Maude of Toronto, laid the *Good News* up in the mouth of the Humber, closing a career in lake navigation, honourable on his part and hers, and took the train for the west. He built up an express and drew business in Vancouver, and moved on to Port Moody, B.C., where he now has both anchors down. But, as he writes, "I often think of Toronto and the lakes.

"At times," he says, "I have clippings sent to me of 'Schooner Days.' The one about the two brothers' trip to Consecon in Prince Edward County reminded me of the trip I made there forty odd years ago in the *Snow Bird* with Capt. 'Old Andy' Baird.

"Consecon, as you know, lies at the foot of Weller's Bay, and Weller's Bay is a young lake – almost landlocked – in the angle formed by the north shore of Lake Ontario and the great southwesterly projection of Prince Edward County.

"Weller's Bay is difficult of entrance, and is cut off from the lake by a long sandbar and an island. It has smaller islands inside it. It is hard to get into the bay, on account of a narrow shifting channel and no piers, but after you get in there is good shelter and water enough to float a large schooner. The Carrying Place landing, where all traffic used to cross on a wooden railway into the Bay of Quinte, is four miles away from Consecon, down at the foot. I had been into Consecon a few time before on the schooner *Helen*.

"The *Snow Bird*, when I was in her, was a fine little schooner of two hundred tons and larger than the *Helen*. She was bluff in the bows and straight in the sides and pretty flat in the bottom, but she was a vessel that could sail and handle like a yacht, and she was a horse to go to windward so long as the water was not too rough.

"Yes, as you have said, she had her centreboard box on one side of the keelson. That was to give her the more strength. She was a particularly strong-built vessel. I've been in Muirs' dry dock at Port Dalhousie, and seen her opened up. I dare say she was the only vessel that ever really made money for Andy Blair or his son, young Andy, both of whom sailed her. In the fine weather, when Mrs. Blair was cooking, I spent many happy days in her, in the coal and lumber trade.

"But this trip wasn't so happy. We wormed into Weller's Bay all right and docked at Consecon and loaded Barley for Oswego.

"We cast off our lines and stood up the bay, but at dark we had not been able to get outside of Bald Head, near the passage to the lake, so we dropped back and let go the anchor.

"It was getting dark early by this time in the year, and this turned out to be a long, cold night. In the morning we found we had been frozen in.

"At breakfast we were discussing whether we would be able to get out or not. I said "We'll get out all right, but the load won't get to Oswego this fall." Then we left the table, made sail, pounded the ice around the sides with poles and fenders, hove up the anchor, and got her moving.

"Before we got up to Bald Head again the ice had chewed our fenders up and was beginning to tear splinters out of the planking of the hull so we let go the anchor and were again frozen in. And it snowed.

"We lay there for a week, and made two trips back to Consecon for supplies, landing in the yawlboat the first time, and tramping down the shore, and the second time going the whole way on the ice. The ice was four inches thick.

"It looked as though we were there for the winter. So we stripped her sails and rigging, stowed everything in the cabin and forecastle, and left one man, Duncan McIntyre, to keep ship for the winter while Captain Baird, 'Young Andy' the mate, and myself tramped to a train and came on home to Toronto, intending to go back for her in the spring.

"When we had been home for three days, we got word from the insurance people that the ice in Weller's Bay had broken up and the *Snow Bird* had dragged back down the bay in the pack ice almost to the dock where she had loaded at Consecon. So we packed our bags and boarded the train for Trenton and drove down to Consecon. There lay the *Snow Bird* all ready to leave, her sails all bent again by McIntyre and the help of the Consecon people. Ten men got into a fishboat with eight oars and stood by us until we were up to the Bald Head passage. The wind was very light, so we lay in Weller's Bay that night, and started for Oswego next morning, with wind still light, the weather very cold, and a roll coming up the lake promising easterly head winds.

"At three o'clock that afternoon we carried away the eyebolt for the mainthroat halliard, and down sagged the sail. By the time we had repairs made and the mainsail aloft again, the light wind had hardened into a fresh east blow, and it was snowing hard. The Old Man was at the wheel, and plugged her at it, but Long Point was still a long way ahead of us, and beyond that we would have no shelter for the heavy thrash to Oswego. So he let her go up the lake, and never stopped till we were under the lee of Toronto Island next day.

"When we came to anchor under Gibraltar Point we were so badly iced up, in the hull, sails and gear, that it was very hard getting the canvas off her, and when the tug *Frank Jackman* came out for us they had to give us their steam hose before we could get the windlass free enough of ice for us to heave it round and weigh the anchor.

"The *Jackman* towed us in through the old Queen's Wharf channel and left us at the old Northern Docks, about where the Loblaw's plant is now, in Toronto's industrial area. The place was then covered with lumber piles. Next day the snowstorm let up, and it froze hard. The *Snow Bird* was frozen in solid at the dock. In those days when Toronto Bay froze, it froze. The ice would cut thirty-six inches thick.

"We ate our Christmas dinners in Toronto, and that is where the barley spent the winter, not Oswego. Next spring the *Snow Bird* fitted out and finished the voyage, five months after she began it. Her crew had to measure the length of Lake Ontario four times to get her across to Oswego – twice in the *Snow Bird* and twice in the train.

"There wasn't much for Captain Baird in that charter. I don't remember the figures, but 6¢ a bushel was big money carrying barley then, and at that rate the whole freight would be about $300 paid in April for a job began in November, with two tow bills and wages for four to come out of it."

Then Snider makes his own remarks about the Snow Bird, *based on his personal research and his own knowledge of her.*

The *Snow Bird* was always an intriguing item of Toronto's waterfront. At the time Mr. Maude speaks of, she was appropriately painted green and white, later green and blue, and still later black and red. No one, not even the port registrars know when or where she began. "Original building unknown" is the entry in the registrar of British Shipping. The first registered name I have been able to find is the *Minnie Proctor*.

She had been rebuilt in Presqu'ile Bay, as far back as 1863, perhaps by late Capt. William Quick for John E. Proctor, JP, one of the magnates of Brighton of whom a curious legend exists. It was he who renamed her. As the *Minnie Proctor* she was driven ashore at Oakville, and there salvaged and bought by Thompson Smith, MP, who re-named her the *Snow Bird*. This was in 1875. Her official dimensions were 77 feet long, 18-foot beam, 6 feet 7 inches depth of hold, registered tonnage, 82.

The *Snow Bird* she remained for the rest of her long life. It only ended in 1904, when she was frozen in near the yacht club, on the south side of Toronto Bay, filled with ice during the winter and sank about this time in the next spring.

Last action picture of the *Snow Bird* in the writer's mind dates from the summer of 1904, when Major Douglas Hallam and I were working up for the Eastern Gap from Frenchman's Bay in the little *Frou Frou* against a strong nor'wester. Abreast of the jetty, at the cut leading into Ashbridge's Bay, we came upon the *Snow Bird* at anchor close in under the lee of the beach, crying her eyes out. Her pumps were going furiously and the water was gushing in two piteous streams from the hawespipes in her bows, as well as from her scuppers. But her cheery crew – there were only two of them, this time – just waved to us when we asked if they needed help, and hailed back that they had her "almost dry."

Port Milford

It is hard to get farther than ten miles from the water anywhere in Prince Edward County, but Milford was born inland. It was literally the "mill ford" of the Black River and should have spelled itself Mill Ford.

Always progressive, the thriving settlement decided to have a "seaport." Not only that, but to be a "seaport" itself. After all, it is only three miles from South Bay, and South Bay is an inlet of Prince Edward Bay, and Prince Edward Bay is an inlet of Lake Ontario, the side of the county that fronts the rising sun.

The Black River runs between high and timbered banks towards the north shore of South Bay. Its stands of oak and pine gave it its name, and choked it with fallen timbers. Nevertheless, under the drive of Dr. Howey Bredin, Capt. William Ellis, shipbuilder, and other enterprising Milfordians, the river was cleared of logs and dredged to a depth of eight feet all the way back to the Milford dams.

To get rid of the high spots they used oxen, which, chained to scoop shovel and ploughs, would plod along the banks. When they came to the county road winding around from Milford to Waupoos, and crossing the river by a wooden bridge, they were not stuck. The bridge would hardly give clearance for a canal boat. They rebuilt the bridge and its approaches so that it could be run back on rollers to let tall-masted schooners through. Horsepower was used to pull it over and and back.

This was early enterprise as lofty in conception as the Manchester ship canal, though humbler in execution. Ships were built "in" Milford at Cooper's landing. Beyond the village there was an ashery, a little factory shipping potash and soap. The first vessel is said to have been the *Mary of Milford*, a little schooner, put together with wooden pins or trenails instead of iron fastenings. The bank was so high where the *Mary* was built that they had to put her on sleighs and team a mile around to the launching place. There were three *Ellen of Milford*s built in the village, and in 1880 a steamer named *Silver Spray* was built by Capt. John Eagan at Cooper's Landing.

Milford was a port of registry in the 1870s, but not all the vessels registered there were built there, some were built at nearby Port Milford. Port Milford became a settlement almost as large as Milford, three miles to its west, when a cannery was added to the local industries. All in all, Milford and Port Milford were the home ports of over a dozen sloops and schooners, some of very good size.

Port Milford, noted in earlier years for its red mansions, stores, warehouses and schooners, as well as its residents' reputation of industry and honesty, is not at the mouth of the Black River, but some miles south of the mouth in more sheltered waters. It is about three miles due east of Milford, facing the sunrise on South Bay. There is not much doubt that Milford was the reason for Port Milford, and in the 1800s and early 1900s, Milford, Port Milford, and the Black River were very much intertwined. All three places were involved in shipbuilding. Milford was a port of registry in the 1870s.

The first known schooner to have been built at Milford was the *Mary of Milford* followed by the *Ellen of Milford* and then many others including the scow schooner *Jennie Lind*, *J.N. Todman*, *Morning Star*, and the *Plough Boy*, built in 1863. The steamer *Silver Spray*, built at Coles Wharf in 1850, and the schooner *Hibernia* built at the mouth of the Black River for William Ellis and Patrick McMahon, as was the *Goldhunter* with a "100 foot keel of good white oak" and the *Phinneas S. March*.

Port Milford was often called Cooper's Dock, named after Jimmie Cooper the areas leading businessman who owned the *Minnie Of Coopers Dock*. Also built there was the *Jessie Brown*, *Jennie Lind* – the first three-masted schooner, the *Huron*, with capacity of 18,000 bushels, for the McMurtry Brothers, and the second three-master, the *W.R.Taylor*, with a capacity of 20,000 bushels and valued in 1875 at $22,000, and the *Speedwell*.

During the building of one boat, the *Goldhunter*, built for Irish Catholics, someone wrote on the hull in chalk "Deeds Medes and Persians have no fear – No papishers admitted here," whereupon the builder, David Tait, wrote in chalk below "He who had written these lines has written well – for 'tis so upon the gates of hell."

May 1, 1943
Jib Picnic in the *Picton*

Capt. Frank McMaster, of Toronto, later lost with his three-masted *Emerald*, had the smaller schooner *Picton* for years when he lived in Deseronto, and he certainly let no grass grow under her bottom.

On November 4, 1894, the schooner *Picton* lay moored to the docks at Shannonville, that now forgotten port in off the north side of Big Bay, below Belleville and Point Ann. She had taken on the first part of her load (which was barley) at Deseronto, and finished at Shannonville.

The day had been fairly warm and one would have imagined that we would have very favourable weather, for that time of year. But after the noon hour the sky began to have long, white, shooting clouds stretching across it, to dim the blue and to spoil what been so bright a day. About three o'clock the air began to change and a damp, chilly wind sprang up. The sun hid behind a huge black cloud.

The schooner was ready to go out when an old Irishman by the name of Pat Malone, who always worked on the docks, came aboard and said to Captain McMaster, "Are yez goin' out this night?"

The captain answered, "Yes, I believe so."

The old fellow said, "By gorry, ye'd not better, because the devil is settin' his traps for a bad one, I can tell yez."

Ed Rourke was mate and all of the crew except one hailed from South Bay, Prince Edward County. The mate asked the old fellow how he knew. Pat wet his finger and held it up.

"That is snow," he said, "I know it."

The captain stood looking at the sky. Shortly, turning to the mate, he said, "It won't be much get ready to go out."

Soon the vessel sailed down the Bay of Quinte, through the Belleville Reach and around Captain John's Island, and down the Long Reach. Then turning at the Stone Mills of Glenora, she tramped down the Adolphus Reach to Indian Point and so out the Gap to Lake Ontario.

The wind had swung around to the northwest and was freshening fast. When they got outside it was blowing a gale and spitting snow. They kept on until they were almost south of the Main Ducks where they closed upon the schooner *Julia*, sailed by Capt. T.L. Van Duesen. She had loaded grain at Kingston and came out the same night, the converging courses bringing the schooners close together as they rounded the Ducks.

The gale blew almost hurricane force and the snow was coming on heavy so both schooners tried to tack and go back. The wind was so strong neither could make it.

The *Picton* docked at Gananoque, Ont.

The *Picton* careened over until her rail was under before she gave up the attempt. The *Julia* did almost the same. The clouds broke for about five or ten minutes, both vessels sighted one another in the clearing, and with their sails close reefed, wing and wing they both started across the lake together.

The mighty wind, the smothering snow and the maddening, climbing, tossing water gave them a wild passage.

On board the *Picton*, the mate assisted by one of the crew, kept the wheel all night. The waves very often washed over the schooner's yawl boat on the davits astern, drenching him at the wheel.

Once in a while they could sight the *Julia* through the snow. The schooners were both good sailing ships and through the mercy of God they found they were going to make it, for illuminating the sky through the snow clouds they saw the lights from Oswego. The clouds lifted for a short time and both schooners sailed in side by side, wing and wing, not shortening sail till right at the pier to overcome the backwash.

The mate said he had sailed in many a storm on salt and fresh water, but he was never in such a blinding snow or seen such a treacherous sea and never saw anything so welcome as Oswego Light.

It being the last trip over, both Captain McMaster and Captain Van Dusen were presented with new fall hats in Oswego.

The *Picton* was there for three days and then went to Charlotte to load coal for Deseronto. Again, as they were ready to go out, the wind freshened to a gale. Captain McMaster – who had been uptown, came aboard and told the mate to get ready to sail. The mate said, "Captain, this looks pretty bad to go out in." But the captain, proud of his new hat and his good little ship, said he was going just the same. The *Singapore* of Kingston was in a hurry to get home. Captain McMaster felt his plain *Picton* could show Singapore what a real hurry was like so out he went, setting both topsails.

"We'll soon be back here with that tied up and not much below it," said George Bongard to Edward Rourke as they sheeted in the fore-gafftopsail home. His words came true – but not altogether.

When they were ten miles out the wind came around straight ahead and the captain's new hat blew overboard. He found that they would have to turn back. Under great difficulty they turned the schooner around and headed again for Charlotte. They came back tearing like a raging fiend. The fore-gafftopsail sheet had jammed in the sheave of the gaff and they couldn't get the foresail off her. They tied up the main gafftopsail and lowered the mainsail, but had to leave the rest to hang or blow out. The press of headsail on her drove the straight-backed schooner through the water like a torpedo, the seas marching over her in threes as though she were a submerged dock. It was impossible to shorten sail further after they entered the piers.

Captain McMaster was a grand hand with a vessel, and he zigzagged from side to side to take the way off the *Picton* in the shelter of the harbour. Yachts filling the basin, ready to be hauled out, drove him from the east side. The slag piles, old timbers, and concrete blocks of the old iron foundry site stopped him to the west. He had his anchors ready, but was unable to drop them lest he overrun them in the shallow water and tear the bottom out of the *Picton* on the flukes. He tried to catch the quarter of the large schooner *Straubenzie* moored in the river, and the fluke of the *Picton*'s port anchor gouged her bulwarks and tore out five stanchions, and the line he got on to one of her timberheads snapped the timberhead off and hurled it twenty-five feet in the air, almost killing one of his crew.

They blew the horn for the bridge but before the tender could get it swung, ripping the gear of the swing gear and tearing her fore-topmast out and damaging her jib boom, all her jibs and her foresail badly, simply stripping her bowsprit. The topmast snapped short and struck the windlass whelps, or it would have gone through the deck. Her jib boom of stout hickory held, but it was almost sawn through by the ironwork of the bridge.

It cost poor Frank McMaster all he made in both trips to pay for the bridge and get his vessel in repair, and his crew quit after this second experience. Most of them left and came home on the steam barge *Saxon*, with Capt. John Vanalstine, to Smith Bay west of Waupoos Island.

Captain McMaster picked up a crew in Charlotte and got the *Picton* into some workable shape and brought her home to Deseronto looking like a brindled muley cow, most of her headgear being still missing and her remnants of forward sails patched like a log cabin quilt and matching the scrapes and scratches on her battered bows.

Snider's fascination with Prince Edward County started early in his sailing and reporting career, and never left him. His description of "The County" (as it is called by residents of Prince Edward County and those counties that border the Bay of Quinte) was always glowing. "When you wake up in the morning you are not sure if you are in heaven or Prince Edward County." Many a weekend was spent talking to the good folks around Picton, Milford and Cherry Valley. Some of his best stories are about the schooners and crews who sailed out of the county. The history of the county is old, and in its heyday very much dependent on schooner traffic. As late as 1944, over 20 million cans of produce from its canning factories were shipped via Canada Steamship Lines from Picton harbour. The story of Nerva *and of Moses Dulmage have been made into a local opera.*

March 15, 1947
A Prince of Prince Edward

Drowsing while the March sunshine stirs the sap in Prince Edward County's sugar trees, the all-but-vanished Port Milford dreams of ninety-nine other springs in South Bay – of the black dog of the mountain that snuffed at the cemetery gate, of the wood burning steamboats, of the barley-hungry schooners, of the canning factory boom, of the ruck and roar of warplanes and artillery practice in the last war, but most of all, it dreams of the man who built the red-brick house on the high bank.

Jimmy Cooper came to South Bay from Kingston a hundred years ago, a barefoot boy with a pack on his back and an idea in his head.

South Bay was the whole stretch of water now charted as Prince Edward Bay, between the finger of Point Traverse, prolonged by the False Ducks, on the south, and the thumb of The Rock, or Cape Versey, on the north (a high-coloured promontory with the profile of Napoleon, or Queen Victoria, according to taste). You find fossilized golf balls of prehistoric coral there, estimated by Dr. Lighthall to be four hundred thousand years old.

James, however, was not one to waste his time on golf. He came to the county a hopeful lad without a penny to bless himself with. He departed fifty or sixty years later for a better land (if there can be a better land than Prince Edward) a white-bearded stalwart, leaving behind his empty pack and a full purse, many who called him blessed, a mellow red-brick mansion still overlooking the bay, stores, warehouses, wharves and schooners, a port, since fallen into decay (Port Milford), and a reputation for industry, honesty, and benevolence which has become a legend.

Jimmy's original pack was filled with cotton and wool and worsteds, pins, needles and crochet hooks, buttons and braid and handkerchiefs for the farm wives of the county. He extended his range of wares and took what he was offered in exchange, the scanty pennies and scantier shillings of pre-Confederation days, butter and eggs and chickens, pork and beef, roots and grains, and cordwood and timber, as his trade grew.

His brother William came to help him, prospered, married, and built a stone house. They needed transport to and from Kingston and the islands – the Ducks, Waupoos, "the Isle of Tantee in the Bay of Quinte," and all the South Bay shore. So they hired or bought vessels, little scows and open boats at first, then bigger scows like the *Jessie Brown* and the *Jenny Lind*.

James Cooper may have had "a piece," as it is called, in many schooners, for Coopers Dock was a favourite building place on South Bay.

Here Jack Tait built the two-masted schooners *S & J Collier*, *Marysburgh*, *Ontario* (a rebuild) and *Sea Bird*, *Collin Gearing*, and, probably, the *David Andrews*, although the latter is said by some to have been built on Timber Island.

These were all three or four times as large as the *Jessie Brown* or *Jennie Lind*. They traded into South Bay for cargoes of lumber, cordwood, apples, fish, and grain – especially barley – and brought back manufactured goods and coal from the United States. They were not limited to South Bay trading, but carried fruit, hay, coal, and stone to Toronto, and some went to the head of the Great Lakers for grain, squared timber, or iron ore. These long-haul bulk cargoes were profitable only for large vessels. An unforgettable sight about 1870 was sixty-four schooners tossing at anchor between

Point Traverse and Timber Island, at the mouth of South Bay, riding out a prolonged westerly gale. By day their tapering spars made a leafless forest, by night their red and green side light and yellow anchor lights, binnacle lamps and cabin lights looked like Picton on Christmas Eve.

At Coopers Dock also was built the first three-master in Prince Edward County, the *Huron*, of 18,000-bushel capacity, by the McMurchy brothers. Old timers looked askance at her for they knew she would take twice the load of the earlier vessels in which they had shares. But the clock won't run backwards, and in 1877 George Dixon, who had built the *Speedwell* here two years before, launched the *W.R. Taylor* the county's second three-master, capable of carrying 20,000 bushels. She was valued at $22,000. She was wrecked in Lake Michigan, recovered, and rebuilt and enlarged at Port Robinson and rechristened *Stuart H. Dunn*, after a Quebec timber trader.

The Cooper store had a basement flush with the bay at the back, where heavy wares like farm implements, anchors and pianos could be stored. Its upper storey was flush with the bank-top at the front, where the customers drove up for the weekly mail. It served the east half of Prince Edward County. You can still see its ruins.

They built wharfage along the bay, where the cordwood they bought and sold fuelled the newfangled walking-beam steamboats and the later bay propellers like the *Iona, Resolute, Reliance, Water Lily*. The lantern on a pole to guide the steamers in

Snider Collection, Marine Museum of the Great Lakes, Kingston

Stuart H. Dunn fully rigged three-and-after, with square sail set, being towed out of Toronto Harbour. This is one of the vessels on which C.H.J. Snider served as crew in the 1890s.

was the only light Port Milford ever had. Milford Village, some miles inland up the Black River (properly spelled Mill Ford a century ago) was older than Port Milford, and has survived it. Several vessels hailed from Millford, or Mill Ford, among them the schooner *Mary* and steamer *Silver Spray*. The *Silver Spray*, was built there just before the last war.

Skeletons of sunken schooners now line the sunken wharves of the port James Cooper brought into being. The last to lay her bones there being the *Fleet Wing*, which entered into rest after a stormy passage from Toronto in 1906.

James Coopers' greatest achievement was not his fortune, or the various Cooper enterprises, but the home he provided for half-a-dozen motherless and fatherless little girls who came, one by one, pigtailed and hollow-eyed to his red brick mansion on the brow of the bank, and graduated from it years later trained in sewing, cooking, and home making by "Jimmy's" motherly housekeeper to become the happy brides of prospering farmers or vessel owners in the county.

March 17, 1945
Blue Bottom of Last Century

Forty years ago, turning the southeast corner of Adamsons grain elevator at the foot of West Market Street we came on a great hulk of a canal-sized schooner unloading coal for the Elias Rogers company upper deck, which occupied about half of the block east of the Church Street slip. She was three-masted and had three yards on the foremast, a squaresail yard with an old black sail bunched to the mast by brails and two yards above for the sooty upper and lower foretopsails, which, unprotected by sail-covers, gathered more grime with each bucket of coal hoisted aloft to the A-shaped frame then used in loading.

Square topsails were by this time going out, as they involved too much gear and scared away the degenerating lake sailor who couldn't handle himself aloft. A square-rigger often had to pay 25¢ a day more to get men, and a square foremast cost as much to rig as the four-and-aft bowsprit, mainmast, and mizzen combined, with their eight or nine sails among them. So the prospects were that these blackened square topsails, and a bulging squaresail, would be the last of their kind in this vessel, and when they wore out the upper yards would be taken out of her. At most a bat-winged raffee would be left for "square" canvas to box her off when she hung in stays.

Her bows were bluff, her stem straight up and down, and her stern overhung her rudder hardly at all so that when the canal gates closed on her she would fill the lock so completely that there would hardly be room left for water in it to float her out. The register gave her length as 140 feet between stem and sternpost, her beam 23 feet, her depth of hold 11 feet 7 inches and tonnage as 384, about as much as the Welland Canal could accommodate until the locks were enlarged.

What made her different from others then carrying coal to Toronto – apart from her square topsails – was her paint. She was the first vessel we had seen painted blue. And almost the last, for in fifty years there were only two others, a canal boat on the Rideau, and a war casualty in the harbour of Hamilton, the *Bermuda*. Blue is a favourite colour for yachts and many of them look smart in it. But it is no colour for a working vessel. Sailors call it unlucky, and owners know it is, for in large areas this paint seems to fade and check quickly, perhaps from the reflected light rays, and requires constant renewal.

This schooner wasn't blue all over. Her bulwarks and top planking for three or four strakes down had been white. Below this down to her light watermark, royal blue had been laid on with a heavy brush. On the schooner's quarter was the name in yellow letters *Grantham* which in our childish innocence we supposed was pronounced "grant'em."

Such was our first acquaintance with the topsail schooner *Grantham* of St. Catharines, built by Abbey at Port Robinson for T.L. Helliwell of St. Catharines in 1874. Our last was at the LYRA regatta at Kingston in 1898, where foreboding about the fate of those square topsails were promptly fulfilled. The *Grantham*'s three yards were laid side by side in a junk pile near the Kingston Yacht Club, and she herself, shorn of all tophamper and pro-jecting bowsprit, and even of her bottom-blue, was a dingy lighter at the wharf of the Donnelly Wrecking Co., waiting for the old passenger paddle steamer *Eurydice* (ex-*Hastings*) to tow her to the next stranding where a wrecking tug and lighter might be needed. *Sic transit gloria navis*. For the *Grantham*, like so many others, "had been a fine vessel in her time," and the pride of Grantham Township, for which she was named.

September 1, 1945
Why the Topmasts Were Sent Down

Schooners continued to have their uses on Lake Ontario for forty years after the barge era began to clip their wings but a drastic change swept their fleet of lake vessels in the 1880s, after the newly-formed sailor's union established a minimum wage of $1.50 for full-rigged vessels. Down came the topmasts in fleet after fleet, in came the jib booms, up came the timber tugs from their daily chores to begin towing the dehorned droghers and grain carriers all the way to the head of the lakes and back, and propellers began to be built, to tow "consorts" that once sailed on their own.

Among the first to feel the axe were the new schooners *Hydrabad* and *Bangalore*, built by John Power for A. Munn and Co., wholesale grocers and ship chandlers in Kingston.

"When I saw fine new vessels like that sending down their topgallant yards, topsail yards, squaresail yard, topmasts and jib booms, and stripped to a foresail or nothing all," said Peter Beaupre of Portsmouth to the writer this summer, "I said to myself, 'There's no future in this sailing vessel business,' and I went to the prison for twenty years."

Mr. Beaupre did not mean that he committed a crime and got himself locked up. Far otherwise. As the sailor son of a sailor family – his father built the *Oliver Mowat,* he sailed in her and qualified as first mate for bigger vessels – he felt that it was a crime to shear the tall three-masters of their wings. Being of good character and well-known in this community, he became an officer in what they refer to in Portsmouth as the "the penal institution." Retired after many years honourable service, he now keeps an attractive hotel in that Kingston suburb once known as Hatter's Bay. Slim, erect, and still of stalwart frame he is a fine specimen of the lake sailor of sixty years ago.

Turning schooners into towbarges was hailed all along the waterfronts of the lakes as a "sharp move" by owners – these "capitalists" to whom is assigned the role of villain in economic drama – to beat the sailor's organization for better wages and better living conditions. There is some truth in this charge, for the new wage scale did not apply to barges and steamers at first; sailors would hire for 25¢ less in a vessel where there was "no climin', no work above the deadeyes nor forrad of the knightheads nor aft of the davits, nothin' to do but steer and pump and eat her meals." But Dave McReynolds, of the RCYC launch, used to say he would sooner set or furl gafftopsails all day long than drag in one wet towline.

Actually, this change to towing was only a part of the demand for speed which produced the steamship, the express train, the automobile, the airplane, and now the atomic bomb. D.D. Calvin tells, in his interesting exposition of the empire his grandfather founded and ruled from Garden Island (*A Saga of the St. Lawrence*) that as the firm prospered it found that it had to handle twice as much timber in a season, and had to make the choice between doubling its already large fleet of schooners, or making its existing fleet do twice as much work. Calms, headwinds, and gales prolonged schooner voyages, sometimes from days to months, and when they had to go to Lake Superior they had to be towed either by tugs or by horses through two canals and three connecting rivers. From 1870 onwards, the Calvin firm had made a practice of towing their schooners from Garden Island to Port Dalhousie or Hamilton if the wind was light. Then twenty chartered tugs to get them up Lake Erie. In 1882 and 1883 they used their river steamer *Chieftain* to tow all the way to Lake Superior for pine. That year they launched their first propeller, the *D.D. Calvin*. In 1884, the *D.D. Calvin* – double the *Chieftain's* engine power – was carrying more timber herself than any of the canal-sized schooner-barges she towed.

Thus the schooner fleet was reduced to low rig or no rig, for apart from the saving in wage rates and the number of sailors needed in the barges, the windage on yards, topmasts and "light sails" made the schooners harder to tow and was a waste of coal and horsepower. Once the light sails and their spars were removed the descent to "sheer hulks" was rapid. The *Norway*, re-rigged without topmasts after her disaster in 1880, continued to sail under "three lowers" while in tow for twenty years. The *Oriental* had only a foresail when she was lost below Port Dalhousie in 1888. The *Denmark* was shorn of all her spars and even her decks, and doors cut in her bow fitted her for use as a freight-car ferry between the Island and Kingston in 1896. The *Prussia*, which once spread fourteen sails to the breeze (she was square rigged on the foremast), was stripped of everything above the deck. So was the capsized *Jessie Breck*, when she survived as the barge HM *Stanley*.

By 1890, or thereabouts, the steam barges *Armenia* and *D.D. Calvin*, and tow barges *Valencia*, *Ceylon*, and *Augusta*, five vessels in all, carried twice as much timber as the six schooners employed between 1875–83, and in almost half the time. So the change from windjammer to towbarge, while properly regretted by all true sailormen, justified itself in economics – although we sometimes doubt whether economics, like other fine words, butter any parsnips. Ontario lost something when men like Peter Beaupre turned their back on the lake.

Towards the end of the century good old lake carriers like the Muir schooner *Antelope*, the Conlin and Norris schooner *Augusta*, the St. Catharines' schooner *T.R. Merritt* and the American schooner *Reuben Doud*, all of which had been cut down to barges at one time or another, were refitted as full-rigged schooners and enjoyed a few years of full-sailed happiness, carrying coal to Toronto. It was hard to find spars for them and sailors to climb the spars, and the spurt did not last long. The big old Lake Erie schooner *G.C. Trump*, which had sailed to South Africa forty years before, and fallen to barge rig by 1913 (she was then the *Arthur of Toronto*, carrying coal for the Elias Rogers Co.), was refitted as a schooner again during the Great War. Before it was over she had made three round trips between South Africa with lumber, although she was aground for a week in the St. Lawrence rapids on her way down from Lake Ontario.

The Great War sent many of our surviving lake schooners to salt water. Few got there, and none came back.

Oswego, N.Y., was probably the most important port for Canadian schooners trading on the Great Lakes. It was the entry port for the Oswego and Erie barge canals that would take Canadian barley and grains, and lumber into the major markets of the U.S., particularly during the days of Reciprocity. Oswego was the source, along with Port Charlotte (Rochester), of coal to heat Ontario's homes.

Snider has described many wrecks at Oswego, including one of the several schooners on which he was crew. A number of those stories are recorded in following chapters. Here is a description of the harbour based on his accounts.

Oswego — a Dangerous Place

Oswego has been, by its very nature, a dangerous port for sailing vessels for some two hundred years.

It is a port at the southeast corner of Lake Ontario. Nearby, the east-and-west shore of the lake turns, and eventually runs almost due north. There are three natural forces, all hostile to the mariner, working in league with each other. The three forces are: Lake Ontario, the Oswego River and the west wind. To this has been added a fourth: the backwash from the man-made breakwaters.

West and north-west winds, which have the widest sweep on Lake Ontario, pile up tremendous seas against the Oswego corner and the rebound from the stony coasts are like roof peaks. Against this pours in the Oswego River, plunging over a long series of falls (around the locks), running as high as eight or nine miles per hour at times as it enters the lake.

The breakwater was the beginning of a new "outer harbour," and gave more shelter to the inner harbour, but the sea it set up in a westerly gale could be felt five miles out in the lake.

"The more backwash, the more breakwater; the more breakwater, the more backwash," is the history of Oswego harbour for two centuries.

It is the major port on the U.S. side of Lake Ontario. It was, and is, a great port, but the backwash remained, and still does.

The main harbour light is situated about a half-mile from shore at the outer end of the west arrowhead breakwall. Until long after World War II, it was a manned lighthouse.

Before the advent of power on sailboats, and before steamboats and powerboats, which has enabled modern day vessels to take Oswego, or leave it when conditions are bad, there were many vessels lost on the beach under Fort Ontario, to the east of the Oswego harbour entrance.

To illustrate the dangers of the harbour, I quote an account from the *Oswego Palladium-Times* of an incident which occurred in December 1942.

"On December 4, Karl A. Jackson, first-class boatswain's mate in the coast guard and keeper of the main light (at Oswego), signalled after three days alone in the lighthouse that he wanted relief, so the 38-foot picket boat, power driven, pushed out from the coast guard station with two relief and plenty of crew to fend her off at the difficult landing.

"The sea was running high, but the boat made the lee of the light, landing two men on the breakwater for Jackson's relief, and picked him off, though he had to jump for it. Little did any of them think Jackson was jumping to his death when he landed in the cockpit. The picket boat then backed away from the wall, to return to the station. When the clutch was pulled out of reverse and the engine put in forward gear it stalled. The boat drifted rapidly towards the east light, in a tremendous sea, between the lake waves and the river current, the engineer working furiously to get her started. Twice the engine coughed and sputtered out. Lieut. A.J. Wilson, who was in charge (he was also Oswego's port captain) – ordered the anchor over the bow. It weighed 125 lbs. Two men crawled out of one cockpit on to the ice-covered fore deck and got it over, the boat pitching and rolling violently.

"The anchor held – for a minute and a half. Just long enough to slew the launch into the trough of the sea and bury her under an avalanche of water. The inch and a half line parted. The boat spun away, the plaything of wind and current.

"If the north wind had its way, she would have blown into the harbour. If the current had prevailed she would have washed it to possible safety past the east light. But neither wind nor current won the war and the backwash settled it by picking the boat up and tossing her on the rocks at the very end of the breakwater, where the east light stands, rolling her over as she struck. Of the six men on deck all, including Jackson, were drowned. He clung to the broken line as the shattered hull drifted past the fatal rocks, but lost his grip. The two who were caught below – one working vainly on the pump and engine and the other in the wheelhouse by order – were spilled out and tossed onto the breakwater. Lieut. Wilson, buoyed up by the air in his oilskins, swam strongly, but could not make it. Nixon, second in command, and one of the survivors, tried to pull him out of the icy water but could not lift him."

The story goes on to detail the heroic efforts of another Coast Guard boat in saving the survivors who had to scramble along 1,600 feet of the ice-glazed rock of the breakwall.

Wind. Sea. Current. The reason that experienced sailors are very wary of harbour entrances in a gale or storm.

January 16, 1943
Wrecked at Oswego Was Fate of Many

How often has "Schooner Days" had to end the story of a stout laker with the location "Wrecked at Oswego!"

That was the end or experience of dozens of the old sailing vessels. One recalls, naturally enough, the first vessel he sailed in, the *Albacore*, which was wrecked at Oswego in 1900. She ran the *Fred L. Wells* and the *T.R. Merritt* a close race for the distinction of being the last sailing vessel, wrecked there, and won it. The *Merritt* struck, rolled over, and came in on her beam ends some miles above the harbour, in the same gale.

Young Capt. Charles Redfearn, now long retired from his last command, the big Canadian National carferry *Ontario No. 1*, was sailing the *Albacore* at the time. Before midnight, the mate called him from his watch below, and said it was blowing pretty hard, and he thought they had better get the mainsail in, for it was a very heavy sail to handle. When Captain Redfearn had turned in it was a light-to-moderate evening and quiet, though the glass was low. We were in for a backlash of the hurricane that destroyed the *City of Galveston*.

They put the crotchtackles on the mainboom and got the sail down between the lazy-jacks with great difficulty, but that was not sufficient relief. The *Albacore*, flying light, was tearing off twelve knots and the remaining sails threatened to leave the boltropes, so they ran down the outer jibs and started to settle the foresail. Captain Redfearn took the halliards, which was a two-man job. She was rolling hard now, and in one surge the throat halliards jumped the thumbcleat and took Captain Redfearn aloft with them, burning the skin of his wrists and forearms. It was as though he had been flayed alive, but in spite of these terrible burns he saved his men from death under the descending gaff. The foresail was badly torn before they got it stowed on the boom. Then the fore-staysail blew clean out of the boltropes. The new standing jib was now the only sail left. It held and saved the ship from losing steerageway and broaching to.

By this time the lights of Oswego, where the *Albacore* was bound, were shining up ahead, and in a few minutes the schooner was racing past the end of the outer breakwater. Steam was up in the donkey boiler, and she blew for a tug. The big harbour tug was away with a tow, but the late "Hunky" Scott came down from inside with the little tug, and as the *Albacore* rounded up, he caught her line and tried to drag her into port across the wind and against the river current.

It was an anxious moment, with safety a few hundred yards ahead and destruction gnashing its teeth down to leeward, the *Albacore* still rolling wildly from the confused sea, but gaining a little smoother water with each fathom.

She sagged off to leeward, taking the tug with her. Scott remembered what had happened to the Oswego tug that tried to drag the *Flora Emma* in off that same lee shore. She got into shoal water herself, bumped the bottom, burst a steampipe, lost the *Flora Emma*, and washed ashore herself – a complete wreck. Her captain was drowned and the vessel she tried to save smashed to as many pieces as the cargo of lumber she had on deck.

Perhaps another ten minutes trying would have got the *Albacore* in, perhaps it would have put both tug and schooner on the beach. The tugman would not take the chance. He put the axe to the towline. Captain Redfearn was not surprised or bitter when the *Albacore* blew side-wise across the tug's stern lantern and raced for Fort Ontario's boulder-strewn beach. He was so burned up already with those frightful ropeburns on his arms he had no indignation left. He knew Hunky had used his best judgment, and that was that. He called the crew to hang on to windward, so as to be clear of falling spars, and next moment the *Albacore* crashed on the boulders.

Her blocky bows of four-inch oak plank came down with one hard crash, and she slewed around broadside. Her jib booms were pretty well over the beach when the racing waves sucked back in the dragging undertow. When the seas broke she seemed hundreds of yards out. She came in almost on the Oswego Lifesaving Station's doorstep. In next to no time the lifesavers had shot a line with their rocket gun. It was made fast on the foremast and the breeches buoy was hauled out. The woman cook was the first saved. Captain Redfearn, with the flayed arms, the last.

He was rushed to the Oswego Hospital, treated for the burns and shock and kept all night. Next morning, bandaged and discharged, he left the hospital. The first man he saw on the windswept street was bearded Capt. Dolph Corson, of the *T.R. Merritt*.

"Hello captain, where's your ship?" asked the whiskered one of the beardless boy.

"On the beach," said Captain Redfearn ruefully.

"So's mine," said Dolph, also ruefully. The *T.R. Merritt* was the finest vessel he had ever had. She was a hopeless wreck five miles to the westward.

The *Albacore*'s experience was a sample of what befell dozens of schooners, both Canadian and American, at the mouth of Oswego harbour.

Snider's dedication as a marine researcher of the schooners of the Great Lakes started in his early youth. He made notes of the schooners he saw in Toronto harbour and elsewhere, made sketches of many of them, and talked extensively to their crews.

In 1948, Snider reported "Forty years ago we started to seek remnants of those honourable sailing vessels which fought on either side in the War of 1812 on the Great Lakes. A harmless folly of extreme youth, with the emphasis of extreme. To date we have found a dozen of the two hundred ships, brigs, sloops and gunboats that took part in that conflict."

His finding and the recovery of HMS Nancy *at the Nottawasaga River has been extensively recorded. Some of his other findings were recorded from time to time in his "Schooner Days" columns.*

"Go," said the inner urge, "find the bones of a sylph."

This did not mean a moth, a fairy, or a slender, graceful woman, or any of the other meanings of that word in the dictionaries.

There was a Sylph *on Lake Ontario in the War of 1812, probably the world's largest schooner in her time, measuring 340 tons.*

His search for the remains of the American man-of-war Sylph, *was spread over many years, and was documented in a series of four weekly columns which not only detailed the extent of his research, but gives an excellent description of the building of the vessel, her usefulness, and her history. This culminated in the column "Axe to the Root of a Mystery."*

September 18, 1948
Axe to the Root of a Mystery

On Clayton's westside waterfront, in front of the Otis-Brookes Company's long-established lumberyard, a row of black dots bobbed in the backwash of the stiff west wind. From our deck – we were anchored off a few hundred yards, as close in as safety permitted – the black dots looked like the rung-heads or upper ends of the floor timbers of a wreck, and a long black line indicated a keel or keelson.

Were these the bones of the long sought *Sylph*, man-of-war of 1812, that we had come two hundred miles to see?

Eagerly we pulled ashore in the longboat.

Foiled again. The black dots were only the wet ends of planks, the "keel" or "keelson" the string piece of a little submerged wharf.

Young Larry Brookes, grandson of the founder of the lumber firm, stood on the foreclosure to welcome us. His father was still stormbound on Amherst Island by the same gale there that had brought us down.

"Look," he said, "would this be what you are after?"

High and dry above the receding waters, in the spot where it had lain since dredged up twelve years ago to the Brookes firm's cost and inconvenience, was enough heavy wreck timber to sink our little longboat and a dozen like it. It was in two sections, each held together by heavy bolts of blacksmith iron, three or four feet long and ranging from one inch to an inch-and-a-half in diameter. There were also eight- and ten-inch hand-wrought spikes or ship-nails. The large section was made up of five main timbers, each about twelve inches square, one of them twelve feet long, the others perhaps half that length. The other section was made of similar pieces with smaller ones attached. All ends were broken off short by a sharp, quick fracture.

"We had to dynamite the heap when it was dumped here by the dredge," explained Mr. Brookes, "to make the pieces small enough to handle."

This was plainly the deadwood of a large wooden sailing vessel of the nineteenth century or earlier. It was not as sound as the timbers of the *Nancy*, built in 1789, but it had been exposed to worse conditions having been sun-dried and frostbitten for ten years after a century of submersion.

A crosscut saw went into a square foot of it like a hot knife through butter at first, slowing to the pace of cutting a dry-frozen ice cream brick in the middle, and fell through the outer shell again almost by its own weight. The outer faces were crumbly with years of rain and sun after long submersion, the core was still wet, and showed a deep purple hue, drying to indigo blue. Good white oak always does that if it stays long enough under water. Irish bog oak, submerged for centuries in the peat, comes out solid black. Each tibmer, by its grain, was a heart-piece – the oldest, strongest, hardest part of an oak tree. They bad been growing on the shores of Jefferson County, N.Y., one month in 1813, and furrowing the waters of Lake Ontario the next. The sour smell of white oak sap was still in it.

In vessels, deadwood is not the superfluity it is in metaphor or the forest. It is an essential. *Webster's Dictionary* defines it as a "a mass of timber built into the bow and stern of a vessel to give solidity." It is the timber foundation upon which the whole structure is reared. From the deadwood, as from the foundation, the shape and size of the structure can be determined with considerable accuracy.

This deadwood was as heavy as that of what we used to call an Old Canaller, meaning not a canal boat, but a schooner built to the limit of the lock of the "Old, " or second, Welland Canal. The present is the fourth. These old canallers were large enough and strong enough to traverse all the Great Lakes and the Atlantic Ocean, as many of them did. They had carrying capacity of up to 750 tons dead weight. Their measured tonnage, or tons registered, ran between 320 and 350 tons, on dimensions varying little from 140 feet over all, 26 feet beam, and 11 feet depth of hold. Their loaded draught was eleven feet, and light draught four. They were comparatively shoal, for they had to negotiate limited canal locks and harbours. They were really intended for a nine-foot draught limit, and sailed well when loaded to that, but they could load down to eleven feet or even more.

This deadwood probably belonged to a vessel 11 or 12 feet deep in the hold, and with greater draught of water, but not 140 feet in length over all, and possibly more than 26 feet beam. Her shorter length would reduce her tonnage, her greater beam and depth increase it, so that her registered tonnage might be as much as an Old Canaller's, but her carrying capacity would be less. This would depend upon the relative sharpness of her model.

The deadwood offered definite information about her shape. The lowest member of four parallel timbers, on which we assumed might be the keels to which the other three had been bolted together vertically, had a groove or scoring in it, meant to take the lowest edge of the lowest outer plank of the hull – the garboard strake. This groove called the rabbet (or rebate) indicated three-inch planking. This might be light for a "full canal sized vessel." They some times run to four-inch planking and five inches in the bilges.

The deadwood timbers, impressive as they were, were not heavy for a canaller, though heavy enough. Averaging twelve inches vertically, with slight variations, they were ten inches across, suggesting that they had been slimmed down for greater speed through the water. In the same way, the comparatively light planking suggested speed, not cargo capacity.

Enough remained of the natural crooks and the mortices to indicate that the vessel had concave garboards and clean lines aft. With her framework rising at sharp angles. All this suggested a deep sharp vessel, built for speed, and built very strongly, without any waste of bulk or weight, so that she would not be pushing one unnecessary ounce or sliver of wood through the water.

The wish was father to the thought, but we did think this was the wreckage of the *Sylph* and will continue to think so until offered proof to the contrary.

The evidence to hand shows that the *Sylph*, after her war career and commercial adventures, was sunk in the bay at Clayton near this spot and was visible here as late as 1877, and this wreck had been a menace to navigation from then on until dredged out ten or twelve years ago.

The descriptions tallied. The *Sylph*'s tonnage was 340 when she was a man-of-war, 236 when she became a merchantman. Tonnage of naval vessels was usually kept "up," because their building was paid for by the ton, so the builders measured them as "large" as possible, while the commercial vessel's tonnage was kept "down," because the owners bad to pay tolls and harbour dues on it. It makes a large difference whether you take the actual length of the vessel or the theoretical length of the keel and subtract an allowance for the beam, and whether you take the outside measurement of the breadth, or only the distance between the inner skins of the two sides.

We know the *Sylph* was comparatively deep, for the American commodore thought she drew twelve feet of water with her guns and stores in. That would be right for a shape standing-keel schooner of around one hundred feet length that did not use a centreboard like the flatter-bottomed Old Canallers.

Drop keels, ancestors of the centre-board, were used by Lieutenant Schank, Royal Navy, in 1774, and were adopted by the British Admiralty in 1790. In 1796-98 dozens of British men-of-war brigs were using them. Centreboards began to appear on Lake Ontario six years before the *Sylph* was built, the first being tried out in a Niagara-built skiff at Oswego in 1806 or 1807, but we have no record of them being used in any American man-of-war on the lakes, or in any but small vessels during the *Sylph*'s lifetime. Had she had a centreboard, Commodore Chauncey would have mentioned it. We have earlier discussed the probability of the centreboard having been used in the *Toronto Yacht*, built at the Humber in 1799.

It may relieve readers anxiety (if any) to record that we turned right around before lunch that day and stormed back across the St. Lawrence and up the Bay of Quinte and Lake Ontario, against the last forty hours of the westerly gales, Without parting a rope yarn in the 3 1\4 day voyage of 420 stormy miles. we moored in the RCYC lagoon at the island with half an hour of our eighty-hour limit to spare. And so heard Big Ben across the bay strike midnight as we drifted off to dreamland.

We went to sleep believing we had accomplished the impossible, viz, finding the bones of that "immaterial being living on and in the air," a sylph. If anyone has another identification, let him speak.

Bridgeport

Originally called St. Mary's, Bridgeport was an important and busy schooner harbour prior to 1856.

Bridgeport was on a large pond west of Port Dalhousie, with a river that flowed north into Lake Ontario, along the river and in the pond were a number of wharves and storage facilities. The Louth Harbour Company, which had wharfage and grain storage facilities on the river, have records still in existence which show the receipt of tariffs for wheat, flour, lumber, tanbark, meats, and ashes (from the burning of the forests and much in demand for the making of soaps), and as many as twenty carts from Smithville lined up to unload grains at one time. The company showed higher tariffs than those recovered at nearby Port Dalhousie, which served St. Catharines at the time. The company had two wharves, each 480 feet long. These may have been at a sight known locally as Squire Clarkes Landing.

Its usefulness as a harbour was greatly diminished when the Great Western Railway built their bridge over the river quite close to the lake in 1856, which resulted in a $15,000 lawsuit.

December 14, 1946
Last over Jordan Was the *Flying Dutchman*

Steer south, true, or south three-quarters west magnetic from the tall, stone lighthouse sending its gleam from Gibraltar Point – yellow a hundred years ago, now green – and you come to a wonderland on the other side of the lake, where three centuries mingle.

You are in the heart of Ontario's "Vineland of the Good," revelling from April to October in bees and blossoms, flowers and fruit, peaches, pears, plums and grapes, corn, wine and cider, honey, root crops, squashes, pumpkins, apples, happy folk and pioneer romance. Here lives yet the old coach lantern.

It is in the log house the Secord brothers hewed out in 1777, when they came, all pow-der-grimed and heavy-hearted, from the destruction of their Pennsylvania homestead in the bloody rancour of the American Revolution. Peter Secord, who killed wolves and bears for the bounty in 1817 when he was 102, may have been one of these lads.

The settlement is said (*Page's Atlas*) to have been begun here in 1755 by Germans from Pennsylvania and New York, but the same authority later says the township of Louth was settled in 1787 when wild land could be bought for 30¢ an acre. By 1817, when Peter Secord was selling wolf scalps, it had two grist mills and five sawmills. This place was called "The Twenty" when Mrs. Simcoe used her water colours. Twen-ty Mile Creek and Twenty Mile Pond, being twenty miles from Niagara. Later it was Louth Harbour and Jordan Beach.

Here Mrs. Simcoe landed in 1794 and drew a picture for her diary.

And here is the building place of the *Flying Dutchman*.

If you have "steered small," as we used to say in schooner days, you will hit the keyhole to this treasure chest with embarrassing accuracy. A wall will stop you, for a concrete causeway under the Queen Elizabeth Way now spans the entrance through which Mrs. Simcoe sailed. From the lake you would not now guess there was an entrance at all. A double-line of piling, bent in the middle, shows there was wharfage here once, but it is only when you get over – or under – the causeway that there bursts on your view a pond broad enough to harbour the British Navy, running back for two miles, to the limestone ridge which swings all the way from Flamboro to Niagara.

Keep on steering south true, and you come to narrowing shores where the river pours itself over the ledge at the foot of the escarpment. You will leave to port sunken white oak evidences of a prosperous pioneer wharf, and a landing stage once served by the old mill road. The old mill itself stands close to the waterfall, all silent and dark.

On the starboard side (which is west, for we are on the south side of Lake Ontario and directions seem left-handed to north shore dwellers) are traces of an ancient set-tlement, which red-brick houses have succeeded. Below this, somewhat nearer to the ponds outlet to Lake Ontario, is a low, rounded hill, still green in Vineland the Good, even in December. Like many others, it is called the Hogsback. The little fold or valley beside it forms a runway to a tiny bay, and here in the year of grace 1862 the keel of the *Flying Dutchman* was laid, of good Twenty Mile oak, and here she was planked of Twenty Mile white pine – the same priceless timber whose squared faces in the Secord log house show the original axe marks clean and undecayed after a 169 years.

The earliest register of lake shipping available, which one Robert Thomas compiled in 1864, gives Bridgeport as the building place and port of hail of the *Flying Dutchman*, Richard Gilbert her builder, Moses Overholt her owner.

Why Moses called his argo the *Flying Dutchman* is more easily understood after a glance at the old atlas. Moses Overholt was listed as a merchant in Jordan, the Overholt farm is in the name of "J. Overholt" in an atlas of 1876. Other names in the old Jordan list of inhabitants, Christjohn Schrober, the shoemaker; Rudolph Nonsinger, carpenter; Jacob Linenbank, glazier; Soloman Wismer, cooper; Peter Zimmerman, blacksmith; emphasize the "Pennsylvania Dutch" connection. Many of the early settlers of Louth township did come from Pennsylvania, the Secords among them, and some were Mennonites, a sect founded by a Frieslander. Some were of Low German ancestry, but a few were Holland Dutch. The Zimmermans were said to be French from Alsace. All were sound, thrifty settlers and made Louth a garden of Eden watered by the Jordan, if we may be permitted to muddle Old Testament geography.

So far as is known the *Flying Dutchman* was the last sailing vessel built in Jordan, though the port was in use for exactly fifty years after her launching. The *Flying Dutchman* did not retain "of Bridge Port" long on her stern. She was soon on the St. Catharines' register. By 1871, she was owned by Henry Ferguson of Toronto and hailed from here. In 1873, Dexter Eccles of Wolfe Island, and John S. Grange of Napanee, bought her, and she went to the Bay of Quinte grain trade, for which she was very well fitted.

September 17, 1942
Riding It Out with the *Queen of the Lakes*

Capt. William Head, master of the *Ocean Wave* of Picton so many years ago that few living men recall that vessel, grinned affably when asked if he had ever been wrecked in the fifty years he followed the water. He is now 87.

"No," said he. "That has been the lot of better men than me in plenty. I guess I was lucky. But I've been near-wrecked, if that interests you.

"I gave up vessel sailing after twenty years of it, and went fishing out of Point Traverse for another thirty years. But in May 1907, I think it would be, my brother-in-law Capt. Peter Ostrander, needed help for long voyages, and I went back to sailing, going with him as mate in the three-masted schooner *Queen of the Lakes* of Kingston.

"The Richardsons, the grain people, owned her, and they wanted Peter to take her up to the west end of Lake Erie to load corn for Kingston from the west side of Pelee Island. Our crew was made up of Prince Edward County men – Peter Ostrander, master; William Head; myself, mate; Elmer Ostrander, my nephew, who was later drowned; Cab Walker of Milford, Johnny Bowernan of South Bay, and Andy Foster. My sister Amanda was married to Captain Ostrander, and she came along as cook. We made two voyages to Pelee Island.

"The second trip in this month of May we got loaded and started back and got as far down Lake Erie as the O (Rondeau Harbour) when it came on dirty from the northeast, and we had to get back behind the long sandspit of Point Pelee for shelter."

There are two Pelees on Lake Erie: the parsnip-shaped point, jutting out like a dagger from the north shore for twenty miles; and the island, large, sandy, fertile in fish, grapes and corn, lying some miles southwest of the point. The great quarter-circle enclosed by the point and the Essex county shore is known as Pigeon Bay, from the vast quantities of wild pigeons that used to feed on its shores.

"We rounded Point Pelee and ran up the back side of the point and let go our anchor in smooth water, but well offshore. To the north of us, and nearer Kingsville in the corner of Pigeon Bay, we could see the riding light of another schooner, sheltering like we were.

"At midnight the northeast wind dropped. We had hopes of getting away in the morning at daylight, but before we had turned in, the wind was howling again, and this time from the south-west. This put us on a lee shore instead of in shelter, for the wind had the thirty mile sweep of Pigeon Bay. We might have slipped our cable and so got out with the loss of chain and anchor, but it was a question if we could clear the tip of Point Pelee, and we could not have weathered Southeast Shoal. The passage between is shallow and changing and the sea came running in with the new wind like a series of rooftops adrift.

The only thing to do was to trust to the Lord and our ground tackle. We had two good anchors and we gave her the second one, and all the chain cable we had. Then we backed up our paulpost and windlass, on which the strain came, and with our big new river line, leading the parts aft to the capstan amidships and leaving them taut.

"I never saw a worse sea, nor one that made so quickly – Lake Erie's shallow water always does.

"The *Queen of the Lakes* was a good old vessel, worthy of the name she had been wearing for fifty years, and a good seaboat. She rode true to her anchors and faced wind and sea like a prizefighter. When the biggest ones swept upon her she would drop her head down and bore through them until the jibtopsail on her jib boom end, twenty-five feet up in the air normally, was plunged underwater. Then she would lift gallantly over the roller, tossing her jib boom fifty feet high in the air and keeping her decks pretty free.

"In one of these springs she settled back on her haunches till the yawlboat strapped across her taffrail on stout oak davits, was plunged under the seas. The strain snapped one of the davits. The boat, full of water, broke adrift and vanished into the darkness. Our last chance of leaving the *Queen of the Lakes* alive – and that a slim one – vanished with the boat.

"But our anchors held.

"Daylight showed the other schooner four miles above us, in as bad a plight as we were or worse. For a mile out the beach to leeward of us was a boiling belt of white surf, yellowed by the sand stirred up by the trampling seas, bursting, retreating, reforming. To windward far as the eye could see, battalions of breakers, tearing towards us in an endless calvary charge, all the horses white and riderless.

"The schooner above us was a white fore-'n'-after, an American, perhaps a little bigger than the *Queen of the Lakes*. We learned later she was named the *Grace L. Gribbie*. She was jumping like a bucking bronco, and her Stars and Stripes were streaming upside down from her main truck. She was in vehement distress of some sort, we could not tell what, and wanted help. Our boat was gone, beaten into barrel-staves on the beach, but we could not have helped her if we had tried.

"Her paulpost, the big oak timber eighteen inches square against which the windlass backs had broken at the deck under the terrific strain and the windlass barrel – with no paul to check it – was turning around like a rolling pin, letting her anchor chains surge through the hawsepipes in the eyes of her. Before they could knot or shackle the bitter-ends of the two chains together under the deck, both lengths had roared out through the openings and she was adrift!

"Her captain was game. It was blowing so hard few sails could stand the pressure – seventy-two miles an hour by official records – but he had a new foresail, and with great labour he got a part of this hoisted and so got her under some control. But she could only sail before the wind, or with it on the quarter; and the beach was ahead of her.

"We feared for a while she would drift down on us and so sink us both. But she answered her helm enough to drive clear. We could see the two men grinding at the wheel, hear the captain's "Port!" and "Starboard!" "Hard over!" and "Hard down!" as she blew past.

"Could she weather the point? Not a chance. With that wind and sea, and that canvas, though it was brand new. The foresail split and blew out in small pieces like gull's wings. She smashed in on the beach two miles below us, and in twenty minutes had completely disappeared. Masts, spars, and all, she was just a long stretched string of broken wood. Only two of her crew of seven reached shore alive.

"We watched our pump wells carefully although the way we were standing on end it was impossible to tell much from the sounding rods. Our bottom and sides and decks were tight, but she began to leak. We found some water coming in through the quick-work of the stern and transom, which was light and not used to being sub-merged. But we also found the water was coming in from far forwards, She was being cut down from her anchors.

"The terrific strain of the chain cables was gearing out the iron hawespipes – each a hundred-pound casting or heavier, the big, round, eye-like tubes through which the cables lead – and sawing down through the heavy oak chocks and timbers, which the hawespipes passed through. There have been cases of vessels having their planking cut through to the water's edge by the surge of chain cables. Given time enough, iron will always wear through wood. The *Ocean Wave* once tore out her hawespipes until they slid down her chains till the anchors stopped them.

"We had loaded some cordwood for the galley fire for the return voyage, and we got this wedged under the chains in the forecastle head, so that when they sawed as she jumped and dived they bit on the cordwood instead of the chocks and hawsepipes. That saved her from being further cut down, and we kept the leak under control by the pumps.

"After that, three enormous seas swept us in succession, filling our decks as high at times as the bulwarks, and threatening to swamp us. And our anchors started to come home. Foot by foot we backed up until we began to feel the effects of the tremendous undertow and backwash from the beach. After that the anchors held again. But the motion, if possible, was worse.

"All day long it blew, with never a let up. At midnight, just when it had begun twen-ty-four hours before, the gale let go. Next morning the lifeboat from Leamington or somewhere came alongside to see if there was anything they could do, and we learned the details of the *Grace L. Bribbie*. We got our house into better shape, hove up and sailed on our voyage again. At Port Colborne we got a punt to serve as a yawlboat till we got to Kingston.

What Is a Shellback?

A shellback is defined in the Oxford dictionary as "A hardened sailor" or "a marine turtle." I do not know the definition of a "hardened sailor."

Webster's International describes a shellback as "an experienced sailor, often an elderly man" or "a person who has sailed across the equator."

For some hearty Canadian sailors, the season never ends.

The Shellback Club is an organization of sailors that has, for over 60 years met for mutual refreshment once a week, when the regular sailing season is over. The club has no constitution, no rules, and no debts. There are no dues, membership lists, or records. Membership is open to all gentlemen sailors who can afford the price of the meal, which is minimal. It has been an institution since its keel was officially laid in 1934. It's motto: "Being in All Respects Ready for Sea."

At each meeting, guests and their introducers lead in the singing of an old sea shanty: one of the traditions of the club designed to keep the old tunes alive, and to recapture the spirit in which the old Shellbacks sang on sailing ships. This is followed by another tradition, that of a yarnspinner telling a tale of the seas, or the vessels that sailed them.

Snider was an active member and regular attender at the Shellback luncheons, a fact reflected in the mention of the club in his column.

November 14, 1942
Lake Fishboats

The Shellbacks sang "Rule Britannia" with their shanties at the meeting at Ellen Bradley Grill Wednesday, for the war news was good. And the yarn of the day was the best of the season yet. It was spun by Stanley Baby, who is an enthusiastic admirer of the sailing fishboat which survives a few yachts, and Mr. Baby has one of them. She used to flourish in hundreds, on all five of the Great Lakes.

"As handy as a fishboat; why, she'd tack under a reefed foresail."

That used to be the lake sailor's highest encomium for a big lake schooner of particularly fine performance. It was praise indeed.

Yachtsmen recognized the fishboat's merits, and forty years ago yachts were built on their lines. J.H. McCaffrey's big black *Carlotta*, forty-feet long, was the finest we had in Toronto. The National Yacht Club brought down a fleet of five Collingwood skiffs one season. There was the *Herring Gull* and the *Merry Mac*, and W.J. Commerford's *Tainui*, and the Clark Brothers' *Pappoose*, and the *Elk*, and the *Maybelle*, and Fergus Kyle's *Billy Kid*, and others.

They had an advantage of being able to go wherever a rowboat could row – two feet of water would float them. They were not expensive, they provided plenty of room for their inches, they were fast – except working to windward – and they were safe if properly handled.

They had to be sailed on the trigger, with someone always ready to let the foresheet and jibsheet run and get the ballast to windward. That needed more crew than a ballasted keel boat, where you could cleat the sheet down and let her take it till the mast went or the sail blew out of her. Two men could and did handle any "mackinaw," as they were all called down here. But a dozen men found room in one.

That sort of pleasure sailing went out as the motor car and auxiliary engine came in. There are a few macs or near macs – some of them just schooner-rigged lifeboats – around Toronto yet, and a revival is going on where pleasure boats of the "Collingwood skiff," "Huron boat," and "Mackinaw boat" type are being built.

Photo by J.W. Bald, Archives of Ontario

Collingwood Harbour, 1880.

They were all "Macs" to us.

Because we thought they originated in the Straits of Mackinaw we called all our clinker-built two-masted craft of the fishboat type macs or mackinaws, whether they were sharpsterned like the Collingwood skiffs, square-sterned like the true mackinaws, or with overhangs like the Huron boats. The preference here ran to the square stern and straight stern or clipper bow. Mr. Baby described one boat which he found an excellent sailor, and was a variant on the prevailing type. She had a flaring spoon bow and was designed to trip by the stern, so that she had a raking keel and was deeper aft than forward. Most macs were as level on the keel as a lifeboat.

Mr. Baby's talk was a most interesting one, and he is not responsible for any errors which may appear in this report of it. If there are any, they are uninformed additions to what he said.

In their heyday their number was legion, the speaker said, and they flourished in sizeable fleets until the advent of the Great War. They constituted a factor of lake shipping for more than a century.

Their modelling was developed for the work in hand and for the waters of their plying. The ultimately developed types were fast, weatherly craft of beautiful lines, fore-and-aft rigged and most of them sparred with two masts. Their foremasts were stepped well forward in cat-boat style and their mainmasts just aft of their centreboard boxes.

Usually the foremast was two or two and one-half feet more lofty that the mainmast, and the spread of canvas fairly well equalized between fore and main spars. The

Archives of Ontario

Collingwood Harbour in schooner days.

mainsail having less hoist but longer foot and loftier peak than the foresail. They had long bowsprits, and often innocent of forestays, and usually only one shroud or leg of rigging was sufficient staying for each side of each spar. They were shallow of draught and on occasion could be run ashore on sand beaches.

There were several hull types, Mr. Baby said, and those of Collingwood skiff model were probably the most numerous. He surmised that most of the lakes fishboat models were evolved from English or Scotch types by British boatbuilders who had migrated to Canada. There were also flat-bottom pound net boats on Lake Erie and square-stern mackinaw boats that were chiefly used on Lake Huron, and sloop type that was used only on Lake Michigan, of Scandinavian origin, for the mainmast was almost amidships, as in the old longships of the Vikings and Norse fishcutters net.

The square-sterned boats were not called mackinaws by the fishermen. That solecism arose with yachtsmen.

The lake fishing boats were picturesque in their numbers and in the manner of their faring; and they went unchallenged until about 1880 when steam tugs could fish five or six miles of nets as compared with thousand-yard sets of their smaller sailing sisters. The cost of their building and powering was disproportionately greater than the cost of equipping and operating the sailing craft. So the tugs did not at first make any great difference. Later, they ousted a good part of the sailing fleet from Lake Erie waters and eventually gasoline boats ousted both from all the lakes fishing grounds – and all the romance from the fishing industry.

The old time fishermen, he said, were a jolly, hard-working, unaffected breed. Superb sailormen in their chosen calling, who loved to race and to test each other's seamanship, and who feared neither winds nor weather in the staunch, speedy fishboats; home-loving, church-going, trustworthy, and respected members of their community.

William Watts of Collingwood, is credited with developing the Collingwood skiff-type of boats to its greatest degree of excellence. He built a great many of them and his son, Frederick Watts, carries on the boat-building business he established at Collingwood. The Watts principle of boat building was to build a half-model, shape and mould it to perfected design, then scale it accurately and build the boat from the laid-down scale. The McGaw Brothers of Kincardine built many of the square-stern Lake Huron fishboats, but not as many or as famous ones as did Henry Marlton, of Goderich.

The Marlton boats, Mr. Baby said, were considered standard of length, weatherly qualities, and sailing ability. They were designed for a trade that took them many miles off shore on the "spine" which runs down Lake Huron, north and south, and often when they were beating back from their fishing grounds in the teeth of a snarling northeaster they needed all the excellence of build and design that their creator had lavished on them; and their crew blessed his handiwork as they battled fierce gales under close-reefed foresail and with two men steadily bailing to keep their boat afloat.

Marlton also built fine, large clipperbowed schooners and he is said to be responsible for the innovation of the clipper bow or cutwater stem in fishboats. Originally all had plumb stems, with a rounded forefoot and slightly raked sternposts, so that they were almost as long on the keel as on deck, and the rudder was hung outboard. Marlton also built fishboats with overhanging sterns, the rudder coming up through the transom. The *Belle Jean Anne*, built by the McGaw brothers in Kincardine was on the lines of the Marlton boats, cutwater stem and overhanging stern, but she was a distinct novelty. She had three masts all of the same height, with a pole topmast on the main, on which she let a large lug topsail on a yard, crossing the topmast, like Breton fisherman used in the English Channel. And she had two centreboards, one ahead and the other abaft the mainmast.

Poletopmasts for racing kites were not unusual with the fishboats, but the *Belle Jean Anne* was the only three-master ever heard of, and the only fishboat with two centreboards.

Snider ran a series of articles on the Spences of Saugeen, and about the founding of the towns of Southampton and Port Elgin. As they were written there was some inevitable overlapping of information. A composite of the material is of necessity lengthy, but worth the reading.

February 1936
Spences of Saugeen

O up and spak an eldern knight,
Sat at the king's right knee:
"Sir Patrick Spens is the best sailor
That ever sailed the sea."

So runs the venerable ballad, and one can well-believe the eldern knight had grounds for his assertion when one thinks of the Spences – old Captain John and his four sailor sons – who used to sail out of Saugeen, or Southampton as it is now called.

Captain John of that name was born at Birsay in the Orkney Islands the year the Battle of Waterloo was fought. When he was fifteen, in 1830, he was apprenticed to John Hay of Stromness to learn boat building. Stromness boat building was no mean branch of marine architecture a century ago, for from that little town, across the island of Pamona from Kirkwall, on the Scapa Flow, went most of the whale ships of the then-flourishing Greenland fishery.

Hundreds of whalers fitted out in Stromness for the Greenland Sea and the Hudson's Bay trade, and they used thousands of whaleboats. The local fisheries used hundred's more – "yolls," "skaffies," "sixerns," and so forth, as the native types, descending from their ancestral Viking ships, were called.

When John Spence had served his six years he shipped on the good brig the *Phoenix*, of London, probably as cooper or carpenter for the whale fishing in the

Davis Straits. Being now of man's estate, 21, and a skilled workman, he made a contract with the Hudson's Bay Company to work for them at York Factory [Manitoba] as a ship carpenter.

His first job was to refloat and repair an English ship which had gone on the rocks in the company's service. He got her off, repaired her, sailed her down to Ungava, and discharged her cargo at Fort Chimo [Quebec]. It being too late to do anything further that winter he made a voyage to England from Ungava and returned to York Factory in the spring.

After building several boats for the company there he was sent to establish a post 150 miles up the George River. This done, he was called to build more boats at a high inland post above Fort Chimo. When one was completed she was laden with furs and brought down to the brink of a very high cataract. Here the furs were baled in canvas and portaged 3 1/2 miles and re-embarked in canoes and paddled down to the fort on Northwest River. The newly built boat was left above the cataract to carry goods up to the upper post next fall.

Captain John's time was completed, but the company prevailed upon him to stay at Fort Northwest River and build two more boats. In the spring he was engaged to sail one of the company's trading vessels along the Labrador coast between Rigolet and Kipicot, two trips a season to Sandwich Bay, where the goods sent out from England were landed. In 1848, after three seasons of this hard life, Captain Spence, now 32, decided to see this Canada on whose outer fringe he had been fried and frozen for a dozen years. He came to Quebec, and from there to Kingston. Here he met his future wife. Although they made their home far to the west, the Limestone City would always claim them. Capt. William Spence, one of their sons, died there last summer.

In the spring of 1849, Captain John pushed west. But his search was not for the "gold in Cal-eye-forn-eye-o" which then had the forty-niners flocking, but for a good spot for fishing and trading with the Indians. After a roundabout trail he found the Saugeen peninsula sticking up like a sailor's thumb between Georgian Bay and Lake Huron: pine and hardwood all over it, lake trout and whitefish all around it, and Indians all through it. Others may have been there before him, but he was one of the first two white men to settle in the wilderness. A Captain Kennedy, who came with him, was the other.

They walked back through the bush together to Owen Sound; brought a canoe there, and went to Colpoys Bay, site of the future town of Wiarton. From there they portaged to the Sauble River, and then paddled down Lake Huron to the Saugeen. Here they built their shanty, and where their shanty was built the present town of Southampton stands.

Nearby, in Lake Huron, was a group of small islands where the whitefish came in millions at certain seasons. In the fall the herring came in tens of millions. The group is known on the chart as the Fishing Islands.

All summer they worked at making barrels, hiring what coopers they could find to help them. The wood for the barrels was right at hand on the stump – virgin oak, elm, pine, cedar, beech, maple, and hemlock.

They also built, or bought, fishboats and a little vessel of some sort; perhaps the *Ellen of Saugeen*. When the time for the fall fishing came on, Captain Kennedy sailed down to Goderich for a cargo of salt, after leaving Captain Spence with the summer output of barrels at Whitefish Island and Main Station Island (part of the Fishing Islands group), ready for the season's catch. The old stone trading post still standing on Main Station Island was built by these two captains.

When Captain Kennedy got back with the schooner swimming deep with salt, bad news awaited him. A government man – may their shadows ever shrivel – had been around and seized all the barrels. He claimed they were cut on "government land" and cut without a license. The fishing had been good, the catch was already for salting, and here ruin threatened the partners' first year's effort.

Courageously, they resolved to salt the catch in bulk in the schooners hold and take it that way to the Welland Canal where they hoped to dispose of it to St. Catharines merchants.

They got down Lake Huron and Lake Erie all right, escaping the expected freeze-up, but the long open fall was their undoing. The fish sweated in the hold, and when they at last reached St. Catharines they not only failed to sell the cargo but they had to hire teams to haul it away from the reeking hold, and lay the vessel up for the winter – with the hatches off.

Nothing daunted, they returned to the conquest of Saugeen, after a few weeks in Kingston. All next summer they made barrels where Southampton later grew. In July, Captain Spence brought his bride up from Kingston, and the settlement knew a woman's influence. In the fall the fishing prospered. The partners had taken the precaution of securing licenses for the timber they had cut for barrels, so they made a profit on their season's operation.

But Sir John Franklin was lost and strong men who knew the ice were called to find him. Captain Kennedy, being skilled in Arctic navigation, was engaged by Lady Franklin for the purpose. Captain Spence thus lost one partner, but Captain Kennedy gained another. He did not find Sir John, but he married Lady Franklin's niece. Captain John carried on, and Southampton and Port Elgin grew up around him. In the spring of 1866, in partnership with George Allen, he bought the schooner *Patton*. Bruce county was being farmed to some purpose by this time, and there was grain, lumber, cedar posts, cordwood, and tanbark to be carried to Goderich, where the *Patton* would load salt for the fishery. Towards the end of the year George Allen was drowned off Inverhuron, and so Captain Spence sold the Patton. In her place, during the winter he built a tidy little schooner of 4,500 bushels capacity, which he called the *Nemesis*. Perhaps he had that government agent in mind when he named her after the Greek goddess of vengeance; perhaps she commemorated an old ship of his Hudson Bay days. There was a nemesis attached to her, of which he little dreamed, and which he little deserved.

The *Nemesis* was appropriately painted as black as the midnight of vengeance the Hellenic deity suggested. A figurehead carved like a Chinese dragon, with gaping jaws and gnashing teeth made her seem the embodiment of wrath when she was storming through the water. Her stem was straight, up to the cut-water knee from which the dragon sprang, and she was low and rakish and two-masted. Altogether, in appearance she was a proper pirate barque, and one would expect the skull-and-cross-bones at her main-truck, she was, in reality, a most peaceful craft, principally engaged in the prosaic and profitable trade of carrying cedar posts and cordwood from Georgian Bay to Goderich or Detroit.

This was in the great block-paving era of civic development in Canada and the United States. Remember the old, smelly, bumpy, rutty pavements of cedar blocks? They replaced the original mud roads and macadam, as the lake towns grew to cities. They were all paved with cedar for a while, but the while was not a long one., Theoretically, cedar is imperishable. Practically it went to the dogs in five years, under the scorching suns and winter frosts, and continual wettings and dryings of city service in the trying days of horse traffic and watering carts. London gets along well with wooden blocks, squared and chemically treated, and laid on concrete. But the cedar block cargoes which the *Nemesis* and a hundred other schooners carried got little treatment beyond the buzz saw. Sometimes they were "laid" without even the bark being removed, and often with no "bottom" but a sprinkling of sand over the native mud. No wonder they didn't last.

But while the block-paving craze was on, paving contractors made fortunes and vessel owners did well carrying forest products to the growing cities. The *Nemesis* was one of the fleet in this trade on Lake Huron.

As some of Capt. John Spence's little boys were able to toddle up the gangplank he took them sailing with him – Johnny, Harry, Will, and Aleck, who was nicknamed "Cappy." He made sailors of them all.

"Old" Captain John of Southampton and Port Elgin, did this. He was so known on Lake Huron long before he died – and he lived to be 90 – but he was Old Captain John to distinguish him from his son, Capt. Jack Spence, who also sailed vessels when he grew up. Two of his commands, which his father owned, were the *Wanderer*, and the *White Oak*, both of which came from Lake Ontario.

All the Spence boys sailed with their father in the *Nemesis*. It is a long time since she was ploughing the waves – sixty years – but there are men still living who sailed with John Spence and his sons in her.

The Town of Collingwood became an important shipbuilding centre in the days of steamships on the Great Lakes in the twentieth century. Its founding and its story as a grain terminal in "Schooner Days" was the subject of several of Snider's columns.

September 23, 1937
"Riddle of the Sands" Gave Collingwood a Railway

Lord it did blow on Georgian Bay last week!

A black shower and then a rainbow in the morning – "all sailors take warning" – then squall after squall from the northwest sometimes just wind, sometimes with driving rain that felt like birdshot.

As far as the eye could see, from the dim bulk of the Giant's Tomb, across to the concrete castle of the new Collingwood grain elevator under the royal blue stripe of the Caledon mountains, the bay was a mass of frothing billows. Like a feather bed with the ticking ripped from the top. The long lathered likeness of white foam all but concealed the pale green of the water.

The great crescent of sand which makes Wasaga Beach so popular in the good old summer time, with hundreds of motor cars, diving rafts, surfboards and launches, and thousands of bathers and sunbaskers, was deserted and bleak. Its only patrons were groups of young grey gulls, parked head to wind for a quick takeoff from the wet sand, and some snipe and sandpipers, trotting about the shallow wind-whipped pools, whirling away like dried leaves whenever they tried the air.

Ploughing along the soaking margin one came at length to the end of the ridge held in place by course grass, where the Nottawasaga river, after paralleling Georgian Bay shore for miles, diagonals its way out and pours its forest waters into the Great Lakes chain.

Here, on the flat sandspit which it has marked for nearly a century, the outline of a large wreck shoed sharply as when I saw it on my first visit twenty-five years ago. From stem to stempost the waterline of a vessel of old Welland Canal size was still traced perfectly by the continuous line of timber ribs. We had just been looking at the remains of the *Nancy*, heroine of 1812, and the contrast was noticeable. This wreck was almost twice the length of the *Nancy*, but her ribs had not been as stout. They were cased in oak plank. This was of double the thickness of the *Nancy*'s two-inch planking but not as well-preserved as the latter, though the *Nancy* was sailing sixty years before this wreck came ashore. Rusted bolts of the back-links of a set of chainplates on the starboard side told a sailor that the ship had been a two-master. Ragged remains of a centreboard box, with the centreboard still in it, edged-bolted and cross-strapped with iron, stamped the wreck, old as it was, as nineteenth century. The *Nancy*, launched in 1789, shows no centreboard. This useful appliance for keeping a ship from drifting sideways came into the lake schooners between 1840 and 1850, although it was used by the British navy much earlier.

The wreck has been a riddle to many a summer colonist at Wasaga Beach. Charcoal remains of their corn-roasts and council fires in the sand-filled bull proved the depth of their deliberations upon their identity and her fate. Like many another, she has shared the purely apocryphal glory of being the "payship of the British Navy, sunk to save her from capture by the Americans" – something which, so far as has been proved, never happened anywhere. Yet legend persists.

While the wind screamed and the sand and spray stung the ears that listened, this is the story the gulls and the sandpipers told of the wreck as they splashed in the pools.

In the winter of 1850-51, five survey parties explored routes for the Ontario Simcoe and Huron Railway, which eventually ran from Toronto to a northwestern terminal. The railway coach was then more of a novelty in Upper Canada than the Cambria was last week. Up to this time the province was entirely dependent upon water traffic and waggon roads for the transport of passengers and freight. The first railway train in Ontario departed from Toronto to Aurora in 1853.

These survey parties were seeking a route which would give a projected railway from Toronto connection with Chicago and the American West by a steamer service from some point on Lake Huron or Georgian Bay. Toronto had been fixed upon as the beginning of the line and there was furious competition over what was to be the other end. Land speculators were just as keen in 1850 as they were when Churchill, Prince Rupert, or Port McNicol blossomed on the map in our century. They had foreseen what Kipling phrased later, that fortunes were to be made by every man who knew where the next ten cities of Canada would arise. Some of them would stop at nothing to secure the selection of their own holdings as the chosen spot – or to prevent some other site being chosen.

Of the five survey parties, one tried for a Lake Huron terminal, either at the mouth of the Maitland River, where the town of Goderich was rising, or at the mouth of he Saugeen where the Spences and other hardy fishermen had built the huts which later became Southampton. A second tried for Victoria Harbour on Georgian Bay. A third went through with Meaford for its objective. A fourth explored the mouth of the Nottawasaga. The fifth considered the possibilities of terminal thirteen miles farther west on Georgian Bay, where an unnamed village nestled at the foot of the Blue Mountains.

The village was not quite nameless. It was faced by a few rock islands, known to mariners as the Hen and Chickens. You will see advertisements in the old Toronto papers, advising that the schooner *Sophia*, or the steamer *Ploughboy*, perchance, will accept passengers and freight for the Hen and Chickens, sailing from Toronto on or about such and such a date, weather permitting. Later, when the town of Collingwood arose in the vicinity, the original settlement was known as the Old Village.

This was the spot which put up the hardest fight for selection as the terminal. Its strongest rival was the Nottawasaga mouth. It was called Van Vlack in the great sawmill days, when rafts of logs by the mile were floated down the Nottawasaga to the big mill at its mouth, and the banks of the river rang to the bite of the axe on the tall pines and the wine of the saws reducing them to millions of feet lumber. Van Vlack has now vanished and Wasaga Beach has taken its place, with summer hotels and cottages sheltering thousands in the season.

In the old days settlement at the mouth was scanty, but for many years a few settlers had fished there for whitefish and sturgeon, cut timber, staves and shingles, and grown a little grain on the sandy acres. It had been a depot since the War of 1812 when Noah Freer used to send the supply of pork and flour and powder and uniforms for the northern garrisons up Yonge Street, across Lake Simcoe to Barrie, and along the Willow Trail to the Nottawasaga. It was here that the *Nancy* was loaded for Mackinac, and it was here she was burned. In the next generation a McAllister brother built a sloop here from timber cut on the banks, its ironwork forged from sword-blades and bayonets picked up after the *Nancy* battle, its timbers plumbed by a bob made from the lead bullets found in the sand. Here, also later, later indeed than the time of this survey – John Potter of Oakville built the large brigantine *Queen of the North* in 1861.

Sir Stanford Fleming conducted one of the surveying parties, presumably the Nottawasaga one, and was impressed with the merits of that route, as giving the shorter amount of rail haul. The length of building time was the main objection to the Lake Huron terminal suggestion. Frederick Cumberland conducted the Hen and Chickens exploration. The name Collingwood, commemorating Nelson's colleague ("See how that noble fellow Collingwood brings his ship into action!"), was suggested for the sight by David Buist, as the survey party broke a bottle of whiskey on one of the rocks.

With the survey reports in, activity to secure the selection of one site as against the other rose to fever height. The tip went around the Hen and Chickens place would be chosen. There was an auction sale of town lots on Front Street, Toronto, with eager bidders. The townsite boomed. Five steamers, including the fatal *Lady Elgin*, later run down in Lake Michigan, were secured from Buffalo and other American ports, to operate on routes north and west from Collingwood as soon as the railway got there.

But the Nottawasaga route had stout partisans.

The rumor came back that as this was the shorter line, and the river would make a better harbour than Collingwood, the line was going there. Some Collingwood speculators were in a panic in 1852.

Then someone unknown chartered the large two-masted schooner *H. B. Bishop* of Buffalo to go to the Nottawasaga to load grain. The Nottawasaga partisans hailed this with delight. The *Bishop* was one of the finest schooners on the Great Lakes at this time. She was 121 feet 10 inches long on deck, 24 feet 19 inches beam, 9 feet 5 inches depth of hold and registered 263 tons. She had been built by Fred N. Jacob of the great wooden shipbuilding firm, Jacob and Banta of Buffalo in 1847. Opposite her name in the Buffalo Customs House register is the laconic entry "Wrecked, 1852."

Nottawasaga added the chartering of the *Bishop* to their accumulated evidence that the Nottawasaga mouth was already a port, had been a port for forty years, and was the "logical location" for the great city which the newfangled railway was sure to produce. They did not stop to examine whether there was a schoonerload of grain in Nottawasaga Township. Maybe there was, but the *H.B. Bishop* could carry 18,000 bushels, and a thousand-bushel crop was good going on the bayshore farms at this time.

The Collingwood claimants said nothing. Some of them looked black and tried to turn over their lots quick before the boom burst. Others seemed remarkably unperturbed. Or so the Nottawasaga proponents thought afterwards.

True enough, the *H.B. Bishop* did go to the Nottawasaga to load grain.

As one of the new type centreboard schooners she could get into the narrow rivermouth without trouble on a quiet day with the wind from the north or east. She only drew four feet with the centreboard up. But if the farmers teamed enough grain to the river bank to fill that nine-foot hold she would be drawing ten feet of water or more, even with the centreboard up. There was not ten feet in the river. There was certainly not ten feet all through the entrance, so she could not get out.

The *H.B. Bishop* anchored offshore and waited for the farmers to ferry their grain out in bags, on scows or in the schooners own yawlboat. Thousands of bushels had to be picked up this way along the shores of the Great Lakes before the harbours were developed. The grain could only be handled when the water was smooth and a vessel might have to wait days or weeks to compete her load. At the first sign of an onshore gale, she would have to weigh anchor and beat off to shelter, coming back when conditions permitted.

She was hanging on, out in Nottawasaga Bay, when a nor'wester broke on her in full fury. The *Bishop*'s anchors dragged through the soft sand like the shares of a farm cultivator grooving the loam. Pointing west with her useless anchors out to the north of her she walked in broadside on. She must have had very little grain in her, for she drove up so high that her crew were able to jump ashore. Seemingly, her centreboard was down when she struck and buckled under her. The remains of the lower part of it are still wedged in the box, and the sides of the box are bulged out as though the board – really a dozen heavy oak planks, bolted together edge to edge – had pried it to bursting point when she struck the beach.

So far as is known, no lives were lost in the wreck of the *Bishop*. But the schooner herself was a complete casualty. So was the Nottawasaga terminal project.

The Nottawasaga claimants exclaimed bitterly, that the schooner had been wrecked "on purpose" and scowled across the water at Collingwood as the author of a plot to discredit the possibilities of their potential port. The theory was propounded and spread that the trip of the Buffalo schooner had been engineered by those interested in the selection of Collingwood for the end of steel and that the wreck was part of the plan to blacken the Nottawasaga internationally. Maybe they were right. Right or wrong, it did.

Collingwood certainly lost no time in pointing out the hazards of the Nottawasaga and the battered hull of the big lower lake schooner was impressive evidence. It was left there like a corpse jangling in chains, as a warning to all who plied the lakes. The treacherous sands which had trapped the pioneer bedded the wreck in so completely that she could not be released without a steam dredge, and they built up bars around her so that the waves could not break her up. When her bulwarks, decks, and upper planking disappeared before the battering of the water, the shore of the winter's ice, and the baking of the fierce sun, her oaken ribs traced a gaunt warning in the smooth sand.

As they do to this day.

Whatever the reasons for the wreck of the *H.B. Bishop*, her fate sealed all possibilities of the Nottawasaga being the railway terminal. Within a year, steel was pointing its two inflexible fingers into the former nest of the Hen and Chickens; the Old Village was disappearing under the new Collingwood; a grain elevator was going up and lake schooners by the hundreds and steamers by the dozen commenced to wear the well-known groove in Georgian Bay, Lake Huron, and Lake Michigan between Collingwood and Chicago. Cordwood and lumber out; grain, pork, beef, and flour back, were the cargoes for decades. It all poured through Collingwood on to the clanging freight cars of the busy railway, for the short-cut across Upper Canada to the sea.

Friend Nosey O'Brien again provides the impetus for another sailor's story of historical fact about sailing on the Great Lakes in "Schooner Days." "Beaver Mormons" illustrates just how well Snider could retell a story in a most interesting way, and at the same time give an insight into another facet of life in "Schooner Days."

June 22, 1935
The Beaver Mormons

"Was I ever wrecked on the Beavers?"

Old Nosey O'Brien repeated my innocent question with the same intonation he would have employed if asked whether he had ever been cremated.

"How would I be alive here and talking to you peaceful now if I'd even been ashore on the Beavers, let alone wrecked on them? What man ever lived to tell that tale and the truth?"

Nosey was of great age when he so deposed at the close of the last century. He had known and survived the Brooks Bush Gang out of which young Brown was hanged for the murder of Thomas Sheridan Hogan, in the old covered bridge across the Don. He, Nosey, had fought in every forecastle and waterfront bar between Montreal and Michigan. That was where he left most of his figurehead and won his name. But to escape with life from the Beavers was, to his way of thinking, impossible.

"Leastways," he added judicially, "it was so thought in my time."

Eighty and Ninety years ago, when such Lake Ontario fore-and-afters and brigs and barques broke into the new trade to Chicago, Lake Michigan was the most dreaded of all five of the Great Lakes, and the vicinity of the Beavers was the most dreaded part of all Lake Michigan.

With reason. Such names as Sole Choice Point, Poverty Passage, and Death's Door, still surviving, explain some of the reputation of the lake. It was almost all unlighted; its shores were shoal, its jaws were full of islands, it was a place where the cyclones of the prairies let off steam.

It was also the portal to the Golden West, then swarming with thundering herds of buffalo, tribes of Indians and whites who painted the frontier posts to match. Chicago itself was still noteworthy as the scene of the Dearborn Massacre. It had not yet achieved fame with its Great Fire or its gangster gunmen, but its gamblers had established a reputation for speed on the draw.

The whole state of Michigan had only two hundred thousand inhabitants in 1840. It was rather a law unto itself and the lake swarmed with timber pirates, who built their own hookers on beaches where they set up their portable mills, and cut their cargoes in defiance of government dues and government licenses. Fur traders still fought one another and the Indians, and bartered moonshine whisky and gunpowder and blankets and trade goods which had never paid duty for beaverskins and fox pelts and deer hides. In short, there was no king in Israel, and every man did that which was wrong in his own eyes and got away with it if he could.

Into this revolver republic in the 1840s burst Jesse James Strang. Wisconsin-born convert to the cult of Mormon. Strang was baptised into the faith in 1844, the year Joseph and Hyrum Smith, the original prophets, were shot in the Carthage jail by a lynching mob. Strang had visions and revelations of such potency that he gathered together a thousand followers, and in 1847 they descended upon the Beaver group of islands near the entrance to Lake Michigan at the Straits of Mackinaw. Thereupon was added another peril to Michigan navigation.

Although the group is always called the Beavers, there is only one Beaver Island. That is the big one of the lot. The others are known as Garden, High, Trout, Hog, Gull, and Little Beaver. When the Mormons came, the islands, like the settlers themselves, were heavily foliaged. Pine, hemlock, and hardwood were as plentiful as Mormon babies or Mormon whiskers. The Beavers had already attracted a few hundred Gentile settlers. They farmed and caught Lake Michigan whitefish, and cut fuel for the sidewheel steamers which used to waddle their way from woodpile to woodpile up and down the lakes.

Strang and his invaders gave the woodcutters and fishermen a rough ride. Everybody on the island, he decreed, had to obey the laws of Mormon, and the first verse of the first chapter was a 10 percent income tax. It was hard on a chopper blistering his hands for $10 a month to have to whack up $1 for the edification of the Angel Moroni, and just as hard for the fisherman who got a hundred bucks ahead at the end of the season to have to pay off ten simoleons for the education of the horde of young Mormons, whose multitudinous mothers soon populated the island. Harder still for a sailor who happened to wander ashore while the steamer wooded to part with a tenth of his last month's pay, just because it was in his pocket.

If anyone, Mormon or Gentile, failed in his tithe, retribution fell on him. The least that would happen would be a bad beating. His woodpile might be ablaze, his nets would be slashed. Or he himself would disappear.

The colony seemed to have a Cheka or OGPU* like the Soviets in Russia. Nobody, not even the Mormons, knew or admitted knowing, who these disciplinary individuals were. They were called Destroying Angels, a terror alike to the Mormons and the pioneers. It was not known whether they were Strang's acknowledged lieutenants, who were called the Twelve Apostles, or whether they were superior to him.

Like the Mormon outlaws, known as Wolfhunters in Utah, the Destroying Angels of the Beavers got the blame for every act of violence and outrage which occurred in Mormon surroundings. The Beavers already held a reputation for shipwrecks. But new wrecks were blamed upon pine knots tied to cows horns to simulate riding lights of vessels safely at anchor. No ship that got ashore among the islands ever, according to lake legend, got away again, and whole crews were supposed to have been wiped out by Destroying Angels who used shotguns instead of swords of fire.

King Strang – he had himself consecrated King of Zion in 1850, the third year after his landing – was more than a visionary. He was a vigorous, pushing man of 34 when he came to the Beavers. He had organizing ability and used it. There was a good natural harbour at the north end of the island, near a lake he named the Sea of Galilee. Here he established a town, modestly calling the place Saint James, after himself. The river from the Lake or Sea of Galilee was, of course, called the Jordan. He built a large wooden temple for their worship, with the pulpit removable so that the temple was on week days the town hall. Temperance was rigidly enforced upon Mormon and Gentile. Destruction of cargoes of cornjuice was one of the "crimes" alleged against him and his angels. He began a system of education, for the colony was, of course, polygamous, and little Mormons and Mormonesses seemed to sprout up overnight. To provide schools and maintain the temple, King Strang clamped down on "tithes" harder than ever. Wherever he smelt a dollar he saw a dime for his kingdom. And proving that he was a patron of the liberal arts, as well as the ancient and modern one of tax-

---

* Both organizations were earlier versions of what was eventually to become the KGB.

ation, he established a newspaper, the *Northern Islander*, published in St. James, with about as much freedom as Adolf Hitler would accord the press of 1935.

Strang I, King of Zion and Emperor of all the Beavers, might have done very well if the Destroying Angels could have been kept in hand. They, or bad actors masquerading in their name, went too far when they held up a U.S. mail steamer which was wooding at the islands, and forced the treasurer of Charlevois County on the mainland – in whose bailiwick the Beavers lay – to turn over the public funds.

The old iron gunboat *Michigan* – still afloat, my hearties, and known as the *Wolverine* now, though her plates were rolled in Erie, Pa., ninety years ago – was the "Mountie" of the Upper Lakes in those days. In her annual patrol she heard weird tales at Mackinac of what was happening on the Beavers so one fine morning she steamed into the harbour of St. James, and anchored. She was a paddle wheeler, and barquentine rigged, and her sails – square and fore-and-aft – drove her faster than her engine.

Did she want wood? She did not. She wanted King Strang and the Twelve Apostles. And she got them, and steamed away to Detroit with them and their whiskers under hatches.

But the grand Sovereign of the Beavers was no fool. He pleaded his own cause before the courts. The Mormon vote was something to be reckoned with in the Middle West in 1850s. King Strang and his hairy hidalgos were released and returned to the Beavers in triumph.

Outrages multiplied. Brigham Young's application of Jedediah Grant's doctrine of blood atonement was staining the sect with the reputation of murder and assassination in the western states. The Mountain Meadows massacre of a hundred immigrants from Arkansas was on its way. In the Beavers, apparently, a subterranean civil feud developed.

Things were so bad that one dark night the gunboat *Michigan* again anchored in the harbour in complete silence, coming in noiselessly under sail. She landed a squad of marines, deputy sheriffs, and law officers – all heavily armed. At daylight they called on the King. He wasn't at home, nor were his apostles. So all day long they searched Galilee and Jordan from Dan to Berersheba, and in the afternoon they came upon King Strang in a cave on the banks – and apparently very glad to see them.

They marched him down to the wharf. He seemed relieved to have such a bodyguard, and laughed and joked as they drew near the landing place where the *Michigan*'s boats lay.

The wharves were all piled high with cordwood for the fuelling trade. As the procession passed between two of the long piles, men armed with shotguns leapt forth and fired at King Strang point-blank. He fell, and coughed away his life and his kingdom among the blood-soaked cordwood.

The shooters were afterwards said to be Destroying Angels, punishing the King for his secret sin. The Mormon mob didn't recognize them as ministers of justice, but fell on them and would have rent them limb from limb. They were hunted all over the island, and only saved their lives by swimming out to the *Michigan* and hiding aboard her. They were taken to Mackinac as prisoners – but never came to trial.

The Gentile population of the Beavers rose in their might, and, helped by immigrants from Michigan, drove the King's followers forth on the long trail for Utah. And so, for generations, the terror of the Beavers has departed from Lake Michigan.

Reader response to Snider's "Schooner Days" column was never greater than during the controversy of the Sunnyside Amusement Co.'s proposal to burn the last working schooner on the Great Lakes, the Lyman M. Davis, *as a spectacle to attract a crowd to the amusement centre in the year 1933. The protests delayed the burning until 1934, but as had happened so often before to famous landmarks and relics, the* Lyman M. Davis *was destroyed as a spectacle for momentary pleasure and profit for the greedy few. The* Lyman M. Davis *was not the first such spectacle, and probably not the last, as "Schooner Days" reports.*

March 3, 1934
Passing Hails: The *Lyman M. Davis*

"This poem of my wife's and the cartoon which I am sending are our contribution towards the saving of the *Lyman M. Davis*," writes Loudon Wilson of Royal Oak, Mich.

The Last Lake Schooner
The Lyman M. Davis

Shall you destroy the last old schooner,
Put from your sight that work well done,
Of thousands of sailors, builders, captains,
Who laid the foundation of years to come?

She is built of the stuff of which they were made.
Strong and reliable, swift and true,
She is fit to represent them now
To let posterity give them their due.

For the profane lust of callous eyes,
For dishonoured dollars of vandal crowds,
Shall her faithful decks be consumed by fire?
Shall devouring flames creep up her shrouds?

Let no her tall masts warp and fall
On her blackened keel sink beneath the blue
Preserve this grand ship of the colourful past
And the future will ever be grateful to you!

G. Harrison Wilson

July 26, 1941
Sending a Schooner over Niagara Falls: Once She Was a British Man-of-War

They had some fool ideas of fun a hundred years ago, among which "Schooner Days" begs to include sending somebody else over Niagara Falls. The objection applies whether the somebody else is a man in a barrel or a pig in a punt. Recently the secretary-manager of the Port Huron Chamber of Commerce, Mr. H.A. Hopkins, who, of course, merits no such criticism, gave an historical instance in a broadcast. It was an account of how the old schooner *Michigan* went over the falls in 1827. And it was taken, after various transcriptions, from an old letter written in Buffalo, September 9, of that year.

"The schooner *Michigan*, as you have already learnt from me, was the largest on Lake Erie, and too large in fact to enter the various harbours on the lake, and being somewhat decayed in her upper work, the thought struck the owner, Major Frazer, formerly of New York, that she would answer the purpose of testing the fate of a vessel that by accident might approach too near the stupendous cataract of Niagara, and also the fate of animals that might be caught in the rapids of these swift rolling waters, and carried over the falls.

"The proprietors of the large public houses at the Falls, on both sides of the river, and of stages and steamboats, made up a purse to purchase the schooner, aware that they would be repaid by the company which the exhibition would attract; and in this calculation they were not deceived.

"For several days previous to the September 8, the stages came crowded, as well as the canal boats, so much so that it was difficult to find a conveyance to the Falls: and such was the interest that the descent was the only topic of conversation among all classes. On Friday night, September 7, wagons filled with country people rattled through the town, and on Saturday morning Buffalo itself seemed to be moving in mass towards the grand point of attraction. To accommodate those who could not find passage in carriages, five steamboats had advertised to leave here on Saturday morning, and great numbers chose this conveyance ...

"The *Chippewa* was appointed to tow down the pirate schooner (as she was termed) the *Michigan*: which service she performed. I took my passage in the boat, and we got under way before the others, passed through the basin at Black Rock, and about a mile below the Rock took in tow the vessel destined to make the dreadful plunge. As soon as we got under way the scene became interesting. The sun shone in full splendor, the waters of the Erie were placid, there being scarcely a ruffle upon its surface, and a few miles astern of us four steamers crowded with passengers, and with bands of music on board, were plowing their way down the rapids of Niagara.

"Our little boat towed the *Michigan* as far as Yales's Landing on the British shore, within three miles of the Falls where she anchored: and at this place the *Chippewa* landed her passengers as well the *William Penn*, and they were convened from thence to the Falls in vehicles of all descriptions. The three other steamboats landed their passengers on the American side.

"Three o'clock was the hour appointed to weigh anchor on the *Michigan*. The task of towing her from Yales's Landing to the rapids (and a most hazardous one it was) was entrusted to Captain Rough, the oldest captain on the Lake. With a yawl and five oarsmen, of stout hearts and strong arms, the old captain got the schooner under way, and towed her till within one-quarter of a mile of the first rapids, and within half a

Sailing Ship 'LYMAN M. DAVIS'
Lying at Sunnyside Beach, Toronto

Archives of Ontario

Lyman M. Davis, as she lay at Sunnyside Beach, Toronto, waiting her execution by fire, 1934.

mile of the tremendous precipice – as near as they dare approach – and cutting her adrift she passed majestically on, while the oarsmen of the yawl had to pull for their lives to effect their own safety. Indeed such was the fear of the hands, as I have understood, that on approaching near the rapids they cut the tow line before they had received order from their commander. And now we approach the interesting moments of the exhibition.

"The high ground on both sides of the American and British shores were lined with people, having a full view of the rapids and of the approach of the vessel. And now it was that a thousand fears and expectations were indulged, as the *Michigan*, unguided by human agency, approached, head on, the first rapid or descent, and apparently keeping the very course that the most skilful navigator would have pursued, having an American ensign from her bowsprit, and the British Jack displayed at her stern.

"She passed the first rapid unhurt, still went on, making a plunge, shipping a sea, and rising from it in beautiful style, and in her descent over the second her masts went by the board, at the same moment affording those who had never witnessed a shipwreck a specimen of the sudden destruction of the spars of a ship at sea in case of a wreck. Expectation of her fate was now at highest. She swung round and presented her broadside to the dashing and foaming waters, and after remaining stationary a moment or two was, by its force, swung round, stern foremost, and having passed to the third rapid, she bilged but carried her hull apparently whole, between Grass Island and the British shore to the Horse Shoe, over which she was carried stern foremost and launched into the abyss below.

"In her fall she was dashed into a thousand pieces. I went below the falls immediately after the descent, and the river exhibited a singular appearance from the thousands of floating fragments, there being scarcely to be seen any two boards nailed together, and many of her timbers were broken into atoms. Such was the eagerness of the multitude present to procure a piece of her that before sunset a great part of her was carried away.

"I believe I have neglected to inform you of the animals on board. They consisted of a buffalo from the Rocky Mountains, three bears from Green Bay and Grand River, two foxes, a raccoon, a dog, a cat, and four geese. The fate of these you will probably wish to learn. When the vessel was left to her fate they were let loose on deck, except the buffalo, who was enclosed in a temporary pen. Two of the bears left the vessel shortly after she began to descend the rapids and swam ashore, not withstanding the rapidity of the current. On reaching the British shore they were taken. The buffalo was seen to pass over the falls, but was not visible afterwards. What became of the other animals is not known. Those who had glasses could see one of the bears climbing the mast as the vessel approached the rapids. The foxes, etc., were also running up and down, but nothing was seen of them after the schooner passed over. Two of the geese were the only living things that passed over, and they were taken up unhurt. Major Frazer obtained one, and an Englishman purchased the other for $2.

Respecting the effigies, of which there were several, the only one I saw below the falls was Gen. Andrew Jackson, apparently uninjured, throwing his arms about and knocking his legs together in the eddies, the only one of the crew of fancy that escaped unhurt. There were over 30,000 people in attendance, and you may judge of the situation of affairs when I assure you that I stopped at Forsyth's about 4 p.m. and was unable to obtain even a cracker or glass of water. It was the same on the American side."

Who and what was this schooner *Michigan*, too big for Lake Erie early harbours? Why was she built?

One thing which makes this old letter of particular interest to Canadians is that it may – one cannot say that it did – settle the ultimate fate of the British ship *Detroit*, flagship of Commodore Barclay, captured by the Americans in the ill-starred Battle of Put-in-Bay in 1813. Lossing in *Field Book of the War of 1812*, compiled for *Harper's* in the early 1860s, when memories were still fresh, says the *Detroit* became an American merchant vessel and, not proving profitable, was striped and sent over the falls with live animals on board, in a sort of public festival organized by hotelkeepers. But later historians, a hundred years and more after the time, have questioned this, and pointed out that there is no official record of the *Detroit*'s fate such as an in a custom house or marine registry.

Might it not be that the name of the British ship *Detroit*, already born by two American brigs, was changed to *Michigan* when she was sold as a prize, and used as a commercial freighter? All official entries thenceforward would refer to the *Michigan*. The fact that she was too big for contemporary lake harbours would fit in with this theory. For the *Detroit* was built for battle. The American men-of-war which captured her were also too big for most Lake Erie harbours, and had to floated away from their launching places on "camels" or pontoons. The fact that the *Michigan* went over the falls "with the British Jack displayed at the stern" would indicate a British origin and signal an American triumph, even if the position of the flags was wrong by every know rule: ensigns are carried aft, jacks forward.

It was fool cruelty to send a cargo of animals over with the *Michigan*, which is what we started out to suggest. The "DV" at the head of this 505th number of "Schooner Days" need not be taken as the equivalent of DV, as the skypilots say in the church announcements. The big V is for a big victory with divine help.

"Schooner Days" had its avid readers, whose personal experiences helped give authenticity and interest to Snider's reporting of the many incidents that occurred during "the good old days."

Albert Leeder, who went sailing in the Nemesis, *(the small black schooner built and sailed by Capt. John Spence of Southampton), as soon as he was big enough, sought out and met with Snider, who reports.*

Mary and Lucy

The *Nemesis* was in the cordwood trade from Bruce Peninsula to the salt blocks of Goderich, a run of about a hundred miles.

Another schooner in the same trade was the *Mary and Lucy*. "I knew her very well," said Mr. Leeder, "and we were often in company. One trip the *Mary and Lucy* loaded pine lumber from Georgian Bay for the foot of Lake Huron. When off Chantry Island light at Southampton the wind, which had been easterly, suddenly changed to the northwest and blew such a hurricane that the *Mary and Lucy* was completely unmanageable. She drove helplessly on to the reef south of Chantry Island and stuck, the seas bursting over her, and her crew taking to the rigging to be avoid being washed overboard.

"Sometime through the night the steamer *Manitoba*, a side wheeler of the then Beattie Line, ran in for shelter. Daylight revealed to Captain Sims, her commander, the *Mary and Lucy* pounding to pieces on the reef close by. He lowered one of the *Manitoba*'s boats, and getting in himself, with his purser, and Ross Lambert, the son of the Chantry Island lighthouse keeper, pulled away for the wreck. As the rescuers neared the reef a huge sea, bigger than all the others, piled in and burst around the *Mary and Lucy* with such force that it lifted clean over the reef in to the deep water between the reef and the mainland, with her crew still in the rigging.

"The pine lumber in her straining hull kept her afloat until she grounded on the main shore, a complete wreck, with her spars still standing. She never floated again, but her crew got off safely.

"But alas the brave rescuers. The seas which had such power as to pick up a loaded schooner and toss her bodily over a reef, rolled the steamers lifeboat over and over like a barrel. It, too, was washed over the reef with the three men clinging to it. First the poor purser let go, then Ross Lambert, the lighthouse keeper's son. The upturned boat grounded near where the *Mary and Lucy* struck. Only Captain Sims was alive."

The *Manitoba* was built at Thorold in 1871 and first ran for the Beattie Line out of Sarnia. Later she was with the *Cambria* on Lake Huron and Georgian Bay routes for the CPR. In 1890, Toronto knew her well as the *Carmona*. She had been brought here for what was expected to be a great excursion trade between Toronto, Lorne Park, and

Grimsby. This was early in the summer cottage commuting era, when urban dwellers were founding summer cottages and going back and forth by water. There was not enough business for the *Carmona* (ex-*Manitoba*) and after freelancing with moderate profit for some seasons, was laid up. Last I saw of her she was being dismantled at Port Dalhousie in 1904.

September 25, 1948
Why Ships Capsize

The York Pioneer and Historical Society has asked about the *Victoria* ferry steamer tragedy at London-in-the-Bush nearly seventy years ago, and sailors of 1948 are still asking how a smart, seaworthy, ballasted yacht could capsize in Toronto Bay, as happened only last month. Here is an attempt to answer both parties.

First, the *Silhouette*, a seagoing tumlarin (a twenty-six-foot, double-ended racing yacht), decked over, and ballasted well enough to enable her to carry racing sail in a gale of wind.

Unknown to twelve men aboard she had sprung leak. There was a lot of water in her. Under a puff she heeled over. The unsuspected water in her ran to the lower side and made her heel more. She had not capsized, but she was so much on her side that one corner of her cockpit was below the level of the outside water. So more water rushed into her. A gallon of water weighs ten pounds. It does not take long for two hundred gallons to run in. That would add a ton to her burden. The weight of twelve husky men made a ton more. She had thus lost two tons of buoyancy. The lead ballast under her keel was not enough to lever her back to an upright position against the two ton pressure. It only helped to pull her down. When she went under completely she straightened up, because she was relieved of the weight of the twelve men, now all waterborne, and the water inside of her was no heavier than the water outside. The initial buoyancy of the wood in her hull and spars raised her upright in the water, though the weight of her ballast and other metal held her to the bottom of the bay.

Too much has been said about the sinking of the *Silhouette* already, and "Schooner Days" apologizes for reopening the subject. The conduct of her crew was admirable throughout, and the salvage work was seamanlike, swift, and successful. No lives were lost, and a dunking was the worst that happened.

But the *Victoria* took nearly two hundred lives, and was a deplorable piece of folly.

The *Victoria* disaster occurred in the River Thames, about four miles below London Ontario, May 24, 1881. Lives lost were 197, most of them by drowning, some crushed when an upper deck collapsed on them, and others when the boiler, mounted between decks, broke loose as the vessel lurched and rolled over one side.

The *Victoria* was one of three vessels operated in a ferry service from London to Springbank picnic park. On the day of the disaster about 2,000 people had been transported to the park and in the rush to get home about 553 persons, many of them women and children, jammed aboard this one ship with capacity for 400, although how even that many could be carried safely in an eighty-foot vessel of shallow draft and small tonnage seems amazing.

Shortly after leaving the pumping station dock at Springbank the *Victoria* began to rock. One story was that Ned Hanlan was rowing on the river and someone shouted that he was passing and many rushed to one side to see him. Another version was that two unnamed oarsmen passed and someone shouted that a racer was in progress. Or a little bilge water may have swashed about in the hold.

At any rate, it appears that a rush to one side occurred and the overloaded upper deck collapsed. With that the boiler broke loose and rolled to one side, and the ship capsized. Hundreds were thrown into the water and many trapped under the ship and boiler. It was London's greatest disaster. It brought grief to so many homes.

A monument now stands on the North Bank of the Thames opposite the spot where the disaster occurred. To see the river today one cannot but wonder how any ship the breadth of the *Victoria* – twenty-three feet – could find room to turn over. In fact, there seems reason to doubt that it could have more than tipped a little beyond four degrees.

The fault was not with the vessel, but within the way she was used. To pack 555 human beings – thirty or forty tons of moving flesh – on platforms (representing decks) so high above a keel only three feet in the water, was a hazard madness that would not have been attempted even in the evacuation of Dunkirk. If there was any water in the shallow hull its rippling from side to side would set up a swaying motion impossible to correct. In this case, the centre of gravity, dangerously high through improper loading, jumped out of control as the ship rocked with the motion of its human freight. Then the weight of the displaced boiler and displaced cargo broke the vessel apart.

The remedy against capsizing is to keep weight low and buoyancy high, water out, and bilges dry.

After two weeks of stories about the Olivia *in 1935, and only days before Halloween (one of Snider's idiosyncrasies about spelling was to always spell it "hallowe'en), came the story about the tragedy of Moses Dulmage, which occurred on October 31, 1879.*

October 28, 1935
Hallowe'en off Point Traverse

Come, friends and relations and neighbours I pray,
Please give your attention to the words I now say,
Of poor Moses Dulmage I wish to relate,
How adrift on the waters he met his sad fate.

Dial backwards fifty-six years. It is the last night in October – Hallowe'en – and all the witches and warlocks of the lake are out. You can see them, if you've the fancy, in the flying scud racking across the sky eternally from the westward. You can hear them in the howl of the wind through the rigging, and the rap-rap-rap of the halliards against the mast.

A schooner fleet is sheltering under Point Traverse – "South Bay Point" as it is called in the barley trade. Their cabin lamps and anchor light prick the early darkness with the likeness of a floating village. This southeasterly prong of Prince Edward County is a favourite halt for schooners waiting for weather. The False Ducks, Timber Island, and Point Traverse, at the entrance to the Upper Gap into Bay of Quinte, give a safe lee, with no port dues. Windbound vessels sometimes lay here weeks on end. When their provisions run out the farmers team bags of flour and drive cattle down and slaughter on the beach for them – a "strand hewing," as the ancient Vikings called it.

Tonight, Thursday, October 31, 1879, ten schooners coal-laden for up the lake or grain-laden from the bay, waiting for milder weather for the slant across to Oswego, have dug their hooks into the clay and gravel off the point. Twenty-two more are lying further up at McDonalds Cove and Indian Point at the upper end of the Gap. Among the ten under Timber Island: the *Julia* of Kingston, smart and new; the *Olivia* of Toronto, ancient and twice rebuilt; the *Fleet Wing* of Windsor; and the *Ariadne* of Port Burwell.

Young Moses Dulmage, South Bay lad of sound Prince Edward stock, is one of the *Julia*'s crew. These waters are as familiar to him as the schoolyard in Babylon across the point, where Miss Annie Wright used to teach him before she married his brother Tom. He has played in them, fished in them, sailed in them, since ever he can remember. His father, Phil Dulmage, and his fathers before him, have farmed in South Bay since Loyalists came.

When the *Julia* anchored here, it was like coming home for Moses Dulmage. He knows the *Olivia*, too, her next-door neighbour. It was his uncle, David Dulmage, who rowed out to the blazing *Ocean Wave* twenty-six years before, when the *Olivia* rescued some of the perishing passengers. Though she was built in Bronte and hails from Toronto now, she is owned by another South Marysburg farmer, Nelson Hudgins, and manned with South Bay boys like himself. They are pretty sure to have a bag of hickory nuts in her forecastle, and apples from the home orchard.

So after supper, he braces the *Julia*'s Old Man for the use of the yawlboat.

"All right," says Capt. Tim Hartney, the skipper. "But be sure to be back early. I'm going to get out of here before daylight if the wind shifts or lulls." The *Julia* is bound for Trenton, up the bay.

It is only a short jog down this street of anchored vessels. The sixteen-foot yawlboat, floating high with Moses alone in it, blows along across the two hundred yards of black water like a cask. The boy scarcely needed the single oar, which, schooner style, he plies with a rotary motion in the sculling-notch in the sternboard. He rounds to in the shine of the *Olivia*'s anchor light so as not to drift by before he can make his painter fast. The boys on board catch the rope and drop the yawlboat astern. He goes down with them into the forecastle, where the red-bellied stove is blistering the paint on the chain lockers.

Yes there are hickory nuts. And Prince Edward snows.

And russets. And Murney Ackerman has his young brother Jake along for a trip. A merry time they have, ducking for them in a draw-bucket, with the hazards of swallowing the pail enhanced by the probability of backing into the red hot stove in the crowded quarters. They sing the "Gipsy's Warning" and "Sweet Lily Vail," and tell ghost stories of Zack Palmateers dog, and the Proctor light, and jokes of life in great cities like Kingston, Oswego, Toronto, and Buffalo And they pass around all the home news of Black Creek and Soup Harbour and Babylon and Petticoat Point. Overhead, unheard, the rigging hums and the halliards rap, and the wild wester goes on with its endless task of blowing itself out. It is great to be young and strong, with a keen zest for hard work and home news and hickory nuts.

Somebody pokes a head into their happy inferno and exclaims "B-r-r-r! Blowing harder than ever! Better stay the night, Mose. There's a spare bunk for you any time, you know." It is the *Olivia*'s hospitable skipper.

"No," says Moses, "I promised the Old Man I'd be back in time for an early morning start, and I'd better be going now."

"Want someone to go along to help you get back? This wind's coming away powerful strong?"

"Oh 'taint far. I can manage, thanks."

"Well, mind you keep well up to windward when you're sculling. Your boat's bound to drift a lot."

"I'll mind," says Moses, slapping his young muscles. Unless you have been through the mill, you cannot savour the pride of the young sailor on his strength and skill. To have doubted himself "man enough" for the yawlboat, singlehanded, would have disgraced South Bay and Babylon and broken Moses Dulmage's heart.

"Goodnight fellows," he called slipping over the rail into the tossing yawlboat. "see you in Oswego, perhaps, next trip."

They hear the heavy creak of the sculling oar in its notch, and the scuffle of the yawlboat breasting the short snapping seas.

"Keep her up! Keep her up!" they cry, waving a lantern for encouragement, for they can see she is drifting.

With his back to the bow, young Dulmage flings his whole weight on the sculling oar, and sways his strong young shoulders mightily against the gale. The heavy yawl-boat leaps to windward. After fifteen minutes' battling, with the sweat pouring from him he is alongside the *Julia* riding light and high-sided. He runs forward in his boat to toss the painter up over the schooner's rail. The wind blows it back on him.

"Heave me a line, quick!" he pants.

Aboard the *Olivia* they can hear the wind-borne splash of the rope in the water as his shipmates heave a coil, but before Dulmage can catch it the yawl has drifted away beyond its reach. He runs back to the sternsheets, and gets the oar into the notch again, but before can bring the boat around she has whirled past the *Olivia* and past the lines her crew try to throw.

"Catch the *Ariadne* and hang on!" they shout down the wind to him.

He is almost exhausted with his heavy sculling, and the gale, blowing harder than ever, tosses him past that schooner, too.

By this time he is panicked, and cries in a terrible voice, "*Ariadne! Ariadne!* Help, help, *Ariadne!*"

The *Ariadne* crew have turned in. The captain in the cabin thinks someone is warning that the schooner has broken adrift. He rushes out and pounds on the forecastle. "Rouse out, rouse out, she's dragging!"

But a glance at the bearings of the other anchor-lights show this cannot be. The chain is grinding steadily in the hawsepipe and she is exactly where she was. But astern is still heard the terrible cry: "*Ariadne! Ariadne!* Help, help, *Ariadne!*"

"It's someone adrift!" says the mate.

"Get the boat down, quick!" calls the skipper.

The *Ariadne*'s yawlboat hangs on davits across the stern, hoisted up on tackles. In the dark they make a bad job of lowering it. They forget the plug is not in. One tackle fall jams and the other end of the boat drops. The man who jumped in when they first began to lower nearly drowned. Three men follow him down the tackles and find the boat half full of water.

"Come back!" commands the captain, "Or I'll lose you all. There are half a dozen vessels astern of us, and he's sure to catch one of them."

He adds this uncomfortably, for still the wild cries for help come, fainter and fainter against the beating wings of the wind. At last they cease. Yet again, and ever afterwards, while the *Ariadne* lives, in the whine of the blocks and the grind of the anchor chain and the sobbing of the water alongside, men will hear that agonizing hail.

Moses Dulmage did not catch any one of the six schooners lying astern, although his boat bumped the quarter of the outermost, as the gale whirled it along.

On Sunday morning, Smith, the lightkeeper on Stony Point, on the south side of the lake, thirty miles across from Point Traverse, saw a schooner's yawlboat on the beach south of the light. She was covered with ice. Face downward on the thwarts, with his legs lashed to the seat by the boat's painter, was the bruised and broken body of a young man. His hands were cut and bloodstained, as though he had pounded them to keep them from freezing. Five rods [eighty-three feet] away, in the ice-fringed surf, washed his steering oar, glazed and icicled.

Moses Dulmage had steered all the way across Lake Ontario that wild night, only to perish under the rays of the lighthouse which was his last hope. He had been on the beach since Friday morning, the keeper judged, but had not been seen because he was concealed by ice and a pile of rocks.

Smith was a humane man. He did not know who this stranger was or whence he came. He thought he must be the sole evidence of a wreck in this long series of westerly gales. He drove with the body to Henderson Harbour, old Hungry Bay, and there saw that it had a Christian burial.

The square-nosed schooner *Sea Bird*, three-hundred tons burden and scow built, came pushing into Oswego with lumber from Trenton for JK Post & Co., as soon as the gales let up. Her master was John Walters, of South Bay – "Captain John Walters, a kind-hearted friend" as the ballad says. The *Sea Bird* had been lying in McDonald's Cove during the gales, and Captain Walters had spoken to the *Julia*, and knew her yawlboat was missing. He had also heard from the *Olivia* of Moses Dulmage being blown out of the anchorage.

When in Oswego, he was told of the find at Stony Point. He drove there, saw the lightkeeper, and felt sure he knew the victim. He then drove to Henderson Harbour and had the newly made grave opened, and so friendly hands from South Bay brought Moses Dulmage's body back to the *Sea Bird*.

Sixty or seventy sail vessels had accumulated in Oswego in the prolonged westerlies. Now that the gales had ended they put forth in one great armada closehauled on the port tack. The wind was still down the lake, but mild. The *Sea Bird* led the procession, her colours at half mast, Moses Dulmage's body in its coffin on her deck. Behind her, their burgees and ensigns also half-masted, whether Red Dusters or Stars and Stripes, marched the whole windbound fleet.

The long port tack brought them all up to Point Traverse. Solemnly, slowly, the *Sea Bird* passed the little lighthouse where a red lantern watched over the anchorage by night. On she steered into South Bay for the wharf at Black Creek. Schooner after schooner parted company with her there. Those bound up the lake came in stays and stood out again on the starboard tack; those bound for the Bay of Quinte eased sheets for the Gap. Every vessel, as she parted company, dipped her ensign and burgee in the silent salute, then hoisted them masthead high, honouring the homecoming of the young sailor who would never sail more.

"*Ariadne! Ariadne!* Help, help, *Ariadne!*" That cry, Moses Dulmage's last, echoed through the *Ariadne*'s rigging of dark nights for seven years: until as though magnetized, she too drove in on Stony Point, on the night of November 29, 1886, and beat into staves, drowning her captain, mate, and half her crew.

Moses Dulmage rests well in the little cemetery at South Bay. His fate is still recalled in Prince Edward County by the ballad of which the opening verse is quoted at the beginning of this story. It had many stanzas. They were composed by Mrs. Thomas Dulmage, his sister-in-law.

August 8, 1938
The *Persia* and Her Pet 'Coon

Forty-five years ago when the "new" City Hall was being built, a big trade was carried on in cut stone. Schooner after schooner swam in from Kelley's Island in Lake Erie or Cleveland, Ohio, with big blocks of sombre red sandstone or grey limestone – the *St. Louis* and the *Jas. G. Worts*, both owned by Sylvester Bros., the *Sir C.T. Van Straubenzie*, the *W.J. Suffel*, – the *Columbian* and *South West*, and *Arthur* (all three Americans) and among still others, the *Persia*.

They used, as a rule, to unload at Sylvester's Wharf at the foot of Church Street, where there was a big timber derrick capable of handling the heavy blocks each weighing tons. But the *Arthur* and the *Persia* used to go to Brown and Loves place, just east of the West Market Street slip, where there was also a derrick and an extensive stone yard.

The *Persia* was a regular caller there. In fact, she never came in with any cargo other than stone in her later days, and it was not always cut stone either. Still, she was not a stonehooker, a classification which was reserved for the smaller fry; the little scows and schooners which gathered gravel, hardheads, cribstone pavers, and building stone along the beaches.

The *Persia* was a stone carrier, which was different. She loaded her cargo in one port and delivered it in another for a freight rate of so much a ton. The stonehookers got their cargoes by the sweat of their backs, and sold them by the toise. Freights did not interest them.

In those "new" City Hall days the *Persia* was a chunky schooner of particularly dingy aspect, for with the exception of one thin, white strip, she was painted black all over, even to her mastheads and peak-halliard blocks. For years she went without a maintopmast, a spar whose absence makes the best of vessels look draggle-tailed. She had been built in Hamilton in 1867, and Robert Baldwin of Toronto was her registered owner in 1874. She was a short deep vessel, 99 feet 6 inches long, 22 feet beam, and 10 feet 6 inches depth of hold. She was 196 tons register. She had a slightly curved stemhead which dubiously justified calling her clipper-bowed.

This compiler's clearest recollection of her is the little pet raccoon that used to scramble around her deck. He was chained to a light wooden pail, which kept him from climbing the rigging, but did not prevent his free rambling about below. He was quite clever at up-ending the pail and crawling into it for a sleep. He was a merry little black-masted bandit and a great thief of the crew's apples.

It would appear that the *Persia* was thoroughly overhauled in the winter of 1893-94, to extent of having her maintopmast restored, and in the spring of the latter year she blossomed forth like a "lily of the field" all white and green in new paint. But alas, such finery seemed too much for the erstwhile dingy stone carrier. On her way up the lake with another cargo for Brown and Love's dock, she opened up and went down off Long Point. Her crew escaped in the yawlboat.

Lake Simcoe was navigated by schooners and by steamer from the early days of Upper Canada. In fact it was part of the chain of transportation from York to Georgian Bay. Holland Landing, on the Holland River, Yonge Street as its first major port. Snider's research led to the following column.

November 11, 1950
Schooners on Lake Simcoe

It was a long time ago, seventy or eighty years at the least, but Lake Simcoe, which now floats nothing but pleasure craft and summer cottages, once had its schooner fleet.

They were not large vessels but were full-rigged centreboard craft, with gafftopsails and jibtopsails and the complete seven-piece rig of two masters and fore-and-afters. There were half-a-dozen of them, in size between thirty and forty tons register, and around sixty feet in length. Their carrying capacity was between sixty and eighty tons weight – about equal to that of two railway freight cars.

Persia, unloading stone for Toronto's great buildings, 1893.

They served to carry lumber, shingles, cordwood, country produce including livestock, to Barrie, Orillia, Keswick, Belle Ewart, Beaverton, and Holland Landing, for consumption or further shipment. They got these cargoes and delivered furniture, drygoods, groceries, implements, and machinery, at every farm that touched the two hundred miles of navigable shoreline on Lake Simcoe and its appurtenances – Kempenfeldt Bay, Couchiching, Cooke's Bay, the Holland River, and the Beaver River.

They needed no wharves. Drawing only five feet when fully loaded, and as little as two feet when light, and being equipped with centreboards, they could come close to the friendly beaches – there being few rocks – and lighten their cargoes with scows and rafts, their farmer customers assisting.

There were also, of course, steamers on Lake Simcoe from very early times, in fact fourteen years after the *Frontenac*, pioneer of steam navigation on any of the Great Lakes. The only old-timer we recall was the *Enterprise*, painted gaily in blue and white with black bandings, in the early 1890s. Before her were: the *Ida Burton*, used as a wharf at Orillia after 1875; the *Emily May*, which became the *Lady of the Lakes* in 1874; the *Fairy*, renamed the *Carrie Ellis*; and the *J.C. Morrison*, finest of all, 150 feet long and costing $60,000.

Still earlier steamers were: the *Morning*, built at Holland Landing at the same time and place as the schooner *Sultana*, already mentioned, 1849; the *Beaver* at Thompsonvllle, 1845; the *Peter Robinson*, 1834; and the *Sir John Colborne* built in 1831 – first on the lake and ninth steamer in Canadian waters. She was built at Holland Landing by retired army officers and other settlers there.

The steamers did very well with the passenger trade in stage coach days, and for a time after the railways came in. The schooners also carried passengers, but could not maintain a schedule because of the uncertainty of wind and weather.

"Ontario's Attorney General beats his lawn decorations – cables anchors and iron-work from ancient wreck – into cannon to kill Huns and cash to help their victims." This was part of a news heading in May 1941, before Pearl Harbour – a very dark and gloomy period of our history.

During those war years Snider kept up his regular column about the old schooners regularly, despite frequent absences to England and Europe as a war correspondent. He had seen first hand the devastating impact of the bombings of England and as a result, started the highly successful British War Victims Fund of the Toronto Telegram. *Occasionally, his columns would reflect the war effort, but always relating it to schooners, schooner times, or to old schooner sailors.*

Snider knew Bluff Point, near what is now Oshawa Harbour, well. He had sketched it in 1905, wrote about it several times. In 1935 he wrote about his presence at the finding of the Caledonia's *anchor and gear.*

In the following column he retells the story of the finding of the wreck of the Caledonia, and how it helped our war effort.

May 1941
Caledonia's Gear Goes into Guns for Britain and $$$ for *Telegram* Fund

Studlink chain cable, kedge anchors and ship chandlery cast in Canada ninety-nine years ago, started yesterday on a three thousand-mile voyage to hurl the Hun from Britain's doorstep and heal the hurts of Glasgow, Belfast, London, and every other blitz-blasted British town.

Who knows? It may be a chunk of the *Caledonia*'s anchor fluke that will bring the last black Dornier down, spell the doom of the last yellow-nosed Messerschmidt, or send Hitler and Co. to the place for which hell is a typographical error. In the meantime, the price realized for the ton of hardware – for everything, even iron to stop Germany, has its price – has come to the *Telegram*'s British War Victims Fund, to buck up the dauntless British spirit, and rush aid to the men, women, and children who have been under fire nightly for months that grow into years, in the front line of the war, while we wait safely at home.

Strange things happen to one interested in schooner days sufficiently to do a little spade work on them.

One day six years ago, we were walking the beach forty miles east of Toronto near Farewell's Marsh, which was a schooner harbour before Oshawa even had a pier. Here we found a power truck, and most of the Oshawa Yacht Club in and out of the water, including Col. Frank Chappell and the young Conants, Douglas and Roger, and the-then Crown Attorney for Ontario County, Gordon D. Conant, KC himself, all heaving like a tug-of-war team on a couple of lines which ran out into Lake Ontario like the landing ends of submarine cables.

The power truck was winching one in on its drum, and the human horsepower was operating on a six-part purchase hooked on to the other. Around them and under their feet were coiled seemingly miles of rusted of chain cable, plain and studlink, wet and weedy, and in the tangle, like a pair of fishhooks for catching sperm wales, were two bent and muddy anchors.

Tallying on to the tackle fall with the others, while the soon-to-be Attorney General exhorted all and sundry to "Heave and bust 'er!" we glimpsed a black waterlogged mass of timber up-end like a whale getting ready to sound, and then fall over on its back.

After that the pulling was easier, for the sodden hulk, loosened from the bottom was almost waterborne, and we snaked it over shore boulders and weed-grown beach stones until it was high if not dry, well above the shoreline.

It was a trough-shaped structure, bristling with spikes and iron bolts, and more and more like the business end of a sea serpent as it came into close view. It was grass-grown and covered with warts, where the iron of it fastenings had preserved the immediately surrounding wood. it had leering "eyes" which were really the iron hawsepipes of the wreck, and there were many curious holes where the undulation of millions of waves through many decades had used the metal fastenings as wood files, and had enlarged the original borings to four and five times their diameter. There were other curious frettings, showing clearly the pattern of the studlink cable, which had been wrapped around and entangled around the wreck as it had rolled in its grave for half a century and more.

The wreck was that of a lightly built vessel. The ribs remaining were only four-by-fives, doubled, what was left of the keel and keelson was seven or eight inches square, flanked by sister keelsons five inches wide and eight inches deep, and bolted through the floor timbers with a half- or three-quarter-inch iron bolts. The mortise for the heel of the foremast indicated that spar was fourteen inches in diameter. The planking was two-inch oak. All the dimensions of the wood had doubtless been reduced by the fret and chafe and decay of fifty-five years; the planking may have been three-inch when it was first spiked on. But on the whole the wreck did not seem to be as heavily tim-bered as the pioneer schooner *Nancy*, heroine of 1812. She was of less tonnage. The *Nancy* was not more than eighty feet long. This vessel, judging from the position of her foremast, would be at least 90 feet long, and perhaps double the *Nancy*'s tonnage.

"What's all this about?" we asked Gordon Conant as the power truck caught its breath.

"Its the wreck we found last fall," said he. "This is Bluff Point, and the point used to have a real bluff with a grove of trees on the top of it, even in my time. Now it's worn down to the nub you see, and the trees are all washed away, with a hundred yards or more of the soil. You can find the boulders once bedded in the bluff out past where this wreck was in the water.

"When paddling alongshore in a canoe on a smooth day I saw an anchor below me and then another with lots of chain. We put a pole down to mark the spot, for the water was shallow, and in the winter the ice formed around it, three feet thick. Then we went to work with saws and axes and cut an opening and hooked a line on to the first anchor and got it up with the help of the power truck, and then the same with the next anchor. This left a lot of chain cable frozen on the bottom or wrapped around the wreck that it belonged to. So today we came back for it all and in recovering the chains we stirred up the wreck itself, and you came along in time to heave all that is left of the ship out. Now that I've told you all this will you tell me what the ship was, and how she got here.

This was where poking into "Schooner Days" proved helpful.

"Edward J. Guy, of Toronto and Capt. Joseph Williams, who sailed seventy-years ago, told me this was the wreck of the *Caledonia*," was the answer. "Mr. Guy saw it as a boy, for he was born in Oshawa. Captain Williams was asked to ship in her in the spring of 1880, but went on another vessel instead. When he came back he found the *Caledonia* a wreck here on Bluff Point. She was loaded with coal from Oswego, and in a thick snow-storm and little wind, when they could not see the land nor hear the surf, she struck one morning on the east side of the point. She ran out so far that the crew had no difficulty getting off her. She was sailed by Capt. Hugh Rooney of Cobourg, and he sent for a tug or a lighter, to unload her and haul her off. But before they got her the wind came in from the southeast and blew a gale, and the poor *Caledonia* pounded apart."

"Only one big piece of her is left," said Mr. Conant, "and here's a chunk of the coal wedged between the timbers of it. You seem to have all the answers. Do you know when she was built, or where?"

"Port Credit, 1842, by Jacob Randall, if she's the *Caledonia*. I'm told she is. Randall Street in Oakville is named after him. There were four or five *Caledonia*s. One was the Northwest Fur Co.'s brig. that brought Brock's men to Detroit in 1812. This wouldn't be the one, for she became the American vessel *General Wayne*, and died on Lake Erie. There were two *Caledonia*s launched at Saugeen on Lake Huron in 1843 and 1861, but one's bones are in Racine, Wisc., and the other would be too small to be this vessel. There was another *Caledonia* built at Port Union, but oldtimers say that the one lost on Bluff Point was the one Randall built. Now it's your turn to talk. What are you going to do with the wreck now that you've got it out?"

"Put it on my front lawn."

That is exactly what Mr. Conant did with it. The chain cables, anchors, keelson, iron pump, stem, apron, keelson, floors, frames, and adhering planking, were loaded on to the truck and carried several miles west to Buena Vista, long the Conant family residence above the headland overlooking Lake Ontario south of Oshawa. Here the relics remained in state for six years. Mr. Conant was so proud of them he would not allow them to be painted or touched up in any way. To him they have been priceless mementos of his pioneer ancestor's times.

Thomas Conant, born 1775, was a ship captain and came to Canada with the Loyalists. He was Gordon Conant's great-grandfather. He built a schooner on the beach not far west of Bluff Point. His son Daniel, born 1818, was also a ship captain, and loaded schooners at Oshawa in the early timber trade. It was Captain Daniel's schooner *Industry* which rescued forty Patriots in hiding and ran them to safety at Oswego in the rebellion of 1837, five years before the *Caledonia* was launched. Daniel himself was not a rebel, but sacrificed his vessel to save his neighbours from the gallows. The schooner, valued at $8,000, had to be abandoned off Oswego, and was carried up the lake in the ice-pack and destroyed.

So the relics of the good ship *Caledonia* found an appropriate resting place on the lawn of the present Attorney General and descendant of Thomas and Daniel Conant. On one of her anchors letters seeming to spell the word Montreal appeared. Apparently it had been moulded into the iron when it was cast or forged. There were also figures indicating the weight and the name Wood – possibly the foundry man.

"I hate to part with them," said Mr. Conant, as he personally lifted the last of the loot on to a truck headed for Toronto, "but I'd hate myself more to think that I was enjoying this hardware on my lawn, while men of my stock were being blown to bits for lack of guns and shells to mow the Huns down or were wet, hungry, and cold for lack of the succor the *Telegram*'s British War Victims Fund could bring them."

The bigger anchor weighed 720 pounds on the scales. The smaller was 575 pounds. There were 165 feet of studlink chain weighing 345 pounds, and 112 feet of plain cable weighing 255 pounds. With two hundredweight of bobstays bolts, pump and hawsepipes the hardware from the *Caledonia* went over a ton – 2,095 pounds to be exact.

May 5-12, 1951
Sold under the "Broad Arrow"

Smuggling was something of a native industry in the nineteenth century. Yonge Street wharf was not the head office of the institution, but it got its share of the business.

In the *Toronto Courier* of August 20, 1836, appeared notice of the intended sale by auction on August 30, by James M. Strange of the schooner *Plough Boy* and the sloop *Martin Van Buren*, "they having been condemned for offenses against the Revenge Laws." In other words, smuggling. Among their cargoes were "a large quantity of Young Hyson tea, one barrel of whisky and seven boxes of cigars."

The sloop, named after a president of the United States, was probably an American bottom, whatever her ownership at this particular time. There were several *Plow Boys*, *Ploughboys*, and *Plowboys* in the lake marine. One was of 122 tons and built at

Oakville, and another was 1,901 tons and built at South Bay Point by Jack Tait for S & J Collier of Milford in 1863. Neither of these two could be the smuggler, for she was seized long before they were launched.

Old Capt. W.M. McClain, whose house with the shining silver doorplate stood at 134 Jarvis Street until after his death in 1914, at the age of 91, knew the right *Plough Boy* quite well. He was born in County Monahan in Ireland in 1823, and his parents brought him to York, U.C., when he was four years old. When he was 14 he ran away from Caldecott's School on Colborne Street, in what had become the city of Toronto, pop. 10,000, to escape a flogging for an ill-prepared lesson – and so got a berth as cook aboard this schooner, at $6 a month, which works out to 20¢ a day.

He found that the culinary duties sometimes included sculling the yawlboat away up under the docking of Yonge Street wharf as soon as the mooring were lines were out. He did not notice at first that this rite had to be performed before the customs officer came down to examine the vessel. What was in the yawlboat he was not supposed to know. It might be tea, tobacco or Bibles. Many's the time, he told us, he heard the heavy feet of the law marching majestically over his head as he silently pushed the yawlboat farther into the darkness.

Tea, he said, was the most profitable article to be smuggled for there was a duty of one shilling, three pence – then equivalent to 30¢. Tobacco was profitable, too. All sorts of household goods were brought in from Oswego and the Genesee and Youngstown, by the so-called "Highland Rangers" and delivered as occasion served. Much later on American-refined kerosene, known to Canadians as coal oil, was a profitable cargo.

There was a carter, nicknamed "Handy" by the knowing, who used to work late at night when there was no moon, calling at Yonge Street slip. King Street merchants could replenish their stock of Bohea, Gunpowder, Seu Chong, and Young Hyson tea from "Handy's stable," where the smuggled chests would repose under a stack of hay professedly kept for the refreshment of "Handy's" horse. He was called Ess, a sly intimation that he came before "T," and tea came after him.

It might have been expected that young McClain would come to no good end, but he was not a blithe Irish lad for nothing. He left the schooner when he learned the purpose of those yawlboat manoeuvres and in good time.

Such smuggling as young William McClain unwittingly participated in was only the retail end, small stuff. The big trade was delivered in river mouths, like the Humber, or the Rouge, or Highland Creek, or in the gullies which gashed the face of Scarborough Heights, making good tracks for farm wagons.

Usually the smugglers sent their cargoes in by yawlboat load when they got the awaited whistle in the dark. There were always farmers, bagmen, and peddlers waiting, cash in hand.

The vessel would lie offshore with sails hoisted and anchor ready for slipping at a warning shot or whistle. Sometimes they dumped whole cargoes to avoid seizure, for smugglers could be hanged in those days.

The story of buried treasure in the marsh at the mouth of Highland Creek is said to have arisen from a smuggler having to heave a cargo of imported tableware overboard when delivery to waiting farmhouses was interrupted.

Young McClain, as said, cut the towline of the *Plough Boy* in good time and shipped in the *Lord Nelson* of 209 tons, a much larger vessel. At the end of eight seasons he was master of a schooner of his own, the *Jane Harper*.

She was one of the early centreboard vessels and had been owned by John Harper, the contractor who had to build the new fort, later called Stanley Barracks. She carried stone from Niagara for that purpose; and was built so solidly that when she struck the Garrison wharf by accident, she knocked the whole wharf down, with no other damage to herself than parting her bobstay of tarred hemp. Mr. Harper urged him to buy land on Bay street near Wellington at $20 a foot, but the sailor thought the price too high. He put all he had into the *Jane Parker* and owned her outright from 1844-68. Then he bought the *Clarissa*, 250 tons, along with Capt. Archibald Taylor. They carried cut stone from Cleveland for the new St. James Cathedral, up to 1852.

After dismasting the *Clarissa* coming across from Port Dalhousie with a heavy sea rolling, he sold out his interest. He went up to Port Credit to buy the brigantine *Credit Chief*, eighty tons, owned before by John Robinson.

Mr. Robinson, it chanced, was in Toronto that very day, and the deal fell through. Captain McClain took his wife's advice and put his money into a farm in Essa township, though be knew nothing of farming, couldn't steer a horse, and never learned to plough.

He mastered the equestrian art however, and used to drive fifty miles to Toronto with his grain and roots – this was before the railway came – and he did so well at farming that he had been made a magistrate, and a captain of the Second Battalion of Simcoe County Militia by 1857.

Came the "Trent" war scare of 1861 and Sir Edmund Walker Head made him major in the Ninth Simcoe Militia. After the Fenian Raid of 1866, which he was active in repelling, he received an office in Her Majesty's Customs in Toronto, and from the Esplanade Street windows of the old building, was able to keep an intelligent eye upon the yawlboats (if any) seeking the seclusion of the sewer mouth and wharf planking at the foot of the street.

Captain McClain was a fine old figure to the day of his death with much white hair and beard piercing blue eyes, and a high weatherbeaten complexion – a typical North of Ireland "mon" though he spent most of his life in Ontario. His brother Robert was a partner with him in vessel ownership and owned among others the schooner *Jenny Lind* in 1864. A grandson of Robert is Colonel McClain of Toronto.

Archives of Ontario.